D1341888

THE BIG GENERATION

THE BIG GENERATION

John Kettle

McClelland and Stewart

The Canadian Publishers
McClelland and Stewart Limited
25 Hollinger Road
Toronto M4B 3G2

CANADIAN CATALOGUING IN PUBLICATION DATA

Kettle, John, 1929-
  The big generation

Bibliography
Includes index.

ISBN 0-7710-4517-4

1. Canada – Population. 2. Canada – Economic
conditions – 1945-   3. Canada – Social
conditions – 1945-1965.* 4. Canada – Social
conditions – 1965-   * I. Title.

HB3529.K47   304.6'0971   C80-094446-1

Printed and bound in the United States of America

This book is for Hil, Brett, and David, John C., Murray E., Kate P., Janet A., Bobby B., Jim C., Annemarie S., Julia L., Chris L., John V., Robinnia V., Michael R., Carol B., Sherry E., the Fox, Lynn S., Mark J., Andy B., Thomas R., Shelley W., Judy B., Elliot M., Ben G., Eddy P., Michael K., Lloyd O., Doug T., Val M., Danny G., Frances K., Gary M., Big Mo, Erwin V., Jenny E., Chris C., Mark F., Philip P., Gabriella V., Stephen L., Barb P., Sean S., Carol V., Rhiannon T., Martin Z., Russell B., Jacquie P., Tom W., Tal S., Toby D., Bill B., Jane W., Rhona M., Robbie C., Sarah G., Alison M., David T., Wayne O., Scott M., Chris B., Anne M., Marg M., Mary G., Don W., Dave E., Tom S., Carol B., Chris C., Mary P., Benjamin B., Phil M., Valerie L., Michael S., Richard B., Moose, Harley F., Margo W., Charles D., Lisa M., Caroline J., Jamie C., Anthony P., Fiona G., Sharon M., David W., Eddy K., Gwen B., Ariane, Rod M., Rufus, Pat B., Brenda M., Sheila P., Jack B., Misty C., and the other 6,819,758 members of the Big Generation.

ACKNOWLEDGEMENTS

The idea that a book should be written about the children of the post-war baby boom struck me in 1977 when I was doing a series of articles for *Executive* magazine. Most of what I thought I knew about that gigantic cohort turned out on investigation to be wrong; yet there was almost no one to interview on the subject, scarcely anything to read.

Since then, numerous friends and colleagues in business and government who learned I was writing about the Big Generation have made useful suggestions and dug out unpublished or hard-to-find information. Among them were Jeanne Binstock, Krystyna Borsuk, Harris Boyd, B. Bruce-Biggs, Al Cogan, David Crane, John Cullen, Gerry Finn, Marie Hubbs, Michael Hudson, Herman Kahn, Dave Keith, Irving Leveson, Tony McVeigh, Jane Newitt, Philip Pocock, Henry Pold, Rudy Ruggles, Bob Russel, Mike Sherman, Bill Snarr, Gary Stamm, Susan Vecchio, Dean Walker, J.E. Wicks, Mike Williams, and Marc Zwelling. I am very grateful to them and apologize if I have failed to mention any others who helped. Three organizations – Hudson Institute of New York, I.P. Sharp of Toronto, and the Toronto library of Statistics Canada – were also most helpful.

A generous grant of computer time from IBM Canada allowed me to study the demographic and economic dynamics of the Big Generation in much greater detail than would otherwise have been possible. I had the valued help of three researchers, Judith Adam, Helen Hardman, and Frances Kitaura, and, thanks to the kindness of Bess and Jim Murray, the opportunity to write in rural peace and seclusion. Jennifer Glossop and Charis Wahl were probing, stimulating editors.

The book would not have been started but for my wife Helen. Quite apart from all the typing and research she did on the book, her ideas, questions, and comments added a great deal. What she contributed by way of personal support, only we know: without it, the book would never have been finished.

John Kettle,
Toronto, July 1980.

CONTENTS

PART I

THE
BIG
GENERATION

A SCENARIO

1975

It is eleven o'clock on a mid-September morning in Vancouver and Eric Hobson is still asleep. As he was yesterday at this time, and the day before.

Eric, who is sixteen, got a job cleaning up at a hamburger restaurant in the spring term and worked there through most of the summer vacation. The manager said he would be trained as a cook at the next opening. That was when Eric decided to drop out of school. But for one reason or another – a fight in the washroom over his girl friend, showing up late a couple of times, a hot exchange with the manager about a missing cap – he was fired. It was the week before school opened. It was also the week his father announced he had met a woman, fallen in love, and was going to set up house with her. And proceeded to do so.

Eric cannot stand his mother's crying and angry outbursts and drinking bouts. He comes down from his room in the quiet small hours of the morning, makes endless sandwiches, drinks milk, eats up all the cookies, goes back to his room and his radio, and smokes. He takes meals at home only when he is out of money.

As soon as he gets up, usually around noon, he leaves the house. But at this hour he is still in bed.

At the other end of the country, in Montreal, Maggie Kadar is running down the hall to her history class. It is not a subject she does well at, though she finds the Canadian history fitfully interesting. Chemistry is where she shines, and although she hasn't yet made a firm decision, it is the field she will make her career in.

Maggie—Magda to her family—was born in 1961, five years after her parents made a panicky exit from Hungary. They met in the Hungarian community that sprang up in Montreal after the revolution, married, worked, and bought a small house. Magda grew up speaking Magyar at home, English at school. After each election the Kadars are less sure they like living in Quebec, and their daughters have become reconciled to the prospect of moving west, though given their choice they would pick Montreal over anywhere they know.

1985

Maggie and Eric have been married for six years, and she is wondering how much longer she will be able to bear it. Eric did go back to school and then on to regional college for a cooking course, which he quit in the middle of the second year. He moved to Calgary at the beginning of 1979, starting a succession of greasy-spoon café and restaurant jobs. The Kadars left Montreal in 1979, convinced that Quebec was going to separate. Maggie's father found a job with the provincial government in Edmonton, and Maggie enrolled in biochemistry at the University of Calgary. Her freshman year was the first she had spent away from home; she was married before the spring. Her parents did not hear about it until the summer vacation, when she at last told them she would not be returning home.

Eric works in a steak house, much patronized by wealthy Japanese and Korean oilmen and eastern Canadian tourists. Maggie is tutoring some first- and second-year students and doing research during the summer vacations for an American pharmaceutical company that has opened a Canadian branch based in Calgary.

They have less and less to talk about. He is a cable freak, with a videotaper, a library of blue movies, and a growing passion for the new murderball games and the annual sudden-death Lougheed Cup finals. She plays the lute with a small group – plucked strings and bowed strings – and is currently reading through all of George Orwell, after the success of the 1984-85 man-and-works series on cable. They have no children, entertain little – his friends and hers don't mix – and, after one unsuccessful vacation in New York, now take short breaks in the Central American package resorts.

1990

Maggie Hobson, now Maggie Kadar again, holds a research job at Tomson-Laws Biologicals, the company she worked for as a summer student. She rents a farmhouse near Lethbridge with Marc Thibodeau, a thirty-three-year-old lawyer, and Vincent Narayan, a twenty-eight-year-old out-of-work actor. Maggie spends most of her week at home, using the terminal in the work room. When she has physical experiments to do she takes the one-hour magtrain ride into Calgary or works with a colleague on the spot over the videolink.

Marc uses the terminal and videolink for some of his work, but spends more time travelling and with clients than Maggie cares to. He has become a real estate expert specializing in international franchising. He hops about the west in the small carpter, uses the transPacific hypersonic when his clients are paying, tries to stop in Singapore for a weekend if there is time, and has a secret passion for kinky Asian gadgets, the more chrome and lasers the better.

Vince has not been offered a part in two and a half years. He is a natural sybarite, soft-spoken, elegant even in homemade clothes, a man who can take a morning to make lunch, a sweet-voiced singer. Maggie sometimes thinks she loves him even more than she loves Marc.

After Marc's suicide in 1998, Maggie and Vincent could not bear to go on living on the farm. They moved with two other couples into a house that had been on the outskirts of Lethbridge when it was built in 1929 but is now half lost in a jumble of 1970s shopping malls, 1980s office and service complexes, and 1990s apartment buildings. One couple, the homosexuals Pat and Peter, are in their mid-thirties and have been together for only two years. They run a second-hand video store. The other couple, Frank and Marie-Anne, are both in their forties. They married in their late twenties when they lived in Toronto, have a teenage daughter Elise, and like backpacking, bicycling, and skiing, but are becoming a little less hearty about it. Frank is one of the far too many doctors in town. He works four mornings a week at the clinic and alternate Sundays at the neurasthenic hospital.

The house has two bathrooms and one large room—made by knocking out the wall between the kitchen and dining room— where most of the cooking and eating goes on. Vince, Marie-Anne, and Pat share the cooking unless one of the others is inspired. The three couples contribute equally to the rent and the groceries; transportation units are fetched from the rent-all as needed. Clothing and books move around as freely as smoke or as Elise; but people regard musical instruments more personally and look after their own.

The economy's gradual slide from recession into depression not only pushed more families and households into city commune-homes, it stirred up a buzz of political activity. It was William Marcus, born in 1946 at the leading edge of the baby boom after the Second World War, who first succeeded in mobilizing his generation's political potential. With terminals and videolinks in every home and workplace, canvassing was no longer a matter of trudging from door to door. Marcus ingeniously matched the household telelogs on commercial cable shows, which any advertiser could buy, with the voting patterns on the cable referendums, which could not be analysed below electoral district level. This allowed him to pump a very well-aimed message straight through the cable into three million videolinks. As subsequent history proved, he was close to ninety per cent on target. Within a year, Marcus's new party, Class Action, was swinging more than half the referendums.

Today, many people expect William Marcus to be the country's chief executive within five years. He has survived three attempts to electrocute him, but carries the livid scar of a severe laser burn across his right temple.

2015

Maggie and Marie-Anne and Pat and Peter all think Calgary is getting dirtier, noisier, more decadent. The black market is the highest priced in the west, and since the San Andreas refugees moved across the Rockies, the quality of nearly everything has been watered down. On a trip back east for her father's funeral, Marie-Anne found a certain charm in sleepy, old-world Toronto that promised a pleasanter life. The four of them are discussing a move. What holds them back is that Maggie, fifty-four, now research vice-president of Mitsubishi-Tomson Biologicals, is the only one with a job; and the life of people trying to survive on government support alone is grim.

Before Frank walked out on them, he and Maggie had had one of those rare inspired conversations when insights and what-ifs and recollections of old research click into place. Within a year Tomson-Laws had a patent on what proved to be a highly effective preventive for strokes. The money to develop it for mass production came from a Japanese merger. Other biochemists and companies were working the same territory, and today it is as rare to hear of someone dying of cardiovascular disease as it is to hear of death from smallpox, cholera, typhoid, diphtheria, polio or malaria, plagues that once wracked whole populations.

Pat and Peter have opened a pot'n'trot with a frankly nostalgic 1980s decor, but it is taking time to catch on.

2025

Maggie ran into gentle, idle Vincent Narayan on the Yonge

Street Mall last year, after she and Peter moved to Toronto; the three of them now live in the Eaton Centre, which was converted from a shopping centre a few years back. What is left of its open space retains something of the building's original character; it is now the city's central bartamart.

It is spring, and New Class Action is making a last effort to influence the retirement referendum. Even the Grand Old Man of the original party, William Marcus, now in his seventies, has been persuaded to give up a week of sailing in the Caribbean to campaign. All the citilites have been reserved for months and political plugs flood the 'links. The generation of the post-Second-World-War baby boom is the core of this last-ditch move to restore retirement pensions, but now for the first time they are fighting a younger portion of the electorate that is almost as numerous as they are and much brighter and better organized – a population that most definitely does not want to support the millions who could lay claim to a pension.

2050

Vincent Narayan died this morning, April 26. He would have been eighty-eight next month. In a day or two Maggie will pull herself together and move into a seniorary. These are the government's only support program for the aged.

2060

"Would I have been happier if we had had a child? Perhaps even a grandchild? M-M – What was his name? – Marc sometimes said he wanted a child. Eric didn't. Vince certainly didn't. I don't think I did. I did want to do well. Well, research manager wasn't bad; and in a big Korean transnational company. It's hard now, though. There aren't many of us left. You can't even talk to the people running things now. Funny accents – phony ark-sents. Words you never heard. No soul. No love. Perhaps I would have hated a grandchild. Could I have been happier. . .?"

16

NOTE ON SCENARIOS

When futurists expect an activity to follow its established path they use mathematics to extend the trend line of the past into the future. As inertia appears to be the main component of many activities, the process seems fully justified. It produces a lot of work for computers.

When a break in the trend seems likely or even possible, however, computers are less useful. The most practical approach is to ask what kinds of things could happen and then try to assess their likelihood.

This is where the scenario comes in. West-coast futurists borrowed this device from Hollywood, where brief scenarios or story outlines were submitted to studio executives before scripts were commissioned. Scenarios were just detailed enough to allow judgements about audience appeal, financing, casting, and the like. Scenarios could not give any idea of the texture or flavour of the proposed movie, but they would show up its main strengths and implausibilities.

For futurists, the scenario is a tool that helps uncover future prospects, which the strategist in government or business can then plan for. As in Hollywood, the futurist's scenarios should pass tests of plausibility, consistency of development, imagination, and reasonable characterisation. They are unlikely to foretell the future exactly, but if they are done skilfully enough, they can give an advance idea of the kind of future that lies down the road.

The scenario you have just read outlined one possible future for members of the Big Generation. It introduced some of the possibilities that await this great cohort of young men and women. Dozens if not hundreds of different scenarios could have been presented: stories ending in universal disaster, stories of luck and brilliance and great riches, stories coloured by ennui and disillusion. It would be presumptuous to claim that this scenario is the most likely, but most of its elements are latent in the life and times of the generation. What is certain, as the rest of this book shows, is that their future cannot be like anything that anyone before them has ever known.

CHAPTER 1

BIRTH OF THE BIG GENERATION

*"I was a Depression kid, an only child,
and it seemed like a great idea to have our four."*

Something extraordinary happened in Canada between 1951 and 1966. It has already wreaked havoc in our lives and will go on echoing down the years into the middle of the next century, disrupting and reshaping and rebuilding most of our society and economy in the process.

What happened was that the historic trend of fertility was briefly reversed. From the time of the first settlement of this country in 1604, fertility has been in continual decline, from ten children for each woman to only two or three at the time of the Depression. In the first fifty years of this century, the combination of this declining birth rate and a growing population produced an annual average of only 250,000 births, with little variation from year to year. But from 1952 to 1965 between 400,000 and 500,000 children were born every year. The result was something quite unforeseen: a hugely oversized cohort of people – the Big Generation.

Yet we find it hard to see them at all as a living, persisting phenomenon. Different people have seen them for different reasons at different times. The baby-food manufacturers realized that they were there and then, later, that they had gone away. The schools reeled under their unrelenting advance in the 1960s. The Unemployment Insurance Commission is very conscious of them right now. Yet, apart from one or two journalists, no one has looked at them as an event, a single group of people growing up, maturing, moving through the stages of life. This book is the first to count them and to identify the years they were born in.

The Big Generation consists of the 6,715,000 people born between mid-1951 and mid-1966, plus the 260,000 people of the same age who immigrated to Canada during the period, minus the people of the same age who emigrated during the period, who were not counted but who must have numbered about 150,000, minus the 240,000 who died in infancy or youth. On Census Day, 1966, at the end of the explosion, the Big Generation numbered 6,591,700. That was thirty-three per cent of the total population. One-third of all the people in the country had been born in the preceding fifteen years!

In the fifteen years immediately preceding the Big Generation there were only 4.5 million births; in the fifteen years following mid-1966 there will have been no more than 5.4 million births. On the evidence of the generations before and after, it would not have been surprising if the middle one had been five million. That makes the Big Generation one and a half million over size.

If, instead of bursting out in the quite unlooked-for baby boom, Canada had continued its transition toward a stationary, zero-growth population, which would have produced lower birth rates than ever before, who knows how few might have been born in those years? The number of births each year would certainly not have been much above the annual quarter million of the earlier years of the century. A rough calculation, creating a little new history, suggests there might have been as few as 4.3 million births between 1951 and 1966.

On any reasonable assessment, the cohort of 1951-1966 is between 1.6 and 2.3 million people too large: thirty to fifty per cent over-strength. For the sake of picking one number, say there are four people for every three who might have been expected.

Many people include the children born between 1946 and 1950 in the Big Generation. They do this partly because the birth rates were so high for a year or two after the war, an increase that was noticeable and widely discussed; but the numbers involved were not all that startling. It is true, however, that these people, the first post-war children, are different from earlier generations. But they are also different from the Big Generation in most respects. In any case I would exclude them from membership in it just on the grounds of numbers: they were not as densely packed into the years of their birth.

The first post-war children did have one important effect on our thinking about the Big Generation, however. The publicity surrounding them in the immediate post-war years seems to have exhausted most of the public interest in the existence of an oversize generation. This, paradoxically, adds to the difficulty of seeing the true dimensions of the Big Generation. For instance, several years ago Prime Minister Trudeau observed that all the children of the baby boom had been absorbed into the labour force and had settled down to married life. It may have been true of the people born in the second half of the 1940s but it did not describe the Big Generation, some of whom were then just entering high school.

Another reason that the baby-boom has gone unrecognized or misunderstood is that it was not a world-wide event. In the world's poor countries, which means most of them, there was no noticeable increase in births at the end of the Second World War. The population explosion happened because of the drop in the death rates, not a rise in the birth rates. China was an exception; but the excess of births in the period 1945-1955 cannot have been more than about one per cent of today's population. (That does mean about ten million extra people, so in numbers it is not a trivial increase.)

Most rich countries had gone through the drop in death rates many years earlier, and their birth rates had dropped back to a level close to the death rates well before the Second World War. After this downward shift, known as the "demographic transition," many countries had been again at or near the replacement fertility rate since about 1920. Nearly all of them experienced a burst of births for a year or two after the Second World War, but then the rates fell back to their pre-war levels. It is easier to note the exceptions to this – the Netherlands, Italy, the Soviet Union, Yugoslavia, Australia, New Zealand, and of course Canada and the United States – than to list all the countries where it was true. In those countries that had finished their demographic transition earliest, the population had settled into a fairly even distribution, with about as many people aged forty to sixty as aged twenty to forty or even zero to twenty.

The Soviet Union's post-war boom was dwarfed by the earlier great changes that occurred in its population from other causes. It has the largest proportion of population born between 1925 and 1930 of any country I have been able to check out, and the smallest proportion born between 1940 and 1945. So it is not going to suffer the difficulties that a baby-boom generation poses, though its problems from uneven distribution of population are

21

already fiercer than most countries will ever experience, and they are going to get worse before they get better.

Both Sweden and Japan had small baby booms starting around 1940 and ending in the early 1950s. Several western European countries, notably Britain and West Germany, experienced small baby booms that were concentrated in the 1960s and did not reach their peaks until quite late, typically around 1965.

The only countries that had large post-war baby booms like Canada's were the United States, Australia, and New Zealand. In all the pattern was similar. But in Australia the birth rate was lower and, as a result, the children of their baby boom do not constitute as large a proportion of the total populace. In the United States, too, the ratio of boom children to the total is a little lower; the different patterns among blacks and hispanics moderate the impact of the boom. Black birth rates are higher, and their baby boom came about five years later; the group born after the boom is therefore relatively larger, and as a result the post-boom decline for the whole country is gentler. The same thing is true in New Zealand, where the Maori, Samoan, and Polynesian baby boom came later, was less extreme, and softened the decline from the peak.

So for a whole variety of reasons, none of which had much to do with us, Canada's baby boom turned out to be the most drastic of all.

Even in Canada, however, the Big Generation did not have the same impact across the country. It was not evenly scattered geographically or by social class. In Canada overall there were about six children for every ten adults in 1966; but in Newfoundland there were eight children for every ten adults, and the ratio was also well above average throughout the Maritime provinces, in Saskatchewan and Alberta, and in the northern territories. Thirty per cent of the Big Generation children lived in rural areas, though only twenty per cent of adults did; by contrast, only about forty per cent of them lived in big cities, where fifty per cent of adults lived. Couples with little education had more children than well-educated couples. The generation as a whole was more concentrated than the adult population in poor, ill-educated, rural families.

Time has now slightly changed the Big Generation and its place in society. Two bursts of high immigration since 1966 have added people in the same age group as the generation; annual births after the end of the baby boom continue low. By the 1976 census the Big Generation had reached the collective age of ten to twenty-four, was larger – at 6.8 million – and accounted for twenty-nine per cent of the total population. At the 1981 census the numbers will be about the same.

Members of the generation are just beginning to surface as individuals in the public's awareness, and most visibly in activities in which youth is a big factor. Most professional sports are dominated by the Big Generation. Nearly three-quarters of the 464 players on the National Hockey League 1979-1980 roster were children of the baby boom (the youngest, Wayne Gretzky and Mark Messier of the Edmonton Oilers, were both born in January 1961), and so were close to eighty per cent of the 402 players on the CFL roster. Some of the best thoroughbred racing jockeys, boxers, and professional baseball players are Big Generation members, as are racing driver Gilles Villeneuve, Olympic medal winners Steve Podborski and Gaetan Boucher, the high-jumper Debbie Brill, and the swimmer Alex Baumann.

Big Generation people are becoming prominent in the arts and entertainment, too. The singer René Simard, classical guitarist Lynne Gangbar, many members of the National Ballet corps and soloists Esther Murillo and Kevin Pugh, most of the spear carriers and a few featured players at Stratford such as Margot Dionne, opera singers such as Mark DuBois and Gino Quilico, and poet Susan Musgrave are all of the generation. So are a few fashion designers like Francois Guenet and Debbie Shuchat, and the majority of fashion models. A sixth of the editorial staff on Canada's biggest newspaper, the Toronto *Star*, and the same proportion of the production staff in the Canadian Broadcasting Corporation are children of the baby boom; but one would not recognize many of the names from by-lines or credits.

Five members of Parliament sent to Ottawa in 1979 were in the Big Generation and four of them were re-elected in the 1980 election. The one who lost at the 1980 election was defeated by another member of the Big Generation. Here and there a young businessman has come to notice. Moses Znaimer, the president of CITY-TV in Toronto, is one. But most of them are still unknown quantities, more noted for being spectators and consumers than as stars or producers.

23

Why is the baby boom significant? If three out of ten Canadians happened to be born in fifteen years, does that matter either to them or to those born before and after?

It matters, for two reasons. The first is that life in our society is to a considerable extent arranged by age groups and in the expectation of consistency. For thirty years, from 1917 to 1947, the number of children reaching school age each year was between 235,000 and 265,000. It did not even rise from the lower figure to the higher, it simply varied up or down from year to year. Thus, the experience of a long generation prepared the whole school system to expect that more or less the same number of new children would turn up each September and that the size of the system would not change.

In the twenty years after 1947, the number of children enrolling in school rose rapidly each year until it had doubled. The results were chaotic – too many children looking for too few teachers and classrooms. The school system is nowhere near recovering from it.

The Big Generation's entry into the job market has not had quite as much effect as its entry into school. But the situation is comparable. For thirty years – from 1930 to 1960 – the same number of youngsters reached maturity each year and went looking for jobs. Because of the rising population they actually found it easier and easier to get jobs. But then – from 1960 to 1980 – came the same staggering twenty-year rise in the number of job-seekers, though the increase in the proportion going to college has stretched it out. Again the result has been chaos – too many people looking for too few jobs.

Society is ruled by inertia, using the word in the engineer's sense. Society has tremendous momentum, like an ocean liner. It takes a long time to recognize that something is changing, a long time to figure out what to do about it, and a longer time to alter its practices or accommodations. Wherever the Big Generation has arrived, the people in charge have thrown up their hands in surprise and horror. At each step so far, the generation has been inadequately or improperly or mistakenly treated; and all because it is so much larger as a cohort than any age group before or any ever anticipated.

The second set of reasons that the Big Generation is in trouble is the opposite of the first: there are so few people following behind it. This means, for instance, that when some institution does have the foresight to anticipate the arrival of the generation, it usually also realises that it is a temporary aberration. Why build enough community colleges to take in all the Big Generation when you know that within a decade the enrolment must be smaller? Can we afford the sports facilities the generation would like? Such quandaries abound.

For the members of the Big Generation, the small size of the younger group means that the traditional reason for promotion and advancement, having a group of subordinates to manage, is always going to be less significant. In fact, throughout this century, the Big Generation will outnumber all their juniors. There will be more people hoping to be chiefs than the sum total of Indians.

The bleakest question that can now be foreseen is, who will support the Big Generation in its old age? In a steadily expanding population, there is always a larger group of people coming up behind to look after the dwindling number of older people ahead. In the case of the Big Generation, there can be no such expectation. As it is now constituted, the Canada Pension Plan is a fraud. And there are many other difficulties that will plague the generation all its life.

All in all, the Big Generation is clearly the strongest social phenomenon of our time, the largest, the most extensive, the most durable.

Then why have we not been able to see it? Partly because we have been looking at the wrong things, the cross sections rather than the continuing phenomenon: the school squeeze, youth unemployment, and so on, and not the generation itself. Until now it has not been important to think in the long term, because changes in population have been small enough to be treated as mere fluctuations. But with the Big Generation we are looking at a hundred-year revolution.

When Copernicus showed that the earth and the other planets circled the sun, and that the sun and the rest of the system did not, after all, centre on the earth, contemporary astronomers one after the other went to their telescopes, took their measurements, and saw for themselves that what Copernicus said was true. It was not new instruments that enabled them to see this new fact, but the power of a new concept.

We need a new concept for thinking about the Big Generation. We need to perceive it for what it is, a very large group of people born within a few years of each other, growing up together, entering on new life experiences together, maturing and growing old together, and all the time doing so in a society that is not only several sizes too small, but will not and probably cannot ever expand enough to make their lives fit comfortably. We need to see the Big Generation as an abnormality in the dynamics of population. It is a disproportionately large lump that the country has swallowed and that is now moving along the population profile as it ages, like a pig swallowed by a boa constrictor, only slowly to be digested and absorbed.

We need to study the generation because it is so large, because the unique circumstances of its birth and upbringing make it so different from any previous generation, and because what happens to the generation is going to be the most important part of what happens to Canada for many decades. So far only a few government departments and agencies have taken account of the Big Generation's existence, and then only for a few years at a time, only in a single guise – as students, runaways, trainees, criminals or pension plan contributors. This outlook offers little chance for getting a three-dimensional perspective on the problem of the generation. It is going to be a staggering problem, this generation, before it is through. Wherever they are, someone said, it is raining.

They are going to be an enormously powerful force for change for the next half century and more. They will change nearly everything. They will abandon the Protestant ethic, the work ethic. They will not live vicariously on future hopes and their children's prospects that buoyed up earlier generations; they do not identify themselves and their interests with national goals; their family life will be unrecognisably different. It will not be a question of getting back to normal after they get through school or after they get into the labour force. They will alter what is normal beyond restoration and make a new world, better, perhaps, or worse than the old familiar one, but wildly different.

They will be as different from earlier generations as men are from women, or French speakers from English. The futures of the fisherman's daughter from Come-by-Chance, the sons of the Rosedale professor, and the children of the Estevan farmer are going to be dissimilar because of birth and childhood experiences, but far more akin one to another than to the lives of the parents who bore them.

We stand at one of the great divides of Canadian history. The shape of our future depends on how well the members of the Big Generation understand what they are, what is happening to them, and what is going to happen in the rest of their lives, and how well the rest of us realize our own advantages, note the problems and dangers that the children of the baby boom represent, and do what we can to ameliorate them. For there is no way back and no way out. The Big Generation is here to stay.

CHAPTER 2

WHERE THEY CAME FROM, HOW THEY GOT HERE

*"There's something wrong when everyone's
goal is to have a family of four
and a station wagon."*

The generation gap is at least as old as the Greeks, who remarked from time to time that young people were going from bad to worse, and who yearned for the good old days. Yet human nature does not seem to be much changed after all these declines. One is left with the impression that most of this cavilling between generation is simply the difference between youth and age rather than any real difference between generations. In middle age most of us would probably dispute with ourselves as youngsters quite as much as anyone else did. Real generation gaps are hard to find. But in the case of the Big Generation the gap is real, and it is much larger than such gaps have been before.

Until this generation came along, even in times when social ideas and values were shifting, it was not difficult to maintain continuity; in fact, the complaint of recent generations has been that it was hard to do anything else. Today, it is not unusual for a person of forty and someone of eighty to talk as though they had identical values. Some of these values are simply traits common to people past their youth, and some of this talk is mere sentimentality; but some values really have remained more or less unchanged through many generations into this century.

It is sometimes difficult today to summon up a clear picture of what motivated our predecessors. Geoffrey Vickers, the British futurist, wrote recently, "Until two centuries ago the responsibility of the person was commonly seen as personal responsibility to a personal God.... It was a culture which overestimated what was to be expected of human responsibility. None the less it made human beings far more responsible than they would otherwise have been. Moreover, it endured long after its metaphysical base had begun to weaken. It was still dominant in the England into which I was born at the end of the 19th century."

In much the same vein Noel Annan, born in 1916, wrote, "The strength of the consensus in society was enormous. . . . It was molded from an amalgam of national self-consciousness and a religious code of behavior. . . . The consensus was also buttressed by the strength of authority. . . . With this respect went a corresponding fear of nonconformity."

Annan tells us that throughout the nineteenth century the nobility, the gentry, the middle classes, and the working classes were sustained by an ethos that had been well developed at least a hundred years earlier and that survived until the First World War. Traces of it could still be felt decades later. It required a man to rule his life "no longer under the guidance of God, but of an overpowering sense of civic duty and diligence." He had to serve the institution he belonged to – the ministry, the regiment, the profession – and put it ahead of his family and his private life. "The supreme virtue was loyalty, and loyalty to institutions must be put before loyalty to people, if only because the supreme loyalty which did not need to be spoken of was to king and country."

Both these men wrote of another country, but most of what they said could as easily have been said of Canada at that time, when this country was still dominated by the British influence. Strictly speaking, these are the values of the grandparents of the Big Generation, who were nearly all born between the Franco-Prussian War and the First World War.

The values of the generation's parents, most of whom were born in the years between the two world wars, are easier to uncover; they are all around us. "People in their late thirties and early forties are the last group who remember doing things just because they were expected to by adults," the novelist Renata Adler said in 1978. The parents of the Big Generation belonged to a dutiful generation, raised in a time when the Victorian ethic still lingered and educated in the same values as their own parents.

Canada was also still essentially a rural nation when they grew up, and this strongly influenced their outlook. At the beginning of the 1920s less than half the population lived in cities, towns, or villages; if one considers thirty thousand the minimum population for a big town or city, only a quarter were urban. At the end of the 1930s, half still lived on farms or in places with a population of less than five thousand, and still only a third were urban. A majority of the generation grew up with rural or small-town attitudes: stable, almost unchanging, rather narrowly conformist values that placed a great deal of emphasis on co-operation, sharing, self-control, taking things as you find them, making do.

Robert Douglas Mead, now a publisher's editor in Philadelphia, went to the twenty-fifth reunion of his high-school class in Evanston, Illinois. He graduated in 1946, and most of his class were born around 1928. The experience drove him to try to understand what had happened to his school friends, what they had been and what they had become. The result was his book, *Reunion*. "This was, after all, the group that in the early 50s had been christened 'the silent generation,'" he writes.

After noting the remarkably good health of his classmates as they entered middle age, he continues:

> And the inner qualities? It seems to me that they are aspects of one essential character which we all shared to some degree: the dutifulness, the dislike of conflicts, the concern for what is personal and private, the rather abstract sense of propriety; the eagerness to master techniques that has made us useful public servants but not political leaders.

He concludes: "We were reasonable people. We believed what we were told."

The key to Mead's generation is found in his words and the recollections of his peers:

> We were hardly a year old when the stock market crash[ed]. . . . By 1932 or 1933, many of our parents had lost jobs, homes, businesses; our fathers had started the long haul of indebtedness and constraint that in many cases lasted till the end of their working lives. . . . One of the things you learned about work was a man standing quietly at your door asking if he could do something around the house – wash windows or clean or paint, rake leaves, cut grass – for a little money or a meal. . . . They weren't beggars. They would just come and ring the doorbell and offer to do some work for a meal. . . . The great events of our lifetime, the Depression and the War, were for us not two experiences but one, a continuity. For our parents, in many cases, the War was an

answer: it meant jobs, new business, an escape into the security of the Army or Navy.

That continuous experience of the Depression and the war was the mould in which the character and attitudes of the parent generation were set. Even today, members of that generation clean off their plates, turn out the lights when they leave a room empty, save jelly jars and pieces of string, and continue to perform other largely irrelevant ritual acts of remembrance. Unlike their parents, the between-the-wars generation was not crippled by the Depression; they simply grew up with it embedded in their innards. "The Depression and the War had prepared us, like an army destined for defeat, for the past, not the future," Mead wrote in *Reunion*. Depression children, and some slightly older, grew up to give Canada its welfare programs, children's allowances, unemployment insurance, Canada Pension Plan, and the rest.

It is not too much to say, as Frederick Herzberg, the American authority on work motivation, has said, "The base line for my generation was the Depression. We based our actions for the rest of our life on it." Herzberg was born in 1923.

Surprisingly, Canada came out of the Depression and went into the Second World War as a largely agricultural country. But the war completed the transition to an industrial economy. (I broadly define agriculture to include fishing, forestry, and trapping as well as farming; in industry I include mining, manufacturing, and construction; services take in everything else. As Sylvia Ostry, the former chairman of the Economic Council of Canada, once put it, the output of the service sector is anything you produce that you can't drop on your foot.)

Around the turn of the century, agriculture produced more than either industry or services and employed more than both together. Today, services account for more production and employ more people than both industry and agriculture together. There never was a time when Canada had a truly industrial economy, never a time when industry was the biggest producer and employer. But industry's importance had been growing for decades; it reached a peak around 1953, when it employed about a third of all Canada's workers and produced forty per cent of its output. Both figures are significantly lower today.

31

Along with industrialization came the unravelling of social order and the collapse of the dominance of elite institutions. What had once been the cause of outrageous rebels like Oscar Wilde and the Fauvists became, after the First World War, part of the common assumptions of that small but increasingly important group, people who had gone to university.

That cause was absolute personal liberty. Educated people demanded the right to read whatever they wanted, see and say whatever they wanted, go anywhere, wear anything, live however and wherever and with whomever they desired; and in the end they demanded the same right for everyone else.

Unless you can look back to at least the 1930s, and preferably to the years before the First World War, it is almost impossible to comprehend how completely the walls have been broken down. When did Hugh Hefner produce the first shocking issue of *Playboy*? Was it really not until 1953? And can it have been as late as 1959 that D.H. Lawrence's genteel novel, *Lady Chatterley's Lover*, was first allowed to be sold over the counter? Yet, after that, almost anything was possible, first in books, then on stage, then in magazines and movies, and finally on television. (Older writers wryly recall the days when publishers tried to get their authors to tone down the sexy bits.) Rules of dress were relaxed. The basis of social convention shifted far from the habits of the elite.

This was a world in flux, offering shocks and surprises at every turn, and its effect on the young adults and middle-aged people who emerged into it from depression and war was dramatic. And they made it the cradle of the Big Generation.

What was there about this changed world that caused people to feel so differently about the number of children they wanted? Despite the interest the post-war baby boom aroused in social scientists, it is still a largely unexplained phenomenon.

Right now one of the more favoured explanations is based on the fact that in the generations since the First World War, fertility rates have gone in twenty-year cycles. This, it is said, is because young men's wages in relation to the wages of their fathers' generation have gone in twenty-year cycles: when the young men's wages have been down the fertility rates have been down, and when wages went up fertility was up. The relative ups and downs of young men's wages have been caused by shortages and gluts of young men in the labour force, and these have been caused by the periods of high or low fertility twenty years earlier. Thus, the whole thing is a self-perpetuating cycle.

This explanation, propounded in its most persuasive form by Professor Richard Easterlin of the University of Pennsylvania, is one of a number of cycle theories going around. The trouble with all of them is that they ignore a larger reality: the continuous drop in fertility in North America since the sixteenth century. The real question is not why fertility rates have cycled up and down in the past sixty years, but why they stopped declining at the end of the Depression.

One explanation, which has been offered rather tentatively, is that the baby boom was an attempt to compensate for the shortage of babies caused by the Depression and the Second World War. Unfortunately for that explanation, more than half the parents of the Big Generation were born between 1926 and 1937 and therefore were in no position to have children during the Depression or the war. Moreover, most of those who were of child-bearing age during the Depression and the war were born between 1900 and 1920, and were unlikely to make a baby boom in the 1950s and early 1960s. For that line of reasoning to hold up we would have to suppose that the intentions of the earlier generation were somehow carried out by their children, or that some mysterious agency was at work on behalf of balanced population growth without conscious human aid. Neither of these seems likely.

It is a fact that births started to rise the year the war started. Although most couples probably reckoned that war was not a good time to start or add to a family, there must certainly have been couples who thought about the prospect of the men being away for years and concluded that this might well be their last chance to have a child or another child. Many women fell for a handsome sailor; many fathers wanted to leave a son if they should be killed; many couples thought a child would hold their marriage together through the stress of separation and temptation. War was bound to stimulate births.

Later thousands of servicemen, carrying within them the brutalizing experience of war, returned with a powerful urge to have children. Life is the perfect answer to death. (Napoleon boasted, "My veterans could make up for all the Frenchmen lost in wars in a single night.") The sweet simplicity of a woman nursing a baby was the only image that could wipe out some memories. The longing to make something good, something permanent, must have become almost irresistible to many who spent years in ruin and destruction and endless movement. They had been squeezed into one of the great archetypal male moulds, the Warrior; another, the Father, was the ideal antidote.

The coming of peace produced feelings of euphoria. We had won the war, vanquished evil; we had decisively ended the Depression; we had fought for freedom, better times, and a fair deal, and now the prizes were about to be handed out. Young parents of the 1940s and early 1950s, who had seen how bad things could be, generally felt pretty good about life and their own prospects.

The baby boom happened to all age groups. The fertility rates for fifteen- to nineteen-year-olds went up; so did the fertility rates for forty- to forty-four-year-olds and all the age groups in between. They started to move up around 1940, under the many wartime pressures, but in the oldest groups they quickly dropped back again. The maximum age of child-bearing had been declining for a very long time, and the wartime rise was short-lived for older women. Rising fertility lasted longest for the youngest, women under thirty.

But are the war and the peace enough to explain the baby boom? No, since the real boom took place between 1951 and 1966.

The most convincing explanations now in circulation argue from the way economic conditions affect women's behaviour. William Butz, a Rand Corporation economist, and Michael Ward of the University of California at Los Angeles have concluded that two factors have the strongest influence on whether couples have children. One is family income:

> Other things being equal, couples with higher income will have more children, just as they will have more cars and more restaurant meals. . . . The other variable is the opportunity cost of women's time: in a society where mothers usually take principal responsibility for raising children, the income they do without as a result is a significant part of the cost of children.

The more a woman can earn, in other words, the more expensive it is for her to give up her job and bear and raise a child.

In the years before the Second World War, so few women went out to work that fertility rates would more or less follow the trend of the economy, which dictates men's wages and therefore family income: economic boom, baby boom; economic bust, baby bust. But once women started to take a serious part in the economy, changes in women's wages made child-bearing more independent of shifts in the whole economy. The economy could continue to rise, but rising wages for women could act as a disincentive to child-bearing and override the trend of family income.

Butz and Ward made a rather convincing test of their idea by building a mathematical model of fertility rates in the years 1947 to 1956, when fertility was on the rise, using family income and women's wages to "explain" the rates: that is, they developed equations which, given the income and wage figures, would return the actual fertility rates. Then they fed in women's wage rates and family income for the years 1957 to 1975. The answer the model gave back was close to what actually happened: fertility rates rose for several more years, then plunged precipitately.

Two other American researchers, Professor George Masnick of Harvard and Joseph McFalls, Jr., of Temple University, took a quite different approach to the question of fertility swings, but came up with an answer that was surprisingly consistent with Butz' and Ward's work. They concluded that the key element was birth control:

> The fertility rates of the 1930s represented levels below those that were desired, and were achieved in part because of deliberate use of birth control, in part because of the inability of couples to form viable unions because of economic and social restraints, and in part due to lower fecundity from poor health and inadequate nutrition.

Couples started by intending only to delay child-bearing, but the conditions that would have allowed them to have children never came. "The baby boom in the next generation is due to a sudden reversal of economic conditions. . . . The small young cohorts reaching adulthood found themselves in a favourable position to marry and settle down."

This group did not start out with the goal of having large families, but simply never learned much about contraception. Many, as a result, reached the family size they wanted but were not as skilled at preventing unwanted children as were the Depression parents, who used birth control from the beginning. Similarly, the decline in fertility that ended the boom came about when younger couples who started out with the intention of postponing a family or limiting it, learned the use of contraception early. The Pill was only one of several new techniques that became available to them.

Another element fits into this picture. The baby boom was the work of mothers younger than ever before or since. The only time in Canadian history when twenty- to twenty-four-year-olds had the highest fertility rate was 1955 to 1968, which lags only three or four years behind the period of the boom. Before the boom, twenty-five to twenty-nine was always the prime age for child-bearing, as it has been ever since. The post-war economic boom allowed young men and women to get married and raise a family at a uniquely early age. Over and over again, at different times and in different countries, it has been found that a woman who starts to bear children early is likely to have more children than one who starts late. So it was with the mothers of the baby boom.

Masnick and McFalls make no mention of women's wages, just as Butz and Ward did not refer to the early use of birth control; but it seems strikingly clear that the two explanations describe facets of the same set of circumstances, attitudes, and actions. What is common to both explanations is that for the first time sociologists are looking at the effect of specific economic pressures on a specific group–younger women–rather than merely trying to relate general trends to changes in the birth rate.

There is a final element that seems to fit into the picture. Charles Westoff, the Princeton demographer, has pointed out that during the baby boom a larger majority of women than ever chose not to remain spinsters and the great majority of married women decided against childless or one-child families. "There was a large increase in the proportion of women having at least two children, but the increase in the proportion of women having three or more children played a minor role in the boom: there was no return to the large families of the past." What brought that trend about is unclear. Westoff says "an unpredictable element of what might be called fashion" seemed to play a role in it.

Mothers of the baby boom have told me the same thing in different words. "I was a Depression kid, an only child, and it seemed like a great idea to have our four," one said. "Everybody else was doing it, and we thought it would be fun too," was the way another put it. Rona Jaffe, the author of *Class Reunion*, said, "In the fifties you weren't anything without a man. That's how we got our identity." She was born in 1931, and found herself left out in a tiny minority when she could not talk about children of her own.

If Canadian women had gone on having children at anything like the rate they reached in 1951-1966, the population would have gone on growing at a fast clip; there would have been seven or eight million newcomers in 1966-1981, and many more to follow. But the sharp and persistent drop in births after 1960 had the effect of isolating the Big Generation, leaving them stranded on the demographic shore, a huge prominence rising above their youngers as well as their elders.

The literature on declining fertility is much more profuse than studies of baby booms. (It includes this engaging comment from the chief planner of Costa Rica's family planning program: "With regard to the causes of this fertility decline in Costa Rica [after 1961], some things are known, some are conjecture, and others, well, who knows?") In contrast to the difficulty of explaining the boom, there are innumerable well-developed and well-documented theories to show why women might have fewer children. But that is not really surprising in the context of the long decline in family size and number of children a woman bore in a lifetime. For centuries it has been normal for fertility to go down. For a few years it happened that it rose.

What ended the boom was mostly the reverse of what had started it. The most persuasive explanations are the economic ones, just as they most convincingly explain the start. At the end of the 1950s there was a distinct pause in the economic boom: income leveled off, many families looked for a second income. The potential mothers of the 1960s had different experiences to compare the new conditions with, and the times did not by any means look so good. By 1965, almost perfect contraception was available; the Pill, which was first authorized for use in 1960 and came into common use by 1963, seemed ideal to the young women of the 1960s.

And the time for big families was passing. People had begun to describe population growth as an "explosion," to see it as a danger greater than the H-bomb, to liken the future of human life on earth to the life of insects. In 1964, the futurist Kenneth Boulding proposed that child-bearing should be licensed. Young people particularly accepted the idea that over-population was a major problem that they should not make worse.

The fashion for togetherness frayed and dissolved into new tastes. The anthropologist Margaret Mead wrote at the height of the baby boom, "There's something wrong when everyone's goal is to have a family of four and a station wagon." More and more people agreed. One journalist wrote sarcastically soon after the end of the boom, "If you've been reading the literature of the Population Catastrophe Lobby during the past few years, you may have noted that a relatively high birthrate was the cause of all America's ills. The three-child family was blamed for everything from social tensions to crowded parks."

The crucial difference between the children born around the end of the Second World War and those born between 1951 and 1966 is that the whole of the Big Generation's life experience has been and always will be governed by its size. The early post-war children, the first to appear with their shiny new arts degrees and self-confidence on the doorsteps of eager employees, were very much in demand. When a youngster with a good degree agreed to show up for a job interview in the mid-1960s, employers felt almost flattered. In a few years that attitude disappeared as the number of vacancies went down and the number of applicants increased. But before it did, it had a lot to do with forming the expectations of the Big Generation, their parents and teachers.

The young people at the end of the Big Generation, born around the middle of the 1960s, are different in another way. All through their lives and school careers they heard how difficult things had become. The frustration of older brothers and sisters got through to these youngsters while they were still young enough to be influenced by it. Many, as a result, did not develop the high job expectations of older members of the generation. Between the pre-boom pioneers and the late-boom teenagers there is a large gulf.

But the Big Generation is essentially one great unit, bound together by the circumstances of their birth and by size. In some respects they are like extra-terrestrial beings who have invaded the planet, bringing exotic, even alien, ideas and attitudes. In most of what they do they break sharply with the past. Many of their tastes and ideas have already evolutionized the popular culture, and this is just a foretaste of what is to come.

But even if we do not yet know for sure how they came in such numbers, we do know what made them so different.

PART II

THE
RAISING
OF
THE BIG
GENERATION

Psychologists everywhere now seem to accept that the experiences of childhood and adolescence make us what we are. The early childhood experiences, before the child becomes objectively conscious of himself, are the most formative. The child experiences the world and everything that happens in it subjectively and accepts it uncritically. He has no other experience to compare it with. This is the way the world is; this is how it works; this is given. The Jesuits used to say, "Give us a child for his first seven years and we will have him for life." So did the Hitler Youth. What happens to the child before the dawning of self-awareness, before he goes to school, is crucial to his attitudes and expectations for the rest of his life. Experiences at school, the younger's first and most impressive contact with the world outside home and family, are second only to pre-school influences in their formative power. Nothing that happens after school is likely to have such a strong shaping effect. With most of the Big Generation now through school, we can get a clear picture of the radically new kind of people they are.

CHAPTER 3

THE FORMATIVE YEARS

"Nowadays there seems to be more
chance of a conscientious parent's
getting into trouble with
permissiveness than with strictness."

Until the arrival of the Big Generation, the process of absorbing the world during childhood was in effect the process by which values were handed down and traditions maintained. So long as there were large families with grandparents and other relatives in residence, a strong church, and not too much formal education, and so long as most of the population lived in the country and was occupied with rural pursuits, each succeeding generation of young children grew up in the same environment as did their parents and took in the same ideas and values.

But circumstances combined to change all that for the Big Generation. For the first time in history, a whole generation grew up in a world that was astonishingly, shockingly unfamiliar to its parents. Almost as if the arrival of the Big Generaion had been a signal for change, the transmission of the traditional ethic ceased.

In its place, a whole new set of powerful influences arose to mould the generation. The children born between 1951 and 1966, like all the billions before them, still accepted the world they grew up in completely uncritically, knowing only that that was how things were; but the conditions and circumstances they accepted as the norm were wholly different from anything previous generations had experienced.

Nine influential factors stand out as the most formative forces in the Big Generation's young life.

AFFLUENCE

During the years when Canada was a quite industrial country, the decades after the Second World War, we also went through the

43

largest economic boom in our history, which I suppose was no coincidence. Removing the growth due to inflation and to increased population, the Canadian economy grew an average of three per cent a year from 1949 to 1973. This meant there was three per cent more real buying power each year in every pocket. Household income grew even more rapidly – three and a half per cent a year on average for the quarter century.

That rate of growth, like the growth of a population at the height of the demographic transition, accumulates astounding results. The most noticeable is that income doubles every twenty years at that rate, whereas it took forty or fifty years to double in the nineteenth and early twentieth centuries. The parents of the Big Generation, the between-the-wars generation, doubled their income between the ages of twenty and forty; in earlier times, the doubling would have taken the years from age twenty to sixty-five or seventy. What took earlier generations a lifetime, this generation had achieved by the age of forty.

As the Big Generation grew up, their parents were emerging from the constraints of depression and war into the biggest economic boom of all time. The parents were like orphans who had found the end of the rainbow. They were adults, but they acted like kids let loose in a candy store. They bought cars and boats and cottages; they came home with television sets and self-cleaning ovens and electric toothbrushes and frost-free refrigerators. They went in for detached houses with suburban lawns and power mowers; they started to drink liquor instead of beer and wore different clothes for every occasion. But they still went to church, stayed with the one company until they retired, and bought insurance almost as if they expected to wake up one morning to find themselves back in the Dirty Thirties. At heart, it was not they who were changed by affluence, but their children.

The children of the Big Generation simply saw that last year's was old, and old was bad; cars lasted two years, wrist watches went out of fashion even faster, and toys lasted two weeks. Commercials on television showed bigger and better and richer things year after year, and what you saw on TV you could go out and get; indeed, anything you wanted was almost sure to arrive by Christmas if not before.

Unlike their parents, who had jumped at the chance to deliver papers or wash dishes or cars for the spending money to buy a few cherished toys, the children learned that there was little connection between rewards and work; the "rewards" were benefits that arrived almost as a right, and work was simply a nuisance.

Big Generation children never knew what it was to go to bed hungry, to go without shoes, to be cold, to wear cast-offs, to sleep three or four in a bed, to wear damp clothes until they dried on you. Their parents revelled in the improvement in their standard of living, but the children had nothing to compare it with. This was how it was; this was given. The post-war affluence that so astonished older people had, for the Big Generation, simply become the norm. To them, money meant comfort, and that was perhaps the most potent influence of affluence.

TECHNOLOGY

The remarkable research and development spurred by the war was probably the biggest single cause of Canada's rapid industrialization in the years immediately afterwards; and industry demanded and provoked intense change. An agricultural economy is devoted to continuity, repetition, constancy, the provision of enough; but an industrial economy runs on innovation, novelty, increase, the provision of more. It has been argued that in the years North America passed through its peak of industrialism it also went through the time of most rapid change in its own, or anyone else's, history.

The quarter century after the war was dominated by technology and the technological fix, the belief that anything could be solved with enough money and engineering. The epitome of the technological fix was the US space program, which carried out the unimaginably difficult, enthralling, and almost entirely pointless task of putting men on the moon with well-nigh faultless skill. (The innovations needed to carry out this task-without-a-purpose are still filtering into civil life and changing it, in many cases for the better.)

Every week, it seemed, there was some new technological miracle. This week, man on the moon. Next week, computers. The week after, heart transplants. Transistors. Polyethylene. Colour TV. Jumbo jets. On and on, in a seemingly endless procession of shiny marvels. And all this was the fabric of the children's lives.

The impact of Canada's dip into industrialism was tremendous,

45

probably as deep and massive as the impact of the Depression. But it worked differently on adults with their Depression background, and on the children, for whom this was their first taste of life.

In general, industry secularizes; it breaks down people's attachment to traditional and religious values. The more rapidly industrialization occurs, the more violent is the rupture: if very rapid, as in Iran under the Shah, it can be unbearably violent. It was not that fast in Canada, and the United States' earlier entry on the path of industrialization softened the impact even further for Canada. But the quarter century after the Second World War was enough to finish off the process, leaving Canada, in effect, a completely secular country; in this respect, it was a country different from what it had been between the world wars.

INSTITUTIONS

The post-war years saw a rapid collapse of established authority and a weakening of respect for institutions that once seemed the foundation of the whole society: the church, university, government, the professions, even the family. It is scarcely reasonable to ask why this happened: it had been happening at least since the end of the Middle Ages, since the appearance of science and reason, since the successful Protestant challenge to the universal Church, since mere men removed the divine right of kings, since the French Revolution, since literacy. The mediaeval view of the world, the body of beliefs that explained to people how and why the world worked, had gradually ceased to be persuasive. As Whittaker Chambers wrote:

> The change that ends ages is infinitely gradual, and, for a long time, largely imperceptible. It is a shift in the general angle of vision. . . . The changes of institutions which this shift of vision makes possible, and in which it is embodied – they come much later.

By the middle of the twentieth century, the mediaeval world view had quite gone, and it was time for the institutions once supported by it to go, too. The dissolution of established institutions was no more the doing of Marxists or television than of gremlins. But the unravelling of society was rapid enough to shock most adults.

46

Let us take the decriminalization of *Lady Chatterley* as the key change. The first of the Big Generation children were only eight years old in 1958, and most of the generation grew up largely ignorant of the real meaning of censorship, and with little sense of the inhibitions that were once imposed on society and the young in particular.

In the same way, most of them had little experience of authority. Few adults, whether parents or teachers, wanted to exercise the kind of strict control of the young that previously had been the unquestioned norm. Children might still be taught by their parents to respect the government or the police – or might not, for attitudes everywhere were changing fast – but the lesson was soon watered down or contradicted by the message from the streets and the media. The years in which the Big Generation grew up were precisely the years in which the pursuit of self-interest before community interest was being turned from uncommon indulgence into popular cult. These are all rather abstract considerations to pre-schoolers; but it was certainly at that time in the children's lives that the new attitudes toward established institutions were first inculcated – or perhaps one should say that the old attitudes were, for the first time, not inculcated.

PARENTS

Among the institutions that were so radically changed by the end of the Depression and the experiences of the war was parenthood. Like the other changes, this one had many causes: but rising awareness of human psychology, which may conveniently if too simply be attributed to the widening influence of Sigmund Freud, aided and abetted by Dr. Benjamin Spock, was probably the main one. The parents of the Big Generation made Spock a best-seller. In the words of Jane Newitt of the Hudson Institute, "in large numbers [they] required professional help to deal with the behavioral and developmental problems of childhood and adolescence." The narrowing of the once extended family, which deprived young mothers of the help and traditional lore (and nagging) once available free and at home from grandmothers, aunts, and cousins, made this the first generation of parents to think of going to professionals, or any outsiders in fact, for help in raising their children. Spock's *The Common Sense Book of Baby and Child*

47

Care, published in 1946, and subsequent pocket-book versions sold more copies than any book written in this century. Its influence was greater even than the twenty-five million copies sold, since scores of other writers of advice to mothers absorbed its message and passed it on.

Spock's message was that the traditional style of parenting had produced children who were too repressed and inhibited. "When I was writing the first edition, between 1943 and 1946," he recalled later, "the attitude of a majority of people toward infant feeding, toilet training, and general child management was still fairly strict and inflexible." His book had an immense influence in destroying that traditional approach. In the introduction to a new edition of *Baby and Child Care* written in 1957 he tried to push the pendulum back: "Nowadays there seems to be more chance of a conscientious parent's getting into trouble with permissiveness than with strictness."

Spock recognized that the new style of parenting was itself a major problem, and that parents now needed to be told to act naturally:

> If your upbringing was fairly strict in regard to obedience, manners, sex, truthfulness, it's natural, it's almost inevitable, that you will feel strongly underneath about such matters when raising your own children. You may have changed your theories because of something you've studied or read or heard, but when your child does something that would have been considered bad in your own childhood, you'll probably find yourself becoming more tense, or anxious, or angry than you imagined possible. This is nothing to be ashamed of. This is the way Nature expects human beings to learn child care – from their own childhood.

Spock identified two kinds of parents who got into trouble with the new Freudian theories: people who grew up with no confidence in their own judgement and people who felt they had been brought up too severely.

> They have often read meanings into [the theories] that went beyond what the scientists intended – for instance, that all that children need is love; that they shouldn't be made to conform; that they should be allowed to carry out their aggressive feel-

48

ings against parents and others; that whenever anything goes wrong it's the parents' fault; that when children misbehave the parents shouldn't become angry or punish them but should try to show more love. All of these misconceptions are unworkable if carried very far.

But millions of members of the Big Generation were raised by parents who were trying very hard to make these misconceptions work.

Enthusiasm for permissiveness has now passed its peak, and parents have begun to have serious doubts about what has become the standard way of bringing up children. Attacks on the cult of Freud have reappeared in the popular press. The psychiatric profession itself has split over what really shapes personality, what gives some people healthy personalities, and what makes others mentally ill or unstable. Bruno Bettelheim, a deeply convinced Freudian, wrote recently that, "if, as modern middle-class parents are often advised, affection and approval are guaranteed to the child no matter what, there will be no fear – but neither will there be much morality." James Dobson's book *Dare to Discipline*, with its message of the purifying consequences of punishment, moved up the 1979 list of best sellers. But the revisionism came too late to touch the Big Generation.

FAMILY

Another legacy the parents left the Big Generation was the effect of being born into a large family. It seems to have been clearly established that first-born children tend to be the most intelligent and that intelligence tends to drop with the child's position in the family: second-born children are typically more intelligent than third-born, and so on.

Various researchers, including some who have been quite unhappy with the results of their studies, have found that birth order is more important than social or economic class, parents' intelligence or education, or other possible factors in deciding a child's intelligence. Several very large studies have confirmed that, on average, birth order directly affects intelligence.

Some explanations have been advanced for this effect. A person's intelligence is established by the people he lives with and the stimuli he gets as a baby and young child. The greater the interaction between parent and child, the higher the child's awareness of the parent's world. The sociologist Brigitte Berger observes:

> The intensity of interaction, however, declines as family size increases. In larger families, children – and especially the youngest children – have the social world mediated to them not so much by their parents or by other adults, but by *siblings who are themselves children.*

So not only is the impact of the parents on each child smaller in large families, but their total impact is smaller. More of the process of socialization is carried out by other children, thus helping to create a children's or adolescents' culture for the youngest children to grow up in: a culture Berger calls "tribal, primitive, barbarian."

What this means is that where families are larger, the average intelligence of the whole community will tend to be lower. Perhaps needless to say, it does not condemn any individual to inevitably lower intelligence. Throughout the 1920s and 1930s, families in Canada had been getting smaller; but the baby boom reversed that trend, and the families established in the baby-boom years were larger – typically four children or more – as well as being much more numerous. Thus, part of the Big Generation's inheritance, it appears, is a level of intelligence lower than it would have been if families had been smaller.

There may have been other reasons in the evolution of man and society that would tend to raise intelligence over time, and certainly one could expect the rising level of education to have some beneficial effect akin to higher intelligence, so the Big Generation may not be noticeably less intelligent than its predecessors. The consequences for the generation may be greatest when it is compared with those who are following it, who, as members of families typically half the size of the Big Generation families, must be expected on the basis of the birth-order theory to be considerably more intelligent on average.

But there is another side to a generation that is made up to such a great extent of children from large families. Life in the family is part of the process of acquiring a personality and social skills. One of the important things missing in the small family is the chance to learn to get along with one's peers. Whatever else the Big Generation has missed, it is undoubtedly blessed with experience in getting along with others, in mediating disputes, in team-work skills.

Another sizable inheritance the Big Generation received from its parents was the broken home. In the years after the war there was a tremendous increase in divorce. Old statistics on separation, domestic violence, and other kinds of family breakdown are not available, so there is little to compare the contemporary situation with; but there seems to be wide agreement that the post-war family was more susceptible to collapse than had ever been the case before. The new divorce legislation of 1968 was like the breaking of a dam, letting loose a flood of divorces. The numbers suggest that a great many marriages had held together under duress, or by force of circumstances, rather than in domestic bliss.

Some years later, in the mid-1970s, about sixty thousand children each year were victims of their parents' divorces. Since half of divorces occur in marriages at least eleven years old, many of those children were members of the Big Generation. The number of children known to have been affected by divorces in the 1950s and 1960s is lower, about a quarter of a million in all in the twenty years.

It is not easy to compare the extent of marriage breakdown before the act with what has been revealed since. Many broken marriages before 1968 led only to separations, not divorces, and separations are not officially recorded. But if the rate at which marriages were breaking down in separation and divorce before 1968 was similar to the rate at which marriages were being dissolved in divorce alone after 1968 – a fairly conservative assumption – then the number of children involved altogether in broken marriages in those years would have been more like a million and perhaps more, or, say, one in five of the Big Generation. Warner Troyer wrote in *Divorced Kids* that about two in five are victims of divorce, but gave no source for the figure. Parents Without Partners, an American organization, estimates one child in five lives with only one parent.

As anyone who has been close to children of broken marriages can testify, family breakdown is deeply disturbing to children. At all ages, from infancy to teen-age, they experience great stress, fear, shame, guilt, bitterness, and anxiety. Some, for obscure reasons, blame themselves for the failure of their parents' marriage. Most feel rejected by the parent who leaves; many blame the breakdown on the parent who stays. Getting used to a step-parent and step-brothers and sisters is also difficult, and frequently produces jealousy, conflicts of loyalty, and feelings of rejection and worthlessness: the fairy tale image of the wicked stepmother has become very potent for modern children. A study of more than two hundred exceptionally disturbed and violent children found that only about forty of them had parents who were still living together, and ninety per cent of those surviving marriages were "chaotic."

TELEVISION

The Big Generation is the first in human history to have been brought up from infancy with television. Since there is no way to figure out what this generation would have been like without television or what previous generations would have been like with it, the medium's impact cannot be exactly measured. But few people who have lived through their own childhood without TV and their children's with, doubt that its effect has been substantial. Jeanne Binstock says:

> The emotional impact of television-watching on small children is underrated. Adults know the events on TV are not real life; children do not. Adults are skillful at avoiding painful identification with helpless or tragic people, seen so often in the course of news reporting; children are not. TV single-handedly produced the global perspective of American young adults. . . . These children, relatively powerless themselves, silently identified with all the helpless people being portrayed. . . . Television produced commitment of feeling rather than withdrawal.

In the span of one generation, television, particularly in alliance with the whole array of entertainment and information now so lavishly flowing through radios, phonographs, movie screens, and concerts, has come to constitute what Clifton Fadiman calls "the alternate life." It is, Fadiman says, no longer simply a diversion from the harsh realities of the workday world, good for a little simple relaxation; it is a complete alternate culture. The life of young people is still dominated by the time they spend in school, but the hours spent with television and the other media must be catching up. These are the competing sources of their culture.

Fadiman wrote recently that this alternate life "works on children and youths every day, year after year, teaching them, forming them, conditioning them. And it is profoundly opposed to traditional education." Given the emotional power of the media and the comparatively dry and rigorous style of education, it is not surprising that young people find many of the traditional means and ends of our society and culture – democracy, say, or arithmetic – hard to grasp and harder to get interested in. "Our children are not worse or better than we are," Fadiman wrote. "They are different. . . . For the first time in history, the child is required to be a citizen of two cultures: the traditional and the alternative way of life. Is it any wonder such a division of loyalties should result in the chaos we observe?" Fadiman believes this is a generation of schizophrenics.

CITIES

The move to the cities after the Second World War was rapid: a swift migration from farm to town, from small town to big city, a general shift up the urban scale. With urbanization came suburbanization and, in time, exurbanization, a movement to semi-rural places slightly outside the metropolitan areas, where suburban rather than rural standards of living were then established.

The appeal of the cities is well understood. Cities offer choice: choice of jobs, choice of things to do with spare time and money. Perhaps not so familiar is the appeal of anonymity. There is nowhere so public as a village of a few hundred people, where everyone knows who is doing what, with whom, and where, and even when. There is nowhere so private as a big city.

Farming communities and small towns say, in effect, "This is done; that is not done." They set standards and guard them jealously. Cities have no standards because they can generate no consensus, and they resist the kind of moral policing that goes on in small towns. Country people are angry when movie censorship is lax, city people are angry when it is exercised at all. In really big cities nothing is taboo, nothing unthinkable. Not just one rebel but a sizable group of people is devoted to being, or doing, or thinking anything that is imaginable and plenty that is not. In cities it is impossible to say, as some small towns say, "We don't approve of lesbians," for instance, or "We don't approve of sniffing cocaine," or even "We don't approve of idleness." Not only would it be demonstrably untrue, but there is no central group of citizens who can agree on what they like and dislike, and stop those who want to try something different.

The other side of this freedom is the absence of community support. City parents find it harder to make their ideas stick because their children can always find at least one family that does just the opposite. City parents cannot rely on neighbours to look after their children, as small-town or country families do. The "block parent" campaign asks city parents to act as if they cared in some general way how all children behave and how safe they are. It has not been easy to get city parents to make that sort of commitment.

Both unprecedented freedom and lack of community support had their impact on the upbringing and forming of the Big Generation, the first urban generation in Canada. Those conditions were what they grew up with, and what they accepted as normal, as the way the world works.

MEDICINE

The terrific drop in infant mortality and child deaths after the Second World War was the result of a research effort so successful that it is no longer noticed as the miracle it undoubtedly was. As Herman Kahn and Jane Newitt of the Hudson Institute noted in 1975, some of the effects of medical research in this century have been revolutionary:

> A forty-year period saw the near elimination of the major child-killing and child-maiming diseases in this country. Comparing 1930 to 1968, reported cases of diphtheria per 100,000 population dropped from 54.1 to 0.1; of smallpox, from 39.7 to 0.0; of whooping cough, from 135.6 to 2.1; of polio, from 7.7 to 0.02.

As a result, the amount of physical suffering post-war children have experienced is very small. Like the absence of hunger, cold, damp, and other physical miseries familiar to all those who went before them, the absence of pain is hardly noticed by the Big Generation. Life without pain is normal. They reach for pain killers at the least hint of discomfort, as if pain were an alien experience that would be dangerous if allowed even the smallest foothold; but, in fact, there is little pain to give them even small twinges.

The effect of these eight major influences on the development of the Big Generation cannot be exaggerated. Because of the conditions of affluence in which most of them grew up and their unconscious acceptance of the technological fix, their expectations of what life will bring them in the way of income, jobs, and satisfaction are much larger and wholly different from those of any previous generation. Those expectations are also almost certainly going to be frustrated, perhaps badly frustrated.

Television, the alternate culture of the media, affluence, and urbanization have loosed them from the long tradition of societal and communal involvement. In its place they have a greater awareness of human suffering and, paradoxically or not, a more strongly developed self-interest and concern for personal gratification. The influence of their parents and family life, especially in the context of a collapsing respect for formal authority, has been to increase their own self-esteem and sense of worth.

The conditions in the years of their childhood combined to make them almost a new species. They have acquired expectations that the future will almost certainly not be able to gratify, attributes that will inevitably cause them to build a society different from anything we have known, new values and beliefs that are tantamount to a whole new religion or philosophy.

One thing more – probably the single most important influence of all – helped to make the Big Generation what it has become: what happened to them when they went to school.

CHAPTER 4

SCHOOL DAYS

*"We firmly believe education is a wise
investment, ensuring the future
of our children and creating
a more enlightened nation."*

The Big Generation is famous, so far, only for going to school.

It is famous because its passage caused the schools to recruit the worst-trained teachers in history, to overbuild ruinously, to abandon most of their basic principles and replace them with a set of untried schemes. Now, having almost finished with school, the seven million of the Big Generation are moving on to other pursuits, leaving behind them an educational system in disorder, its teachers badly demoralized, its budgets under bitter attack, its buildings impossible white elephants, its philosophy in rags and tatters.

At the heart of the disaster, however, there lies an amazing achievement.

Between the two world wars, most children did not go to high school. Right after the First World War only about a quarter of all the youngsters of high-school age were actually enrolled in high school; the proportion had risen to little more than a third by the end of the Second World War.

Post-war educators, pushed by parents and politicians, set about raising the percentage of teenagers in high school. Their objective was one hundred per cent. In some provinces, those who would have been in high school anyway, because they were going on to college or university, went into five-year courses ending in Grade XIII. Those who were to be drawn into the high schools for the first time, who would go out to work or into vocational training after school, would take a four-year course ending in Grade XII.

It was a noble idea; and if it had been introduced in the 1920s or 1940s or 1950s, or delayed until the 1980s, it would have attracted little criticism. As it was, the combination of the higher rate of participation among teenagers and the great numbers of the Big Generation moving up through the schools was nearly disastrous. The baby-boom children caused primary school enrolment to double in twenty years; but when they reached high school, and high school was rejigged to enfold not a third or a half of the age group but one hundred per cent of them, they doubled the numbers in high school within ten years, doubled them again in the next ten years, and finally pushed total enrolment in the mid-1970s to five times what it had been a quarter century earlier. By 1976 some ninety-five per cent of the age group were enrolled in high school, though drop-outs had begun to reduce the percentage attending.

Over a quarter of a century, the average schooling increased by half, from eight to twelve years. The fact that the Big Generation were the first recipients of this new high level of education guaranteed it would have the maximum impact when they reached adult life: instead of four or five million people with an average of eight years at school there would be seven million people with an average of twelve years' schooling. Numerically it meant a huge increase in man-years of education presented to the society. But the qualitative difference was larger still, and its basis was in the difference between primary school and high school.

Primary school education is principally concerned with instructing children in what directly concerns the society they belong to. Public school teaches children how to count, how to make change, how to measure and weigh, how to read well enough to understand directions, how to speak clearly enough to ask for instructions. Public school imparts social values: this is what we believe in, this is how we behave, these words and deeds are forbidden, these are the attributes we share. Ever since the days of the little red schoolhouse, public school has taught co-operation, collaboration, and sharing: it has favoured activities involving the whole class.

The legacy of public school is the spirit that is still found in many farming and fishing communities – broad agreement about what is right and wrong, a strong feeling for tradition, a set of widely accepted moral and social values, the desire to share and work with others in the community, and in many cases a readiness to accept good luck or disaster, whatever comes, as fate or God's will.

Traditionally, secondary school has had entirely different goals. Developing independence and self-reliance have been high among them. Students are encouraged to think for themselves, to work alone, to create, to be different. They are taught more about ideas than about facts, with emphasis on the abstract rather than the concrete. It is the fond hope of every teacher that by the end of high school his students will be self-motivating, independent-minded, and creative.

The legacy of high school is the spirit that is found in universities, or among people in fairly demanding white-collar jobs – endless discussion and argument about possible courses of action, a strong desire to challenge accepted ideas, varied personal values and few common social or moral values, the desire to excel and get ahead, a conviction that most of the world's problems can be pinned on someone – often on large institutions.

Before the Big Generation is through with education, between a third and a half of them will also have some post-secondary education: anything from a few extension course credits to a potful of degrees. Only about one in twenty of their parents was ever enrolled full-time in university; at the 1976 census, no more than eight per cent of people over fifty had any post-secondary education, and it is not much of an exaggeration to say that that eight per cent were running the country.

The Big Generation will eventually average more than twelve years of education; but even with just twelve years, the generation is as different from all previous generations as French-speakers are from English-speakers, as young people are from old, as farmers are from city dwellers. This is not just a figure of speech; it is evidenced by innumerable polls and surveys in which people were differentiated by education, religion, sex, age, language, and so on. Over and again education has proved to be the most distinguishing of all characteristics. Opinions on almost any subject vary more among people with different education than among people who differ in any other way.

In a survey on allowing abortion on demand, for instance, only twenty-three per cent of people with public-school education favoured it, but more than fifty per cent with post-secondary education approved. In another poll, asking whether American influence in Canada was too great, thirty-four per cent of those with public-school education answered that it was, while sixty-seven per cent who had post-secondary education thought so. And in a third survey, on whether marijuana should be legalized, only eight per cent of those with public schooling approved, while thirty-six per cent with post-secondary education did. These are essentially the differences between the Big Generation and its predecessors.

Before the Big Generation, Canada was at heart a grade-school country. The Big Generation is essentially a high-school generation. As sociologist Jeanne Binstock says, "The change is about equivalent to the introduction of reading and schools at the beginning of the industrial revolution."

It is impossible to exaggerate the importance of that achievement of putting the Big Generation through high school. At the same time, from the point of view of the educators, the passage of the Big Generation was like being hit by a tidal wave. It is worth taking a close look at what happened, because it was the first public contact between the Big Generation and the world, and it shows very clearly what an enormously disruptive force the generation contains, a force that is only now beginning to be felt in other arenas.

Before the baby boom, the development of education – at least in the twentieth century – had been so slow and the institutions of education so stable that they could be called stagnant. Every September from the end of the First World War to the end of the Second World War, about a quarter of a million youngsters showed up at Canada's public schools to start Grade I. The same buildings and playgrounds sufficed to house them, year after year. They needed no more teachers. Budgets altered little. The school to which parents took their six-year-olds in the first half of the 1940s looked astonishingly like the school of 1918. Often, it was, in fact, the school of 1918, to which they themselves had gone for the first time, holding the hands of their parents. Schools in those days were the epitome of stability; eternal institutions, unchanging and unchangeable. Considering what had happened to banks and big businesses and governments during the Depression, the constancy of the schoolhouse was astounding.

The year the war ended was also, as it turned out, the year the peace of the schools ended. Practically every year for the next twenty, the number of children turning up to register for Grade I each September was higher than it had been the year before. By 1965, Grade I classes were at least twice the size they had been in 1945.

Inexorably, the schools filled out, grade by grade. In the whole school system, from kindergarten through Grade XIII, enrolment rose from two and a half million in 1950 to an extraordinary six million at the peak in 1970.

The school explosion triggered an educational revolution. The continuous increase in school enrolment, coinciding with the post-war economic boom, meant that educators found themselves in charge of a growing portion of the gross national product. The eyes of the country were on them as never before. In 1970, a third of the whole Canadian population was in school, either teaching or being taught. Without doubt it was the country's principal occupation. On the grounds of sheer numbers of bodies and dollars, educators may be excused for having thought it was also the most important.

The pressure to expand the school system arose from several sources, although one predominated–the "human capital" theory, the idea that public investment in education would bring economic benefits to society as well as to the individuals who got more education. The Economic Council of Canada stressed this point repeatedly in its annual reviews. "Education for years to come has to be the Number One priority in government spending," a provincial government minister of education said at the height of the spending. It became common to refer to education in terms formerly reserved for business. It was believed that the increasingly technical demands of sophisticated post-war industry would require many more highly educated graduates, and it was in the schools that the technologizing of Canada had to begin.

As one newspaper put it: "Every dollar spent on education is an investment in the future." That was just what we kept calling it in the 1950s and 1960s. "The investment in education will continue to increase," the Ontario education minister declared in 1968. "The community colleges will show a quick return," an education official said.

Slightly extending the metaphor, parents told their children, "Education pays." The generation that had gone through the Depression had not failed to notice that educated people survived best. "Stay in school, you'll get a great job, you won't have to worry about your life, everything will fall into place," the parents said.

Two other elements helped to propel the expansion. One was

the fact that the flourishing economy was giving people more expansive ideas, among them the notion that education was a luxury they could increasingly afford. In economists' terms, the demand for a more highly trained work force made education an investment good; the demand of wealthy taxpayers for more of this splendid public service for their children made it a consumption good. On both sides of the ledger, education looked like a good thing, and that soon translated into enormous sums of money. In 1950, as the expansion began, education took a mere 2.5 per cent of the gross national product. By 1970 it had risen to nine per cent. Because of economic growth and inflation, the increase in dollars was even more spectacular – from half a billion dollars to roughly eight billion dollars.

The final influence was social or political rather than economic. It was the feeling, driven home by Allied war leaders, by the new United Nations charter, and by popular demand, that education was a civil right. Indeed, was it not one of the four freedoms?

In this heady atmosphere, John Dewey's philosophy of progressive education found sudden prominence. Dewey (1859-1952) was being taught in the colleges of education as early as the 1920s, but it took the unique post-war conditions to make his ideas broadly acceptable. Dewey argued that the schools were failing in their task because classrooms were dominated by teachers who had become skilled in presenting information. That left the children with only the passive choice of absorbing the information presented to them, or not. For Dewey, the first business of the school was to show children how to co-operate and help one another. Teachers might turn red in the face trying to teach, but children would learn nothing that they did not actively take up and use. Dewey held that the instincts and impulses of children, which they expressed in their attitudes and their activities, were the basic medium of education. Schools should help children to accumulate and assimilate experience, for this was how they would develop into balanced and aware adults.

Time subtly changed the emphasis of Dewey's ideas, or at least the way they were interpreted by his followers. Teachers who favoured progressive education discouraged anything like competition among classmates; instead they wanted them to work mainly on collaborative projects. They favoured group activity over individual achievement, average test scores over high marks.

They deplored anything that suggested elitism, a reflection of the egalitarianism that was gaining ground everywhere in the world outside the school. There would be no reward for excellence and not much for effort, none if that effort was intended to give the student personal advantage.

Thanks to the conservatism of Canadian institutions, thousands of teachers who learned about Dewey's revolutionary ideas went through their careers without ever putting them into practice – until the 1950s. Then these ideas began to work their way into the schools of Canada. The route was through chaos.

In the 1950s and even more in the 1960s, the schools were under tremendous pressure to increase the space available for pupils. No sooner had the board of education built a school in a developing suburb than they were out shopping for "portables," the ten-thousand-dollar class-sized prefabricated movable huts that made most school yards look like Second World War army transit camps. By the mid-1960s, the pressure on the grade schools was at its peak, and the high schools were feeling more strain than ever. A survey in Toronto found half the classrooms were overcrowded, with thirty or more pupils; some had more than fifty pupils. Faced with a yardful of wooden cabins, they decided on a revolutionary answer, the flexible or wide-open school.

Afloat on an ocean of money, educators were seized with a spirit of joyous experimentation. Administrators told architects that in the next school they designed they wanted walls that could be moved or, better still, no walls. Without walls, the noise of one class learning to sing might be expected to disrupt another learning to use the microscope, so it was necessary to make the ceilings more sound-absorbent and to cover every inch of floor with carpeting. The fact that the educators had no idea how children would react to camping on broadloom, almost out of sight of walls, did not stop them.

A supporting philosophy of team teaching, multiple group teaching, and multi-class teaching sprang up, and gained its devotees, though not without a struggle. A major problem in making the open-school system work was in keeping track of the children. It was possible for a child to fade away somewhere for days on end without a teacher noticing.

But the enthusiasts, most of whom were administrators, principals, superintendents, and not classroom teachers, kept the experiment going for years. One school put no fewer than ten teachers together in a teaching team and had to resort to surprising measures to guide them. Children were tagged with signs that served to tell a teacher what they should be doing, or at any rate what some other teacher thought they should be doing. This child is wearing a tag with a yellow dot, which means he has not started reading but ought to be ready for it. "So if a child with a yellow tag wanders in, I know he has either been sent here or is interested and has come by himself. I grab him and give him a beginning reader," a teacher explained cheerfully. If the child returned for more, there was a reading program he could be set to follow; if he didn't return, the theory said not to worry, it just meant he wasn't ready to start reading. The spirit of John Dewey hovered overhead.

At another school, built in the mid-1960s after births had peaked, the administrators perceived that what was passing through the school system was not a stream of ever-increasing width but a flash flood. They took the idea of the four-grade tumult, expanded it, and came up with the concept of the fourteen-grade uproar. A gigantic campus would enclose every stage of education from kindergarten to Grade XIII: in this way they would have a chance of adapting the available space as the Big Generation passed through, first letting the elementary school grades have the main part of the space, then switching the emphasis to the secondary school as the bulge of children grew older and moved up the school. It would have to be large – there were provisions for an eventual pupil population of 3,500 – but the cafeteria, auditorium, and library would be equally available to pupils from all grades, and with any luck the whole thing would work just as efficiently when the largest grade was XIII as when it was I.

At least, that is how the inspiration of that particular development can be interpreted now. At the time it came out clothed in a quite different philosophy. "We have a bad old chain in education," the chairman of the school board said. "Universities blame high schools for turning out students unprepared for college life, the high schools blame the elementary schools for deficiencies in students, and the elementary schools blame the parents." The campus concept should increase understanding between the different educational levels, he said, and do away with the chain of blame. "We're looking forward to co-operation in curriculum development, for instance."

No one at the time seems to have questioned the pathetically shallow aim of generating understanding between two levels of education by making them share one cafeteria. No one asked why thousands of children had to be assembled on one field so that someone else, a few teachers presumably, could work out ways of dovetailing two abutting curriculums, which in any case were largely established by the provincial ministry of education. No one pointed out how horrifyingly grandiose the proposed educational complex was going to be, or how crazily out of scale it was with its modest objective. But at least no one proposed going all the way and building it on the grounds of the nearest university.

Another terrifying problem tormented the school trustees and administrators. Teachers! Where on earth were they going to get enough teachers for the great horde of the Big Generation? Even to recruit babysitters for six or seven million youngsters would have been problem enough, but teachers were supposed to be more than warders. So a great manhunt began: first for elementary-school teachers, then for secondary-school teachers; first for qualified people, then for acceptable people, finally in desperation for warm bodies that could be stood up in front of a class.

The Depression had slowed everything down, the economy, the growth of population, and anything else that might have stimulated growth in the schools. Then the war took many of the male teachers away and made it hard to replace them. As a result, the teacher population grew very slowly over the decades of the 1930s and 1940s. The teachers aged visibly. By 1945, half the male teachers in Canadian schools had been teaching for thirteen years or more, and in some places – Toronto, for instance – half had at least twenty-one years' teaching behind them. After the war, the soldiers and munitions workers were changed back into teachers, some of the twenty-year lag was caught up, and the average age and years of teaching dropped back toward more normal levels. Other things being equal, the old growth rate should then have resumed.

As it was, the Big Generation went to school. From 1950 to 1970, the number of teachers in primary and secondary schools grew at an unprecedented pace. Ten to twenty thousand new teachers were taken on every year. The experienced teachers were swamped by novices. By 1965, half the male teachers across the country had a maximum of six years' teaching experience. In places where the demand for teachers and the turnover had been highest, experience was even shorter. In Ontario in 1966, two-thirds of the secondary-school teachers had taught four years or less; in Metropolitan Toronto, half the secondary-school teachers had taught no more than two years. Throughout the 1960s, the only period in which such a thing was ever recorded, women teachers were usually more experienced than their male colleagues.

These were remarkable and disruptive changes. Yet for years they inspired no attempt by departments or boards of education to probe the future. They were treated as if they were unpredictable acts of nature. Although the rising birth record was open knowledge, its significance for the schools seems to have been largely ignored. No one foresaw that enrolment would rise; no one thought about starting the necessary number of new teachers on their courses of training. A veteran teacher at the Ontario College of Education, Professor Charles Phillips, recorded what must have been a nearly universal experience from coast to coast:

> Because of failure to anticipate an acute shortage of secondary-school teachers in the early fifties, the Ontario Department of Education ... had been forced in 1955 to introduce an alternative method of securing a High School Assistant's Certificate by attendance at summer sessions – a desperate measure because the teacher's preparation was inevitably inferior.

Until then, people who wanted to teach high school had to spend a year at the college after they graduated from university. The summer sessions allowed them to cram half the course into eight weeks the summer after they graduated, start teaching on probation that fall, go back to the college for seven weeks the following summer, and come out of it with a teaching certificate. Before 1955, the college had a few hundred students each year seeking their certificates. The summer sessions attracted thousands.

By 1962, more than half the secondary-school teachers in Ontario had been trained in summer sessions. "To many of us,"

Professor Phillips wrote in his history of the Ontario College of Education, "it appears that administrators are unable to take action in anticipation of the future or to foresee the consequences of the belated and short-sighted remedies they devise in emergencies."

The training for public-school teachers was just as skimpy. A young freelance writer called Barbara Frum described what was happening at Toronto Teachers College in 1968.

> High-school guidance teachers counselling students without the marks or drive to succeed at university often advise them to enter teachers' colleges. And with the continuing shortage of teachers, the colleges have been obliged to accept them. The staff has 24 weeks to transform Grade 13 graduates, more than half of whom got less than 65 percent in their final high-school year, into competent teachers able to teach every grade from one to eight, every subject: math, English, science, music, art, physical and health education, history and geography.

Throughout the 1960s, the hardest-pressed provinces were recruiting teachers from provinces that were not suffering so badly. But after a while every province was feeling the pinch, and the recruiters went overseas. In 1967, school boards in New Brunswick, Ontario, Quebec, and Saskatchewan sent recruiting teams all over Britain. The next year teams were combing France, Australia, and New Zealand as well.

Teachers had been slow to take advantage of their scarceness, but at about the time the school boards started recruiting abroad, teachers began to campaign in earnest for higher pay. They learned how to get the ear of the press, and the newspapers were full of articles showing that teachers earned less than the school janitor for an hour's work or, reflecting the "investment" idiom, comparing teachers' wages with the going rates in industry: "The average tradesman would have to drop around $1,000 to take a teaching job in one of the technical schools." For the first time there was talk of strikes. The teachers' federations were still reluctant to call for mass walk-outs, but many teachers were prepared to submit their individual resignations in concert. The 1967 strike of thousands of teachers against the Montreal Catholic School Commission was front-page news across the country.

As a result of the chronic shortage of able and experienced teachers, young and cheerfully ignorant teachers quickly came to form a majority in the profession. Knowledgeable teachers who could have advised caution over the eruption of educational experiments became a minority, either cowed and sullen or angry and derided. At the same time, the optimism and high economic morale of the post-war years carried over into the schools, colouring the tremendous expansion of budgets and physical plant.

The arrival of the Big Generation was a bit like an invasion; not exactly an enemy invasion, but not the welcome arrival of a few friends and relatives either. It was a time that demanded heroic initiatives, bold and innovative answers, gallantry and self-sacrifice on the field.

In short, on every front the educators' defences against the Big Generation were in chaos. And yet all the signs seemed to point the same way. The walls had to come down because the classes were too big. Discipline, stuffy classical studies, and rote learning were perceived as oppressive evils just when the schools were being taken over by young teachers who could not meet the strict demands of the classical classroom. It takes experience and persistence to grade children and their work consistently and fairly. Grades were abandoned. It takes rigour and application to operate a structured curriculum, to hold a class of children of varying capacities to the outline of a pre-planned program of learning. Curriculums went.

People who are unable or unwilling to exert discipline have a strong motive for denouncing it and dispensing with it. People who lack the experience to retain a large, complicated program of education in their minds, to integrate the innumerable strands of human knowledge into a whole piece of cloth over months and years of teaching, are much more likely to support notions of "freedom," "flexibility," and the primacy of the student's impulses.

It was not a conspiracy to destroy a noble edifice, nor was it a campaign to build a new temple of education; most of what happened in the 1950s and 1960s was the desperate response of a group of administrators whose teachers were not equipped for the rearguard action they had been conscripted to fight and who snatched whatever tactics they could from the pathetic weeks of instruction they had been given before they dashed into the campaign.

A few of the more experienced hands resisted the wholesale abandonment of classical principles of education and suggested that it might not be necessary to change everything, all at once, in order to change some things. Hilda Neatby, a professor at the University of Saskatchewan, wrote in 1953 that instead of opening all levels of education to anyone who wanted in, the schools should maintain quite strict standards, so that only those able to learn would be in class. In the upper grades of high school only the brightest five or ten per cent of the population might be able to stay. In the circumstances of a general enthusiasm for progressive education, it was surprising that her book, *So Little for the Mind*, achieved the popularity and press coverage that it did. But Professor Neatby was not only addressing a teacher corps that was on the eve of a massive rout and would not heed her, she was shouting into a wind that was blowing through the whole society; and some of the politest epithets that came her way were "elitist" and "reactionary."

From one end of Canada to the other, the schools introduced such novelties as the "continuous progress method," under which each child proceeds at his own pace, independent of his peers. The new math, new physics, and other innovations placed more emphasis on grasping the underlying principles of the subject than on gaining a practical skill. In some schools, even more remarkable experiments were made: the pupils were given control of the curriculum and could decide what they wanted to study, making as much or as little use of the teachers (or "resource persons," as they were renamed) as they felt inclined; the pupils in some schools could even decide when they wanted to attend, or indeed if they wanted to.

A 1968 newspaper account of a visit to the New School in Vancouver opened like this:

> "What's this?" asked the stranger, "a school with no classrooms, no timetable, no curriculum, no exams, no report cards?"
>
> "That's right."
>
> "I suppose the next thing you'll tell me it doesn't have teachers, either," smirked the stranger.
>
> "How did you guess," beamed the host.

68

The New School was an experimental elementary school for children aged five and up.

In many schools, essays were no longer marked, exams were not set, grades were not allotted; almost everywhere the university entrance exam was dropped. In a few places discipline became the equal responsibility of everyone in the school–pupils, teachers, support staff. One person, one vote. Almost everywhere the strap was abandoned. Whatever seemed stiff, formal, or even definite was questioned, and whatever seemed soft, flexible, and imaginative was welcomed.

What capped the educational revolution was the Hall-Dennis Report on education in Ontario, though it cannot be credited with initiating progressive education or even of supporting its early struggles. *Living and Learning* was the title of the report published in 1968 by a committee headed by Mr. Justice Hall and Lloyd Dennis. In the words of a contemporary educator, Professor J.M. Paton of the University of Toronto, *Living and Learning* was "a popular exposition of progressivism" rather than a "careful analysis of complex problems in teaching and learning." Hall-Dennis urged all the new methods on Ontario schools: continuous progress, no curriculum, no direction by teachers, no exams or grades. Their report declared, with thrilling confidence, "The needs of the child are simply stated. Each and every one has the right to learn, to play, to laugh, to dream, to dissent, to reach upward, and to be himself.... A child who is learning cannot fail." It became famous for its comment, "Our children ... must be made to feel that the world is waiting for their sunrise."

The 1960s ended with politicians, administrators, and teachers claiming all the world as their parish, like John Wesley; their ambitions boundless, their confidence seemingly unshakable. "There is a growing acceptance that, perhaps through education in its broad sense, we can do more to unify this country than in any other endeavour," a provincial minister of education said. (As it happened, he was soon to become the premier of his province: it was William Davis, speaking in 1968.) Education, they felt, was the best and in many cases the only way to solve the problems of people and nations struggling with a world grown complicated. In 1967, journalist Harry Bruce tried to sum up what it was educators believed education would do for its recipients. He was writing specifically about university education, but the idea went right on up from kindergarten with little change:

> The creed, vastly oversimplified, says that university education offers entry into tomorrow's aristocracy of training and intelligence; university education promises national survival, healthy profits, general well-being, food for the hungry, wisdom for the politically rash, solace for the uncertain, judgement, meaning. The Answer.

The universities and colleges were under firmer and more conservative control. Compared with the thousands of schools and school boards, there were few universities, and they were large and used to numbers. They had handled the returning war veterans with aplomb, finding temporary accommodation and classroom space, absorbing the maturer ex-soldiers into classes of young high-school graduates with skill. In general the universities were run at a more sophisticated and expert level than the schools and boards.

All the arguments in favour of expanding the schools fit the universities. In addition, their administrators had the advantage of being able to track the approach of the Big Generation over a distance of nearly twenty years, compared with only six for the grade school administrators. The 1957 Soviet success in launching the first earth satellite, Sputnik, added to the conviction that the new world of technology demanded more and better education, more workers with higher education, more research, more Ph.Ds. "[The roots of] the bubbling revolution that has recently gripped university education across the country," Harry Bruce wrote in the mid-1960s, "lie in the recognition by government and industry that knowledge is power, knowledge is a resource that ultimately *pays off* in production and dollars, and, as the Bible says, knowledge increaseth strength."

It was considered obvious that education paid: newspaper and magazine articles routinely offered calculations of the value of a degree, either in the difference between university graduates' and high school graduates' starting salaries or in the difference in potential lifetime earnings for graduates and non-graduates. The rush of returning veterans into college was all that was needed to prove higher education was a prize for winning the war, a hard-won right. And this level of education above all others represented one of the most desirable consumption goods in the post-war boom.

So the universities could see the fuse of their own explosion burning, burning, nearer and nearer; and if they were in any doubt the provincial governments told them what to do. The presidents of Ontario's universities were summoned in 1961 and asked what they expected enrolment to be in 1971. The figure they gave, they were then told, was at least forty per cent too low by government reckoning; they must do everything possible to speed preparations for a much larger enrolment. What all the provinces foresaw was a continuing increase in the enrolment rate – that is, in the percentage of people of university age who would actually enrol in university. It was the same thing that was then happening so spectacularly in the high schools applied to the much larger coming generation of young people.

Both prospects seemed certain enough. The full-time undergraduate enrolment rate, which had stood at four per cent of the people aged eighteen to twenty-one throughout the whole period between the wars, had risen to seven per cent in 1952, after the veterans had left the universities; by 1961 it hit twelve per cent. There was no doubt the Big Generation was coming; a forecast published by the Economic Council of Canada a few years later assumed, on the basis of postwar trends, that by 1975 the combined undergraduate and graduate enrolment rate (percentage of people aged eighteen to twenty-four) would be twenty-one per cent. This would mean a total of 540,000 students would be at university. In 1951, the total was 64,000.

Old universities swelled and new ones were started all over the country. At the end of the Second World War there were thirty universities in Canada, seventeen of them founded in a forty-year burst between 1838 and 1878. As the Big Generation's advancing shadow fell on the ivory tower, twelve more universities were established in a tremendous seven-year splurge between 1959 and 1966. It was certainly the most intense period of growth the university world had ever experienced or likely ever will again.

If it was hard to find the money and construction crews to put up enough buildings for this expansion, it was even harder to find the professors. They had to be people with graduate degrees, which

71

meant a minimum of six, and more likely eight, years at university before they were ready to become university teachers themselves. But the population that the new and growing universities could draw on in the 1960s consisted of people born in the middle of the Depression – the least numerous cohort of all.

In 1966, the federal Department of Labour reported that only about half the new faculty members taken on by Canadian universities came from Canada. Dr. John Saywell, dean of arts and sciences at York University, one of the dozen baby-boom universities, wrote in his annual report:

> In a sellers' market, and with the affluence of many universities (especially in the United States), it proved very difficult to move people with established reputations and almost impossible to persuade distinguished scholars to assume administrative responsibilities.

That year York's arts and sciences faculty sought eight full professors and could hire only two, tried to find ten associate professors and recruited only six, looked for four department chairmen and found none, and did not even try to get chairmen for two other departments. Half the university professors hired in the 1960s came from countries that either anticipated no imminent burst of baby-boom freshmen or had not suffered low birth rates in the 1930s. As another result, by the end of the 1960s, six out of every ten full-time university teachers was under forty – another record, the youngest and no doubt friskiest set of professors Canada ever had.

In the same years a whole new level of post-secondary education was added, the community colleges which sprang up from coast to coast. Called by a variety of names – CAAT in Ontario, CEGEP in Quebec, public colleges in Alberta, regional colleges in British Columbia – they offered training for semi-professional careers such as nursing and computer programming, with diplomas and certificates rather than degrees. They were slotted between the professional education in law, medicine, engineering, and the like at universities and the technical and trades training available in apprenticeship programs and institutes of various kinds. By the mid-1970s, there were nearly two hundred community colleges in Canada with a full-time enrolment of over half a million.

The first wartime and post-war children to go through the lavishly expanded post-secondary education system, those born between 1940 and 1947 or so, were one of history's happiest cohorts. They were treated like the prototype of the Big Generation without suffering the peer pressures its numbers exerted. They were watched with the greatest interest, almost pampered. Far from worrying about job prospects when their education was over, they were courted by corporate recruiters sent to woo them before they graduated. In many minds they had the responsibility for pulling Canada into the modern world. Not surprisingly, they were arrogant, sometimes unruly, occasionally ridiculous, as when they asserted that not only should tuition be free but they should be paid a hundred dollars a week to go to university. Their degrees conferred huge advantages on them: their choice of jobs, markedly higher starting salaries, the excitement of working in an environment that wanted as much as they could give and was grateful to get it.

Including the ex-servicemen, the first twenty years after the war saw half a million degrees granted; that was the majority of all the degrees then held by the whole population. The process of dragging sleepy, rural, ignorant Canada into the twentieth century was well under way, and education was the key to making it succeed, or so people had felt for two post-war decades.

Yet the mid 1960s were the last years anyone could be quite so naively hopeful about the results of education. The surging growth of primary- and secondary-school teachers suddenly petered out–literally, from 5 per cent growth in 1968 and 1969 to one per cent in 1970 and none thereafter.

From 1970 on, there was much more cynicism, much less of that joyous spirit of reform that had run through the educational apparatus. By 1970, virtually all the Big Generation had started school, and enrolment was at its all-time high. The only way to go was down. After years of frantic increase, the trick everyone knew–expansion–had become irrelevant, useless, misleading. As a school board planner nervously pointed out, "The whole system is geared to growth; there is no procedure for decline.

Everett Reimer, an American reformer, observed that education had been transformed from the Answer to a deep problem, organizationally, economically, and socially. It had set out to help people and had become a self-perpetuating empire. "No country in the world can afford the education its people want in the form of schools," he wrote in *School is Dead*.

> There are still people who believe that we could finance the education we need by means of schooling, if only we were willing to give it priority, but this belief ignores the dynamics of schooling. No sooner is universal high school attendance approached than the competition shifts to colleges, at higher costs. There is already agitation for degrees above the Ph.D. on the grounds that the doctorate has become common and degraded. There can be no end to schooling in a world that puts no limits on consumption—where degrees determine people's position at the trough.

In 1970, Sybil Shack, a past president of the Canadian Teachers' Federation, identified "a growing malaise among teachers, a discontent and unhappiness which more and more often was reaching the point of mental ill-health." Education was in upheaval, criticised equally at the family dinner table and on the television screen. The kind of opposition that once occasionally got a teacher fired from a rural one-room school was being maliciously directed against a whole profession on a whole continent, she said:

> We have tried to remake ourselves according to the pattern of the latest psychologists, sociologists, philosophers, and politicians. Since these characters are as uncertain of their ground as we are, we have often found ourselves staggering through swamp land, sinking in quicksand, or dying of thirst in the vast unexplored reaches of the human psyche.

Writing at the peak of the Big Generation's passage through school, Dr. Shack observed:

> Education has truly become everybody's business. For a generation it was looked to as the panacea for all ills. With education would come more and better jobs, the disappearance of discrimination and war.... But the magic formula didn't work. The ills of the world continued. In anger and disappointment the society which had looked to education for the solution is now ready to blame education for the failure.

The disillusionment was widespread. As often happens, when

the mood started to shift, it went in a rush. After 1970 it became hard to find anyone who had a good word to say about the schools or the teachers. Or even about the products of all those billions of dollars and millions of man-years of effort, the students. For the education of the 1950s, 1960s, and 1970s is now widely held to have produced poorly educated young people, who lack either the skills or the motivation to do anything useful for the community that supported the education empire so long and at such expense. (How the schools' failure can possibly be the students' fault is another matter; but whatever the reasons, the public is clearly more antipathetic to recent school graduates than it ever was in the past. When did you last hear young people described as "our hope for the future"?)

How have the schools failed?

A sociologist, Professor John Alan Lee, bitterly detailed how the schools had failed their pupils in an article published in 1978:

> What the [Ontario] Ministry of Education created over the ... years was a failsafe system of education.... The most important lesson taught in Ontario high schools in the past decade was probably never the explicit topic of a single class or assembly. But it was the lesson students learned best: "School is easy and it's almost impossible to fail here. Therefore life should be easy, and failure there equally unlikely. Be sure to have my sunrise ready when I graduate!"

The universities were among the first to notice the deterioration in standards. High-school students once had to take a provincial examination to get into university, but that was before 1967. Since then, each university has had to pick freshmen students as best it could. "We have students coming in who can't write a sentence," Dean Arthur Kruger of the University of Toronto said in 1979, "and we have the highest standards in the province. All the universities I know of have remedial programs."

Basic language and mathematical skills are acquired in high school only by students who seek them. They are no longer compulsory, and of course students are no longer tested at school to see if they have acquired them, though the University of Toronto has now recommended that the province restore the Grade XIII exams.

Politicians also began to react. Among the clearest responses was that of the Quebec government, which in 1977 proposed a broad return to basics in the province's secondary schools. Among the ideas put forward were a longer school year (to compensate for teachers' strikes and professional days, a shorter school day, and other time losses); more detailed provincial curriculums, so that the significance of having taken a particular course would be clearer; a compulsory program of courses with no options in the first three years; and the restoration of homework and exams.

By the late 1970s the government of British Columbia was also almost openly attacking the progressive educators in the public school system. The government helped to finance private schools, thus offering parents an alternative and taxpayers the prospect of some relief; they would not agree to reduce the pupil-teacher ratio, a leading objective of the British Columbia Teachers' Federation; they sponsored their own back-to-basics campaign that emphasized reading, writing, and arithmetic.

Everywhere the drop-out problem got worse, and, ironically, the main cause was the effort to make high school accessible to everyone. By 1977, the Toronto Board of Education found that the four-year high-school course designed for those who did not plan to go on to university had gone badly wrong. The course was attracting thirty per cent of high-school students. By the last year of the course, Grade XII, only one-third of them remained. The course had failed to meet the needs of two-thirds of those for whom it was intended.

Members of the Big Generation began to reach age eighteen in 1969. If the Toronto figures are typical for the country as a whole, then something like a hundred thousand youngsters a year have been dropping out of the four-year course; by 1979 a million or more children of the baby boom must have left school in frustration and anger, to be followed by perhaps half a million more in the next few years.

Would they have been better off if no one had tried to induce them to stay in school? A difficult question, since the alternatives were not all that satisfying either. But they were offered the chance to stay at high school. Educators knew, as one said in 1977, that these new high-school pupils were "looking for something quite different from the traditional academic program of the past. . . . It's been necessary to develop new programs for these students, with new standards." Obviously the new programs came nowhere near what the students wanted. Extending high school has turned out to be one of the most critical ways in which education has failed the Big Generation.

The impact of the decline of the schools on the teachers was appalling – is appalling, because it is still going on, and the reverberations are going to be felt for years. Professor Phillips's oracular lament about administrators who cannot "foresee the consequences of the belated and short-sighted remedies they devise in emergencies" is now echoing ominously throughout the profession.

It is obvious that even inside the profession the right hand does not know what the left is doing. Two announcements were made within a few days of each other in May 1978. One was that the Toronto campus of the Ontario Teacher Education College had just graduated 499 elementary-school teachers. The other was that the Metropolitan Toronto school boards had just fired 469 elementary-school teachers.

The figures were even worse than they looked, because graduates of the universities' five-year teacher training courses, designed to turn out secondary-school teachers, were desperate enough to be looking for, and getting, some of the few elementary-school jobs available. And in May 1978, more than half the class of secondary-school teachers who graduated a year earlier had still failed to get any kind of teaching job, primary or secondary.

All over the country, similar lunacy was occurring, not always with the almost viciously close match of the Toronto numbers, but always with devastating effect on new and experienced teachers alike. Teaching, once the chief occupation of university graduates, had become the sector with one of the worst unemployment records, and with by far the highest applicant-to-job ratios: in 1977, it was reported that there were seventy-three applicants for every teaching job on offer at one Manpower office. Dr. R.W.B. Jackson, inquiring into the consequences of declining enrolment for the Ontario Ministry of Education, said the prospects for high-school teachers were particularly poor. "Some directors I talked to . . . could see no new hirings for ten years. It's just like the 1930s."

The training for secondary-school teachers now takes five years almost everywhere, though for elementary teachers it still only takes two. In defence of the educational authorities, it should be said that there are problems in forecasting future school enrolment, the most obvious of which is the difficulty of foreseeing the future drop-out rate in high school. The problem of forecasting high-school enrolment five years ahead is severe. But elementary-school attendance is compulsory, and drop-out rates hardly affect it. Enrolment for a whole province is easy to predict, as most family movement is from one municipality to another in the same province; only four per cent of primary-school pupils changed provinces between 1966 and 1971, and only three per cent immigrated from another country. Not only that, but the forecaster concerned with elementary-school teachers' training has only to look ahead two years.

So what madness allowed the authorities to accept thousands of young people for teacher training when they must have been certain that thousands of teachers with jobs were going to have to be thrown out of work?

The answer is that it was government policy. "The government has a public policy that qualified students should be admitted, that there should be open access," the dean of education at the University of Western Ontario, Bernard Shapiro, replied when asked why the universities were turning out more teachers than could possibly be needed. The provincial policy was one factor, certainly, though it did not bind the universities. Probably stronger, though unstated, was the universities' own struggle to find students. By the mid-1970s enrolment in arts faculties had dropped precipitately. Yet applications for places in the educational faculties stayed high–two, sometimes even three applicants for every place. The universities simply found it hard to turn them down.

Government open-door policy was a more potent factor at the teachers colleges, which prepare primary-school teachers, and it was reinforced by an even higher demand from would-be students. In Hamilton, the Ontario Teacher Education College got five applicants for every place in 1977 and ten for every place in 1978. Enrolment levels were therefore set in the context of a high demand and a public policy that said qualified students should not be turned down. The impossible employment market, which obviously should have overridden all other considerations, didn't. The colleges and their staffs survived, at the expense of trainee teachers.

Although the frustrated graduates presented a pathetic spectacle, the plight of the employed teachers was even more serious. They were older, more bound to the profession, less flexible in where they could look for other work. They dug in, scared to move. Turnover rates, once as high as fifteen per cent a year, dropped to one or two per cent. Teacher federations began to panic about security in the early 1970s, and tenure clauses started to appear in employment contracts; after two years on probation, a teacher would be given tenure, guaranteeing that he could not be fired except for incompetence or misconduct.

By the mid-1970s the teachers' federations were shooting for absolute tenure for senior teachers and conditional tenure for younger teachers that guaranteed them employment at least for the life of the contract. As the demands came at a time when the school boards' budgets were continuing to rise even though enrolment was declining, the taxpayers vehemently resisted the demands. In several cases, teachers won tenure clauses by accepting low salary increases, which is rather like saying, "If I can't eat well, at least I'll eat regularly, and for the rest of my life."

Most of those who lost their jobs suffered silently, but the anguish was plain. "There's a lot of bitterness, a lot of unreality. Some of them have nervous breakdowns. And a lot of them are asking themselves what they're going to do for the rest of their lives." That comment was made by Sherle Perkins-Vasey, a former teacher who ran a course for teachers laid off in Etobicoke, Ontario.

Although the number of teachers may not fall as fast or as far as enrolment, there is no doubt that tens of thousands of teachers will have to go. Among them, because seniority counts, will be a disproportionate number of the youngest and most recently hired, the oldest members of the Big Generation who were lucky enough to get trained and hired as teachers.

The decline in enrolment also produced some tricky problems of what to do with empty classrooms and, in a number of cases, with complete schools. Administrators in many cities set a rule of thumb that when enrolment dropped to a third of capacity, the school should be closed.

The blows fell unevenly: in metropolises the inner city schools lost thousands of pupils while suburban areas continued to grow. Projections for Ottawa, for instance, show a forty-nine-per-cent drop in city enrolment between 1971 and 1986 and a forty-three-

79

per-cent increase in the surrounding county, Carleton; tens of thousands of children are involved in each place. Calgary thought about closing a sixth of the city's 250 schools, including one attended by a mere seventy-eight children, while the suburbs were growing at a record clip and straining the school construction budget. Toronto contemplated the prospect of tearing down a street of houses to build a new separate school while two nearby public schools were on the verge of closing for lack of students.

Answers were not as easy to find as the newspaper headlines sometimes seemed to suggest. Many areas losing children felt deeply threatened by everything that was happening to them – the deterioration of old residential areas, the spread of office buildings – and the school closings were only a part of it. Downtown Calgary residents feared that the lack of schools would push the remaining families out of the area and hasten the final collapse of their once-flourishing residential neighbourhood.

And in country districts denuded of children, the survivors faced the prospect of a school career on the buses, from kindergarten through the end of high school. When they closed the public school at Kiosk, Ontario, local children were sent to a school thirty miles away. They have a hundred thousand miles in a school bus ahead of them before they graduate from Grade VIII.

The Big Generation had led most school boards to build bigger schools rather than many small schools. It was generally the most economical solution at the time, but the economies of the 1950s and 1960s led inevitably to the heartbreaks and chaos of the 1970s and 1980s. If ten 500-student schools had been built in a neighbourhood instead of five 1,000-student schools, it would have been easier to handle the closings.

One nightmare for many administrators was the fear that the trend would reverse again, and then they would have to try to get back their lost and loaned schools or once more face building new ones. Since most schools are in areas zoned only for residential and school use, the most straightforward solution to the death of a school would be to sell the land for housing, which could then in a few years create the need for a school all over again. The problem of unwanted schools, many still unpaid for, is one that will remain to haunt the 1980s.

For different reasons, the universities' dream of building a new Canada also began to evaporate at the end of the 1960s. Disillusionment was the first symptom of the problem. It can be traced in a sequence of comments:

1966: "University campuses are producing a generation of pocket Leonardos, men who teach, advise governments and business corporations, write scholarly volumes, and help to rescue TV from the miasma of moronity." – Claude Bissell, president, University of Toronto.

1967: "[Large universities are] governed and run as manufacturing corporations. . . . The student feels like a piece of raw material being pressed and moulded into a product to fit an economic slot." – Douglas Ward, president of the Canadian Union of Students.

1968: "It's *our* university, only for *us*. Everything should be directed to making teaching and learning a real live swinging thing – to make minds click together faster. But now, we feel we are just being processed, like Kraft cheese." – Lyn Owen, McGill University student.

1971: "When a graduate of 1971 experiences great difficulty in getting a job and is aware of the fact that a graduate of 1967 secured the same sort of job easily, the tendency is not to simply adjust one's expectations downward, however inevitable that process may be, but rather to feel let down, to feel that somehow 'the system has failed.'" – Edward Harvey, Ontario Institute for Studies in Education.

1976: "My students seem so serious these days. It's hard to joke with them, they're so concerned with passing exams and getting a job." – Biology lecturer.

1977: "Right now a BA means nothing. It's just a piece of paper to prove you may have some brains." – Mary Hutson, drop-out from York University.

1978: "High-school students, take heed! Don't go to university to get a job, because it doesn't train you for one. If you think a BA will help you in the market place – FORGET IT!" – Barbara Borenstein, university graduate, letter to a newspaper.

1978: "I've spent several years working thirteen hours a day so I could do something constructive for society. I don't care about the money—I can make $97 a week from the Unemployment Insurance Commission. But it's ridiculous to feel you have a contribution to make and have nowhere to make it. How did it all happen anyway?"—Barry Silver, graduate in parasitology from the University of Manitoba, unemployed.

1979: "I don't think the world owes me a living, but I did the necessary things to get a job and a decent standard of living. Now I'm not getting it and I'm not happy."—Howard Pinnock, urban planning graduate from Ryerson Polytechnical Institute, unemployed for one year.

1979: "What does a university education entitle you to? I don't think it entitles you to a painless entry into life."—James Ham, president, University of Toronto.

Ham was right, of course. The universities had never guaranteed anyone a job; in fact, it was sometimes argued that they followed too closely their ancient British models in offering only learning for learning's sake, the best and richest consumption good of all. But until the arrival of the Big Generation it had always been implied, or assumed, though not explicitly guaranteed, that anyone with a degree who wanted a job could have one, and society would be grateful to him for taking it. Echoes of this centuries-old assumption can still be heard in the comments just quoted.

It will not have escaped your notice that things started to go sour as the first member of the Big Generation arrived on campus in 1968. "It was around 1968 and in the years immediately following that the growing supply of university undergraduate-degree holders collided with some rather harsh facts about the Canadian occupational structure," Edward Harvey of the Ontario Institute for Studies in Education wrote a few years ago. He was pointing out that no one had bothered to check whether the increasing stream of young people carrying their degrees and diplomas from the post-secondary institutions bore any relation to the requirements of the economy.

In general, that kind of manpower planning is about as popular in North America as five-year economic plans, government-run newspapers, and collective farms, and for the same reason: they are all totalitarian methods that restrict freedom and impose uniformity. Presumably any university administrator, or politician, or civil servant who thought about the matter at all decided that market forces would resolve the imbalances and force a correction. We know now that they do not: the plight of the school teachers is the most obvious, but not the only, proof.

The half million post-war youngsters with degrees were probably more than enough to fill the demand for university graduates for many years to come. Momentum, the fatal slowness of people and societies to see that change is needed, kept up the flow into the universities. After all, many young people had been planning on going to university; it was their parents' dearest hope that they would go; the universities had no desire to fend them off; there was no mechanism by which individual companies could say that they would not be needing any more graduates for a while. That left only government, among institutions, to call halt; but it was and remains government policy that anyone who wants an education and is qualified should get it. It has taken more than ten years for would-be students to realize the situation, and the over-supply is still not corrected.

Even professions as seemingly surplus-proof as medicine and law began to show signs of overcrowding in the second half of the 1970s. In 1977, a Toronto law firm reported that it received a hundred applicants for one job, admittedly a very desirable job. That year, seven per cent of the previous year's graduates from Osgoode Hall Law School were still unemployed, a number close to the national average for all ages and occupations; but nonetheless, the following year, in 1978, there were still 2,700 students who wanted to enter Osgoode Hall, knowing that only the top 330 would be accepted. And in 1979 the supply of engineering graduates exceeded demand for the first time since the Depression.

Young people with degrees, even if they were not doing well, were doing better in the labour market than young people without; but the glory of the university seemed to be irreversibly tarnished. A 1978 study by Statistics Canada said, "New graduates may be competing with graduates of previous years trying to improve their position. It could be 1990 before supply matches demand." That year, 1990, is just about when the last of the Big Generation with a graduate degree will leave university; if Statistics Canada is right, the mismatch between degrees and jobs, from 1968 to 1990, will have coincided exactly with the passage of the Big Generation through university years.

It was the Big Generation, I think, that inspired Richard Needham's parody of *H.M.S. Pinafore*:

> When I was a lad, the teachers said,
> "If you don't go to college, you're as good as dead;
> "without an education you're a stupid slob
> "who'll never, ever, get a decent job
> "(not even as a hitman for the Moose Jaw mob):"
> So I went to college and got my degree,
> since when I've been supported by the UIC.
> (So he took his MA and his PhD,
> and now he's getting married on his UIC.)

In 1977 some unemployed graduates of the University of Manitoba formed the Winnipeg Association of Unemployed University Graduates to protest the left-hand-right-hand stupidity of the policy of open access to education. "There are specific things we want to do, like bringing about a limitation in university enrolment in professional faculties," the group's founder, Vivian Rachlis, said. "If the universities are turning out forty to fifty per cent more graduates than are needed, then they should be made to put on the brakes."

The Big Generation's experience of university has been unhappier than that of earlier generations, who were not schooled to expect easy success. The pressure of competition, uncertainty about the future, and dismal job prospects has made students savage. "It's almost on an animal level of behaviour, the aggressiveness to get marks," Dr. John Evans said in 1977 when he was president of the University of Toronto. Students steal other students' notes, essays, and work books. Library books are stolen, and chapters that are required reading are torn out. "Cheating has now become a part of the university scene," James Daly, history professor at McMaster University, wrote recently. "It is hardly possible now to leave marked papers unsupervised; the best ones may be stolen for use or sale. . . . It is no longer enough to cheat in order to get ahead; now cheating is done in order to keep others behind."

Professor Jill Webster, in charge of disciplining the 17,000 students of Toronto's faculty of arts and science, said not long ago that forgery, plagiarism, and falsified records had reached epidemic proportions and posed a serious threat to the university's intellectual standards. Professor Daly of McMaster commented, "There's no excuse for cheating, but we could say this with a better grace if permissive education had not been cheating students for a decade."

Accompanying the decline of the university was the rise of the community college. By 1978, some colleges were being swamped by Big Generation youngsters who had concluded that jobs came before the life-long advantages of a liberal education, and that colleges were better preparation for jobs than were universities. Humber College's experience was typical of the panic of 1977: the college received 12,000 applications for its 3,800 first-year places. In 1978, Cambrian College in Sudbury found itself so crowded that it arranged to board out some of its students: where the college registrar found space was Laurentian University. Another college studied the prospect of taking over public schools, which were feeling the pinch for a different reason.

Success was not without its problems for the colleges. The people they were originally set up to serve, the less academic students who were destined for technologists' jobs, were in danger of being displaced by students with higher grades who were slumming because of the colleges' record of getting jobs for their graduates. By 1978 a number of colleges found they were getting applications from young adults who had already graduated from university, could not get work, and wanted to improve their chances; at least one application was put in by someone who already had a Ph.D. A number of colleges gave university graduates low priority.

But in 1979 the colleges, too, experienced the first chill of student disillusionment. After more than twenty years of growth, enrolment in colleges for the 1979-1980 academic year was very slightly below the previous year's figure. The reason is probably what Professor John Alan Lee forecast in 1978:

> The temporary shift of enrolment preference to the community colleges has merely postponed their day of reckoning by a year or two. The surpluses of physicians, lawyers, dentists, and pharmacists will soon be followed by surpluses of

journalists, photographers, computer operators, and fashion designers.

If that does happen, the community colleges will then be doomed to follow the universities into their present unhappy condition and even more miserable prospects. The 1960s forecasts of soaring university enrolment held good up to the beginning of the 1970s; in fact, some forecasts were proved too conservative, high though they had seemed at the time. The Ontario universities' 1961 estimate of their 1971 enrolment, for instance, which they had been told was at least forty per cent low, turned out to have been sixty per cent low. But the Economic Council's forecast made a few years later, in 1967, that full-time undergraduate and graduate enrolment would reach 540,000 in 1975, proved to be much too high. The actual figure was 360,000, two-thirds of what was foreseen. The rush to university simply stopped in its tracks.

The thousands of professors taken on in the 1960s in anticipation of the arrival of the Big Generation are now ten to twenty years older, and mostly tenured. Following the protective lead of the school teachers, some of them now belong to quite militant unions. Whereas sixty per cent of full-time university teachers were under forty in 1968, it is now those aged thirty-six to fifty who make up sixty per cent of the staff. The sudden levelling-off of enrolment has meant that the universities have not been hiring new staff during the larger part of the 1970s. They had no funds to do so, as their income depends on enrolment, and had no reason to do so, as they already have more teachers than they can usefully employ. Over the next five years, it is now expected, thousands of professors will be fired, including professors with tenure, who had what was in the past a guarantee that they could stay for life unless they did something outrageously incompetent or dissolute.

Professor Mort Paterson might stand for them in their dilemma. He was born in 1935, has been teaching philosophy at Laurentian University in Sudbury since 1968, was tenured, had a salary of $28,500, and in 1978 found himself with a total of twelve students, ten in a first-year course and two in a fourth-year honours course. Frantically trying to improve the odds on his survival, he set up a correspondence course that attracted fifty students. He said in the summer of 1979:

We're in imminent danger of losing our jobs. Those who

teach in newer and smaller universities are all in the same boat, but Laurentian is going to have to be the first to let tenured professors go. I'm forty-four and in mid-career. There is no job for an out-of-work philosophy professor to go to and it's going to get worse. I think the government should have foreseen this. They could have foreseen this. They could have done a better job of planning, demographically.

The problems create a particularly ironic spiral. The glut of professors exists because everyone could see the approach of the Big Generation. Just like the Big Generation, the professors hired in the 1960s are now being isolated by the vacuum following them. One dean confided to a friend, "I have a faculty that is aging in place." Desmond Morton, vice-principal of Erindale College, estimated that the group of professors in their late thirties and early forties would likely dominate the universities until the beginning of the twenty-first century. Professor S.P. Rosenbaum wrote disconsolately, "The single most serious crisis now confronting universities . . . is the inability of these universities to renew themselves. . . . Slowly but surely stultification is occurring."

One reason the Big Generation does not want to go to university is that the prospect of jobs at the university, long the main employer of people with post-graduate degrees, is very low because of the faculty glut. Once again, the Big Generation finds that its approach made exciting and rewarding opportunities for others, but that when it passes, it leaves despair in its wake, and all the opportunities disappear. The generation made work for hundreds of thousands of school teachers, but now those teachers are out of work or under threat of losing their jobs; and there are no school-teaching jobs for the generation. The prospect of their arrival launched the university boom, but now the boom has collapsed; and there will be no university-teaching jobs for members of the Big Generation.

The present teaching staff is unlikely to step down to make way for the Big Generation. So far the universities have not been successful in persuading any large number of professors to retire early, go on half salary, take part-time jobs outside the university, or resign and go into banking. Instead they have been persuaded that they need stronger and more militant faculty unions. A Science Council of Canada forecast of full-time university professors in 1990 indicates that sixty per cent will be aged forty-five to sixty and less than twenty per cent will be under forty. "The one thing we all have in common, whether we're at large universities or small, is fear," David Inman, president of the Ontario Confederation of University Faculty Associations, said not long ago. One of the most prestigious of all jobs a few years ago is now a disaster area.

The universities before the Big Generation were calm, careful, and sophisticated in running their affairs. Today they are close to panic. When enrolment started to drop, they lost income; but their costs, mostly professors' salaries, rose. They could not, or at any rate did not, cut staff to match income, as an automobile-manufacturing company might have done. But they did some other things that auto companies would have found familiar.

Some of the biggest universities reduced admission standards in their badly hurt arts and science faculties, in an attempt to draw in students who would otherwise have had to go to less desirable universities. The smaller universities, in desperation, began buying catchy commercials on radio stations and spending more money on advertisements in magazines young people see. All universities tried more intensive recruiting tactics, among them telephone calls by professors and administrators to potential freshmen, paying travel and accommodation costs for students who agreed to visit the campuses, and wining and dining high-school guidance counsellors. In 1978, the competition got so fierce that the Council of Ontario Universities set up a special agency to watch out for breaches of the recruiting guidelines.

Even so, by the end of the 1970s the universities faced large budget deficits, and the provincial and federal governments had made it clear they were not going to continue to hand out money simply to maintain institutions that were increasingly short of students. The problems the universities and the colleges face in the 1980s are likely to be severe. Claude Fortier, chairman of the Science Council of Canada, put it succinctly: "To be effective, the universities must attract our best people, provide them with an education of the highest quality, and be able to give them some assurance of a role in society commensurate with their training." All three factors were essential, he added. If the universities could not achieve them, young people could be turned off higher education. "Such a breakdown could occur within the next ten or fifteen years." Since there seems at least some probability that the universities will not be able to do any of these things, Fortier's warning of irreversible damage to society was grim.

Thus it was that the Big Generation wrecked Canada's education system. The chaos of their arrival, the panic to put up enough classrooms and find enough teachers to staff them, gave way to the misery of their departure, the half-empty buildings, the tens of thousands of demoralized and out-of-work teachers.

But many think the system had its revenge on the Big Generation.

CHAPTER 5

A NEW KIND OF PEOPLE

*"It's completely out of control
in there."*

Education, affluence, the impact of Dr. Spock and the new parenting, the trauma of family breakdown, urbanization, the post-war
crusade for universal personal liberty, television, the disap-
pearance of respect for established authority–all these helped to
make the Big Generation unique. Millions of young people have
grown up in the past thirty years with a world view that is totally
different from the image used by any previous generation. The Big
Generation and those who are older co-exist in the same physical
space, but they interpret the details in quite different ways. The
expectations of the two parties, coloured as they are by their pic-
tures of how the world works, are largely at variance. The elders
are baffled by the Big Generation, and the generation has no idea
why it should be thought strange.

Several distinctive qualities created by the special circumstances
of the Big Generation's upbringing and education now define its
unique nature, and most of this chapter is concerned with them.
But in addition to these major structural features of the edifice, as
it were, there are also a number of general characteristics that
might be likened to special colouring or highlights, adding
emphasis to this feature and modifying that one.

Many members of the Big Generation learned at school that as
long as they were trying, they were fulfilling their obligations.
(Hall-Dennis: "The child who is learning cannot fail.") To a considerable extent this replaces for them the pursuit of specific goals;
it redefines the idea of achievement and thus also the idea of success.

As Spock observed, many parents taught their children that
when things went wrong, the fault lay not with the children but

with someone else. The Rousseauist view that man is an innocent being capable of perfect virtue but ruined by corrupt institutions – a belief now commonly held by high-school and university teachers – potently reinforced the earlier lesson.

The generation grew up during the height of the campaigns for absolute personal freedom and for an egalitarian economy – progressive taxation, universal social security – that flourished during the post-war economic boom. Adults could question the social and political assumptions behind these campaigns; but for the Big Generation this was simply the way things worked. The generation took the ideals of personal liberty and egalitarianism as accomplished facts. By comparison, the rigid social behavior of their parents and grandparents looks as formal as the code of the samurai or King Arthur's knights.

The considerable intellectual and emotional autonomy fostered by high-school education added another tone to these ego-bolstering factors.

Another accent was the childhood message many received that it was all right to act out your feelings, including your aggressive feelings. Spock hastened to suggest limits to this idea once he realized how widespread it had become, but that was another canary it was hard to get back into the cage.

Television advertising, indeed the whole gratification-oriented message of TV, both overt and covert, was augmented by the permissiveness of parents and their ability to please themselves by indulging their children's whims. Herman Kahn, the futurist, used to ask college audiences, "Who has ever failed to get anything reasonable that he wanted within a year, and by reasonable I don't meant a yacht or a Rolls but almost anything else?" He claims that rarely was a single hand raised.

Whatever the Big Generation does and whatever specific characteristics it exhibits, these accents of self-esteem, expectations of success, and personal gratification are omnipresent.

Taken together, the ideas are not unlike those of the wealthy and educated in earlier times: the late Victorian esthetes like Oscar Wilde and Walter Pater, and the sensitive Bostonians like Charles Eliot Norton and Bernard Berenson, who scorned the bourgeois materialism of their day; or the rich undergraduates of Oxford and Cambridge in the 1930s who agreed that "the life of the industrialist and businessman was degrading and contemptible," who distrusted power and success, rejected the heroism and ideals of the generation that fought the First World War, and would not vote to fight for king and country. But while those were tiny fractions of the populace, the Big Generation includes one person in every three and is quickly becoming the central faction in the society. This revolution, unlike its forerunners, is a mass movement. The rebels lack polish and refinement, but they will make up for it in impact.

The characteristics that define the Big Generation and its potential can be quickly outlined. It is by far the most highly educated generation in history. Compared to earlier generations, it lives much more intensely in its feelings. Its interests and skills are more abstract and less concrete. The members of the generation are more sharply differentiated one from another. Many are alienated from society, many, as a consequence, choose to live in a society-within-a-society, the youth culture. A significant number of Big Generation people show a marked capacity for violence.

Let us look at five of these characteristics in more detail.

FEELINGS

What has struck older people about all the young since the Second World War, including the forerunners of the Big Generation, is how much they live in their feelings. The Beat Generation at the end of the 1950s–youngsters born no earlier than 1940–attracted the sharp observation of Paul Goodman, who noted that they were "unscheduled, sloppy, communitarian, sexually easygoing, and careless of reputation"; that they rejected the popular culture in favour of Zen Buddhism and the writings of D.H. Lawrence; that "they regard talk as an end in itself, as a means of self-expression, without subject matter"; and that their artistic activities included poetry, painting, "reading to jazz, decorating the pads, and playing on drums. Everybody engages in creative arts and is likely to carry a sketchbook."

Above all was their devotion to whatever heightened experience, their constant exploration for sensation, feeling, getting out of one's self and into a new world. In *On the road*, published in 1957, Jack Kerouac wrote of people "who never yawn or say a commonplace thing, but burn, burn, burn like fabulous yellow roman candles exploding like spiders across the stars." Compare this with Pater: "To burn always with this hard gemlike flame, to maintain this ecstasy, is success in life." The Beats, the post-war pioneers, provided much of the raw material for the Big Generation, even down to language, like "like," "man," "cool," and so on.

Ten years later came the Flower Children, born in the late 1940s or early 1950s. "We read Shelley for inspiration and *Soul on Ice* for the facts," a woman born in 1947 recollected on turning thirty. "At the height of the madness, I, too, heard Allen Ginsberg chant. In a room filled with psychedelic posters and the pungent smells of burning grass, he reached over and touched my hand – a typical sixties gesture of love."

Charles Reich, in his 1970 book *The Greening of America*, chronicled the post-war children's new attitudes, which he called Consciousness III to contrast them with the attitudes of two earlier generations, the immigrants and the men in the grey flannel suits. His generalizations may have been based too narrowly on his Yale students, as some critics have said, but they reflected a broad band of the new ethical spectrum. "The foundation of Consciousness III is liberation," Reich wrote. "It comes into being the moment the individual frees himself from automatic acceptance of the imperatives of society." To Reich, liberation meant that the individual was free to develop his own philosophy and values, his own life-style and culture. "Consciousness III starts with self," Reich wrote, "[and] rejects the whole concept of excellence and comparative merit that is so central to Consciousness II." He was equally contemptuous of social form: "To observe duties toward others, after the feelings are gone, is no virtue and may even be a crime. . . . the new generation looks with suspicion on 'obligations' and contractual relations between people."

Some of these attitudes are typical of adolescence and young adulthood. But they are not inseparable from it. The greater part of what Reich described was characteristic of at most a small fraction of earlier generations: most older people held no such ideas and felt no such urges at any age. In the case of the Big Generation, Reich was describing the dominant ethic.

It was for the oldest members of the Big Generation that the Woodstock festival was put together in 1969, Jimi Hendrix, pot, Janis Joplin, "three days of peace and music," Arlo Guthrie, and all. Before the Beatles, popular music had been more a cheerful banging than an appeal to feeling, but to grip the Big Generation music had to get under the skin, pound like a revved-up pulse, scream, weep, tear a passion to tatters. Music is still the dominant entertainment for the generation, a much more important part of life for them than images or printed words; efforts to censor lyrics, such as are made in some high schools, are surely misdirected.

The huge rock concerts with massive sets, lasers, and strobe lights can attract crowds of 50,000, 75,000, and perhaps more in the biggest cities. Typically, in the late 1970s, the audiences were made up of people born between 1957 and 1964. Those were just the years when Marshall McLuhan started to talk about living in the five-sense sensorium, and now that is what these youngsters are doing. "Most rock shows are just sound, and you're supposed to provide the feeling," a fourteen-year-old says after an Electric Light Orchestra concert, "but ELO is, like, all the senses, they're like a great movie with monster sound."

For the whole generation, school was fun – "macrame and folksinging," one girl described her talents. "Throwing pots and reading astrological charts with flair," another said. Out of school they skied and threw Frisbees: sinuous, sensuous, personal, uncompetitive experiences that are about as far as you can get from the official school sports, football or basketball.

The decline of literacy with this generation is probably over-emphasized. The average product of the high school today and the average university freshman are less skilful with language, know less of the classics of literature, and have a smaller stock of cultural information than graduates of an earlier generation. But to put it all down to TV or anything else is to ignore the effect of the democ-ratization of education, which has consciously reached farther down the academic scale for students. The top tenth of the Big Generation could probably do at least as well as the top tenth of their parents' generation. It is the more broadly based average that compares badly.

But the dilution of literacy has its effect, reducing the rigour of thought, logical coherence, literary standards, and clarity of expression. Progressive education directs young people away from the mastery of structured knowledge and toward the impulsive accumulation of experience; away from whatever might be called stiff or formal toward what is soft and imaginative: astrology and macrame rather than grammar and calculus.

94

There is evidence that at least some high schools were so shorn of intellectual content that bright students were left high and dry. A Vancouver researcher found that children with higher IQs and a greater disposition toward intellectuality did better than their fellows in elementary school, but at the start of high school there was a sharp reversal: the more intelligent pupils' grades fell off while those of the less intelligent remained about the same. The educational system failed to catch the interests of intelligent and questioning young people, the researcher concluded.

Television, with its high emotional impact and low intellectual content, pushed the generation in the same direction, away from the logical and toward the imaginative. It would be harder to say that using marijuana contributes to the generation's generally unstructured, undisciplined, emotional, and non-intellectual style, though users do say it stimulates imagination and the feeling centres; but it certainly is part of that style, and there is no doubt that pot smoking is centred in the generation, whether judged by the age of the people who are getting most of the convictions for possession (twenty to twenty-four is the central group) or by more anecdotal evidence from users.

This is a generation whose emotional needs and fantasies are satisfied where stomach-churning violence and occult mystery meet – in movies like *The Exorcist* and *Alien*. It is a generation that dotes on science fiction, but is equally happy with neo-Saxon myths about Mordor and the Hobbit. It has little time for established religion, but feels comfortable with Hare Krishna, the Moonies, and Scientology. It knows a great deal about Atlantis, the Bermuda Triangle, and ancient artifacts that just might be proof of prehistoric space travel. It can reject the divinity of Christ for lack of proof but believe devoutly in UFOs on the basis of a handful of faked snapshots. "Irrational" or perhaps "enthusiastic" best describes these attitudes.

The generation's sexuality makes parents and other older people very anxious. Their own youth was stamped by the strongest possible taboos about sex, what nice girls did not do, going too far, dire warnings about animal passions, terror of venereal disease and getting pregnant. These youngsters are the beneficiaries of sexual liberation, penicillin, reliable contraception, and abortion.

It may not be an exaggeration to talk of a youth-sex revolution. With improvements in health and diet, the age of puberty continues to fall. The latest data show that a third of all girls now reach puberty at eleven or earlier. A hundred years ago the average age was about sixteen; in 1951 it was about fourteen; in 1955 only a little under thirteen. Now it has dropped quite sharply, and the change is creating problems.

"Until just a few years ago the average girl matured at age fifteen and married at age eighteen," one sex therapist says. "Now they are maturing at twelve and marrying at twenty-two. Ten years between maturity and matrimony is too long for a bodily process to go without functioning." By the age of sixteen, a fifth of British youngsters have had sexual intercourse; in the US, it is a fifth by the age of fifteen. An increasing number of teachers and counsellors think sex education and birth control advice are being started too late.

They are also concerned that the pressures to have intercourse are unwelcome to many emotionally immature but physically mature youngsters; but that these pressures are getting harder to resist. "An intercourse fetish," Dr. Corinne Devlin, head of the McMaster University Medical Centre Reproductive Regulation Clinic in Hamilton calls it:

> Advertising and the media have taught them being sexual is going to bed with someone. It leaves out getting to know someone, feeling good, necking and petting. . . . Kids end up having sex to their detriment. They are being traumatized by it.

Both boys and girls are also getting caught up in prostitution while still adolescents. Several hundred juvenile prostitutes are thought to be operating in Vancouver alone.

The country is more open about sex than it was a quarter-century ago. People want to talk about sex more than they did, read about it more than they did, share it more than they did, do it more than they did – the Big Generation most of all. All kinds of sexuality are out of the closet, homo as well as hetero, group and solo as well as duo, public as well as private. In one of the major triumphs in the liberation of human feelings, sexuality has been made both important and commonplace in the years since the Second World War, just in time for the generation to enjoy it. Even the kinds of sex once thought scandalous are now accepted, with the result, as Robertson Davies put it, that Big Generation homosexuals "want a respectability and domesticity that their gay great-uncles would have scorned as bourgeois."

Year by year, from the Beats to the Flower Children to the Rock Fans, surrender to the emotions has grown more widespread, more open, more admired and recommended. So far the feelings expressed have been love more often than hate, but so far, for most of the Big Generation, life has been comfortable, cradled, supportive. There are ominous indications that life and its unexpected difficulties may tilt the balance toward discomfort and frustration. If it does, the generation's feelings could quickly switch, too.

INDIVIDUATION

An American poll asked teenagers for their most important goal in life. In 1974, about forty per cent said, "The opportunity to develop as an individual," and slightly more said, "A happy family life." When the same question was asked in 1976, almost fifty per cent put development as an individual first and only thirty per cent chose a happy family life. There may be have been quirks in the survey that would make the differences between the polls unimportant. It may not be possible to say much more than that in the mid-1970s, on average, teenagers thought personal development and family happiness the most important goals in life and put personal development first. But when the same question was posed to adults, only twelve per cent gave personal development top priority and eighty per cent chose happy family life. The difference between those born before the mid-1950s and after is striking, and appears to be more than just a difference in ages. The Me Generation, as Tom Wolfe called it, is not just a faddish attitude but the distinguishing mark of a new ethic.

Abraham Maslow defined a hierarchy of human needs, which formed a pyramid. The first need had to be satisfied before the second could be explored and so on. He described five levels:

5. Self-actualization
4. Esteem
3. Belonging: love and intimacy
2. Safety: avoiding pain and discomfort
1. Physiology: water, food, sleep

A person will struggle for water and sleep before he worries about safety. He must feel safe before he seeks love and intimacy. And so on.

During the Depression, many people were still fighting for satisfaction at the lowest level; but post-war circumstances – affluence, good health care, concerned parents, sensitive teachers – propelled the Big Generation to the top of Maslow's hierarchy of values, allowing them the hitherto rare luxury of concentrating on the development of their own creative and spiritual potential. It has to be regarded as one of the finest moments in civilization; and, as far as I can see, the only problem is that for too many of the Big Generation the stability of their pyramid rests on the struggles of others. With their more abstract and less practical skills, with their inexperience in the techniques of physical survival, and with their unquestioning acceptance that Maslow's levels 1 and 2 are simple givens, they are not capable of rebuilding the pyramid should it crumble.

So enormous is the Big Generation's fascination with self that the number of full-time teachers of psychology in the universities grew fifteen hundred per cent in twenty years; from eighty-eight in 1956 to 1,376 in 1976. From a spot halfway down the list of forty-eight teaching fields, employing notably fewer teachers than philosophy, classics, history, or religious studies, psychology rose to its present eminence as the fifth largest group of teachers, following only medicine, education, mathematics, and commerce. Is this because we all need so much more psychological attention? Or is it because so many more of us want to investigate our own and others' psyches? Answer: yes to both questions.

This is the generation, as Jane Newitt has pointed out, whose parents made Spock a best-seller and in large numbers asked professionals to help them deal with their offspring's childhood and adolescent problems of behaviour and development. The Big Generation now resorts to psychiatrists itself in large numbers and makes best-sellers of guides to self-analysis. "A heightened sense of one's own complexities, an increased dependence on experts, seem certain to be qualities that [they] will carry through life," Newitt concludes.

Grade school socializes, high school individualizes. Going through high school liberated millions of members of the Big

Generation. Or is "liberated" the right word? It made them independent-minded, encouraged them to reject traditions, community values, and conventional ideas; but as part of the campaign against elitism it denied them experience of competition, discouraged any efforts to excel, did not show them how to become self-reliant. So they are free spirits with a difference: few can act independently. Eric Hoffer says, "Everybody wants to be somebody, before he's anybody, even when he's nobody."

Affluence, education, and Freud all contributed to the Big Generation's uniquely high level of individuation. But it can be argued, as does Kenneth Clark, that the whole long course of human civilization has been directed at making each human being separate, individual, free of the constraints of genus, of blood, of tribe, of family. And now suddenly the development is bearing fruit.

ALIENATION

Alienation is the feeling that one is in a group but not part of it. A large number of the Big Generation are in the Canadian society but not of it. They do not share its values or goals; though still resident, they are expatriates in spirit, self-exiled rebels. The country they dwell in is, increasingly, a counter-culture set up in opposition to the dominant, conventional culture or a unique and personal universe with only one citizen.

Paul Goodman described typical members of the Beat Generation as having "(1) attachment to a middle-class home but (2) withdrawing from its values, (3) without growing into other worthwhile values." They were, he said, "on speaking terms with their families but dissent from all their ways." Charles Reich said the Consciousness III generation realized they could live "without the guideposts of the past." In the post-war world, for instance, "a life of surfing *is* possible, not as an escape from work, a recreation, or a phrase, but as a *life*." Surely the image of someone devoting a life to isolating himself from all contact with the world and its human problems and opportunities, submerging himself in an existence defined simply by the motion of rolling waves, is the perfect symbol of alienation.

What made earlier generations part of their communities? The shared values had the central function of supporting social institutions, "king and country," the *civis* to which the citizen owed duty, the instruments of social power. But this is just what the process of individuation liberates people from. A 1978 poll of students in ten Ontario universities asked how much confidence the students felt in various institutions and public figures. The five they felt most confidence in were medical doctors, television news, consumer activists, TV and radio commentators, and newspapers. The five in which they had least confidence were advertising agencies, major oil companies, major corporations, business executives, and politicians. In other words, the students had least confidence in the people and organizations that run the country and most confidence in those who stand back from, observe, and frequently criticize the way the country is run. (The medical doctors, solid establishment figures that they are, are an unexplained exception.) Over ninety per cent of the students surveyed called Canada "a democracy in name only" and thought that "special interests run the country and ordinary people don't count." All of which suggests a high degree of alienation.

Alienation has not just happened, it has been inculcated. The parents of the generation, reacting to the strictness and orthodoxy of their own upbringing, desperately tried not to restrict or direct their children. A hundred times a day they offered choices: "What would you like to do? Which of these toys would you like? If you want to go to Sunday school you can. It's up to you."

A product of this upbringing pondered the results in his sophomore year at Harvard: "They never did force any arbitrary system of values on me – what I find is that with so much freedom, I'm left with *no* value system. In certain ways I wish I had had a value system forced on me, so that I could have something to believe in." There is no release, no growth to be had in trying to revolt against an authority that is not there. As the New York sociologist Ernest Van den Haag put it, "it is no fun to fight pudding."

Geoffrey Vickers says, "Literally, an autonomous person is one who makes his own rules and sets his own standards. He is at the opposite pole from the responsible person," the person who has made some commitment of personal responsibility. It was autonomy, not responsibility, that was nurtured in the Big Generation's homes and schools.

The first result of alienation is not that beliefs evaporate and institutions crumble, but that too many people can no longer make any commitment to them. Then they evaporate and crumble. There is still a monarch, still a *civis*, still a structure of social and economic institutions that functions tolerably well for many Canadians, that was indeed built up by many of them and still looks pretty good to them. They may soon be in a minority, however, and they are bound to dwindle to a small fraction of the whole society. The Big Generation's disillusionment with the underlying beliefs and ethic is what will eventually bring down the institutions.

With many of the Big Generation, alienation has been built into a life style. At the University of Toronto, Jack Quarter identified two distinct types of students in the 1970s, those undecided about their careers, who were forty to fifty per cent of the students interviewed, and the rest. It was the undecided who interested him: they were a new phenomenon, they were challenging the established order, and he began to perceive that they shared many characteristics.

Among the undecided, he found, there was a disproportionately large number whose politics were left wing. They were more principled, had a stronger appreciation of the arts, preferred "soft" esthetic subjects to "difficult" subjects like chemistry and mathematics, "expressed a higher tolerance for ambiguity, a desire for freedom and independence from judgemental authoritarian thinking," preferred ideas and the mysterious to facts and the concrete. The undecided, he also noted, experienced more guilt, unhappiness, and anxiety, and were more withdrawn.

In a paper on changes in young people's ideology, Quarter discussed other researchers' findings. The American poll-taker Daniel Yankelovich distinguished two groups of college students rather like Quarter's decided and undecided; Yankelovich called them the career-minded and the post-affluent. These were the proportions of each class of student agreeing with certain statements:

	career-minded	post-affluent
Competition encourages excellence	71%	48%
Factors important in a career choice:		
self-expression	56%	75%
chance to get ahead	45%	19%
prestige	28%	14%

Finally, Quarter noted that the strongest opposition to the existing social order appeared to be coming not from the poor, as a Marxist would expect, but from the rich; not, in other words, from families that would ordinarily be thought of as "failures," but from "successes."

Some people who have looked at the fear and insecurity that now marks so many university students who anticipate extreme difficulty in finding a satisfactory life on graduation have described their mood as more conservative than at any time since the 1950s. This seems to be simply wrong, a superficial reading of the signs. A Cornell University dean suggests that the sagging economy has "temporarily camouflaged alienation of the youth by forcing more acceptable modes of behavior," but thinks that beneath the conservative veneer, "alienation toward organizational and societal life is about as strong as it was in the early 1970s."

Very large numbers of baby-boom children have grown up with no loyalty to anything but themselves, with no sense that there is anything outside of themselves that deserves their loyalty. They have been explicitly offered the cult of self-actualization as a fit object of devotion. They have been told explicitly that there is no philosophy, religion, or ethos that can command universal attention, that no external "authority" should dictate their standards, and that it should be their highest aim to establish a set of values that suits their own special needs. They are offered more and more choices – and no criteria for making decisions except self-satisfaction. Remembering the pinched, conforming, inhibited world of most of their parents, that is a huge leap forward. But it should not surprise us if it has left members of the Big Generation unsteady on their feet.

Everything has conspired to drive the members of the generation more firmly into each other's company, to the exclusion of outsiders. The frequent talk of sub-cultures in the society – the drug sub-culture, the counter-culture, and the like – masks the central fact that most members of the generation live in one sub-culture, which may conveniently be called the youth culture.

The origin of this intense cohesion was the experience so many members of the generation had of being brought up by their siblings – or, for the older, of raising their siblings – in that "barbarian," "primitive," "tribal" culture of adolescence that Brigitte Berger described. It was intensified by the determined preference of progressive educators for co-operation and collaboration. Out of these unifying experiences have come the various manifestations of the sub-culture.

Woodstock was a uniquely massive and intense event, but it set a pattern for the emotional power, now often riotously explosive, and the hysterical adulation of today's rock concerts, the Nuremberg rallies of our time. The rock culture is the most obviously binding and enclosing part of the alternative culture Clifton Fadiman drew attention to: the music-and-TV electronic culture that engulfs members of the generation and pulls them away from the work-a-day culture of their elders.

We hear less from the media these days about rural communes of innocent hippies, bare-footed, meditative, sensitive to the environment, pot-smoking, and a little smug; but it is a life that seems to be attracting more people today than it ever did when it was heralded in the newspapers. It has bred a mailbox-full of magazines and newsletters, general and specialized. To outsiders, this is probably the least decipherable class of citizens, and researchers are left to ponder the twenty per cent of the Big Generation described by Statistics Canada at the 1976 census as "rural non-farm."

Student activists have formed an intense culture since the Second World War; in western countries it has been more noticeable since 1968, the year the first baby-boom child reached university. That culture may be temporary, but it can be suffocatingly intense: revolutionary, insular, liberationist, self-engrossed.

The rock culture, the hippie culture, and the culture of student activism are aspects of a single culture rather than separate groupings. Membership in one often includes membership in others. A notable feature of these associations is that they are more communal and operate on a larger scale than the clubs and parishes of the previous two generations, except during wartime. In fact, in many respects these are the armies of the Big Generation, which train, unify, and defend it. These strong groupings have arisen despite the fact that the alienated, individuated members of the Big Generation have little liking for conventional social forms. The groupings within the youth culture are, self-evidently, not institutions like churches or tennis clubs, open to all ages; they are age-selective. (Scan the faces at a rock concert for anyone over thirty or try joining a group of student activists if you are over twenty-five.) A recent one-paragraph news item noted that a missing fifteen-year-old girl holidaying in London with her parents had been found "in a hippie commune" in another town. In any previous generation she would have ended up as a prostitute, a store clerk, or a servant; but now there is a pervasive culture that fields runaways. The culture of the Big Generation, in short, has the making of not just an alternative culture but an alternative society.

VIOLENCE

Feeling runs strong in the Big Generation. Through the 1950s and most of the 1960s, when things were going well for the generation, the dominant feeling was love. At the end of the 1960s, which was also the second phase of the post-war economic boom, the oldest members of the generation began to rebel. They felt they were cannon fodder for the big guns of industry; they felt used, manipulated, and excluded from decisions about how their lives were to be run; they felt the joy going out of education. Undoubtedly, later on they also began to feel the first pressures of competition from their peers of the Big Generation and the difficulty of catching up or competing with the pioneering and often brilliant group born in the 1940s.

These students were among the first to question the value of merely having a degree. As student activism spread from Latin America and Asia to Europe and North America, students were rapidly politicized, picked up radical, usually Marxist, perspectives on their world and its problems, and turned violent when resisted. Their parents and others of their generation had assumed that the privilege of going to university would automatically induce feelings of gratitude and dutifulness in the students. The burning of the computer centre at Sir George Williams University in Montreal and similar events deeply shocked the parents' generation.

In any generation adolescence is a time of violence. "On the average, adolescent boys double their strength between the ages of thirteen and sixteen," Toronto psychiatrist Dr. Saul Levine says. "At the same time, there are hormonal changes taking place which release an aggressive drive. Young people have to learn to channel that aggression, energy, and drive into socially constructive endeavours." As more and more of the Big Generation reached adolescence, youthful violence became increasingly prevalent.

Affluence added tools to violence: cars, alcohol, drugs, and guns. But it takes more than just opportunity for destructive anger to burst out. It takes real provocation. And the generation is being provoked on four sides: frustration, overcrowding, alienation, and naiveté.

It entered life in the most rosily hopeful of times, absorbing the optimism, prosperity, and confidence of the 1950s and 1960s, knowing without doubt that this was how the world really worked. But one after the other, the unquestioned beliefs built in during childhood and school days are proving to be miserably, bitterly wrong. Look back at the catechism of beliefs and values taught to the Big Generation. Is their experience in college and the job market confirming their belief that it is almost impossible to fail? Are employers treating their willingness to try as a sufficient response to the needs of the work place? Are professors and bosses and civil servants telling them they are real human assets, important human beings with a wealth of feeling and imagination to contribute? Are people now urging them to enjoy their freedom and autonomy, and treating them as equals?

The answer to nearly every one of these questions is no; and in consequence it is increasingly common to hear members of the generation cry out that they have been misled and betrayed, robbed, cheated, and deprived. Their faith is turning out to be a hollow mockery, and there is little anyone can do to change it.

Many members of the generation are under considerable stress from overcrowding: at home in a few cases, at school or university in almost all cases, and in trying to get jobs. At every turn, four people of the age group stand where it would be reasonable to find three: or more often four hundred where three hundred might have been expected. In particular places – popular college courses, favoured jobs – the overcrowding is worse. A student at Ryerson Polytechnical Institute in Toronto was so angry when another took over the computer terminal he had been using that he stabbed the other student in the arm. "The violence is just a symptom of the overcrowding," an official said.

Alienation has left many members of the Big Generation so cut off from the society and community they live in that normal constraints no longer work on them. They feel deeply rejected. They expected to be able to do something useful and rewarding with their lives and find they cannot. They feel they are not needed, have been sold down the river, have lost their dreams. Equally crippling for at least one in five is the experience of seeing their families disintegrate or break down, leaving them awash in a sea of guilty despair. Thousands of them have been thrown out – thrown away, some people would say – by parents who could not stand the strain of living with the king-size adolescent egos of the Big Generation.

The fourth side of the assault on the generation's confidence is the fact that they have been carefully guarded from anything that might have prepared them to handle the situation so many are now in. The young university students who cheat, steal, and lie to get ahead of their peers are showing plainly that they have no idea how to deal with competition. Instead they panic. And no one is more surprised at the violence than the teachers who prepared that bed of roses for the Big Generation.

So these are the causes of the angry aggression that is starting to flow through society from this increasingly unhappy generation. Clearly it is still a minority that is actively involved; but the extent of the problem is much larger than most people like to think, and the anger and despair are not far beneath the surface.

Vandalism is now reckoned to cost a hundred million dollars a year in Canada. It ranges from setting fires in libraries to smashing car windows and scratching paint in underground parking areas; from spray painting obscenities on subway walls to destroying young trees in parks; from overturning grave stones to invading a private house and trashing it. But the overwhelming proportion of the damage is done to schools.

A study by an Ontario city said, ruefully, that most vandalism was not aimless, but directed at specific targets. A social worker in another city said, "Vandalism is on the rise because young people lack pride in themselves and in the place they hold in their community, so they are turning to vandalism as an outlet for their frustrations." A youth services director said, "If we learned anything from the American experience [in the 1960s] it's that people are looking for some way to participate, they feel they're left out."

Assaults on teachers are being reported more frequently. An eighteen-year-old drop-out went back to his old school waving a beer bottle in the cafeteria and bragging to the students. When a teacher told him to leave, the young man punched the teacher in the head, kicked him in the shin, and finally finished up in jail for two weeks for assault. In another high school, a former pupil who went back to the school was asked to leave; he threw the teacher who spoke to him through a plate-glass window. The student was jailed; the teacher was so terrified he had to be given a year's leave of absence. In a third school, a student asked for permission to leave class early and was refused; the student's boy friend then went into the classroom and beat the teacher up.

Drinking seems to be part of the problem. Students are returning drunk after the lunch break. In one Ontario county, in one term, eighteen students were expelled for drunkenness. The county medical officer of health said, "They were too intoxicated, too disruptive to be allowed to stay in class. They weren't just sloshed, they were unco-operative and vomiting on the floors." The doctor added that he believed for every one suspended there were a hundred who were drunk but not troublesome enough to warrant suspension. Another school board reported more students "going berserk" and making "uncontrollable outbursts."

But most incidents seem to be a form of retaliation against the schools: an emotional response, however twisted, to a perceived harm. "It's people who have dropped out or been expelled," according to Alan Murray, the president of the Ontario Teachers' Federation, which represents a hundred thousand teachers. "They are unemployed. They have nothing else to do. They tend to want to tell off teachers who had something to do with their being expelled."

Psychiatrist James Wilkes put the wave of assaults down to frustration. "Kids are unable to accept and deal with frustrations, because everything around them says mental pain is bad, immediate gratification is good." He repeats a typical comment made to him by an adolescent: "Nobody owns me, so nobody rules me, so I ought to be able to do what I want." Traditional therapy will not be much use in that situation: "It's difficult to change the pattern, because they don't think anything's wrong."

Many teachers were badly shaken by the increase in violence in the last years of the 1970s. A confidential report by one board of education declared, "We must start our long-term activities so that we will not require policemen or security guards in the corridors, signal systems, or riot squads." Other reports speak of hundreds of verbal, physical, and sexual assaults on teachers. One survey of six hundred teachers found that most had been personally involved in at least one violent incident and a fifth had been involved in five or more incidents.

The Big Generation is now a major factor in crime. About half of those jailed in Canada are members of the generation. "There is no doubt the single, unemployed male between the ages of twenty and twenty-four, with a low level of education, and living in an urban setting, is the most violence-prone member of society," John Hagan, a University of Toronto sociologist, said. Almost every assault with racial overtones in Toronto in the last half of the 1970s has involved members of the generation, typically men aged eighteen to twenty-one. The late teen years and early twenties have been the most crime-prone for as long as age-specific statistics have been kept; and of course the mass of the Big Generation emphasizes the situation and would have done even if there were no other factors to take account of. As it is, several elements commonly thought to stimulate crime are increasingly present: hard economic times, unemployment in the age group, and the strains of living with an oversize cohort. Women's liberation has been blamed for bringing more women into crime, including crimes formerly the preserve of men, such as car theft, assault, and robbery. About eight per cent of women in Ontario are aged sixteen to eighteen, but they were twenty-two per cent of the women jailed in 1977.

Wherever violence is a problem, alcohol seems to have made it worse. In one of the characteristically wrong judgements officialdom has kept making about the Big Generation, several provincial governments lowered the legal drinking age just as the generation was looming up. One might observe cynically that it was also just when this substantial bloc was approaching legal voting age. In 1971, for instance, Ontario lowered the drinking age from twenty-one to eighteen. This instantly opened the bars and taverns to nearly half a million young people who were previously excluded and gave earlier access to the rest of the generation in the province as they grew up.

The result was a major disaster. The highway safety committee later reported that drivers between sixteen and eighteen were involved in about six per cent of all alcohol-related collisions in 1967; by 1973 they were in fifteen per cent of alcohol-related collisions. "By 1975, the proportion was a staggering 37.2 per cent and still rising." It was not until the last day of 1978, however, that the legal drinking age was raised, and then only to nineteen.

Drinking teenagers and young adults turned camp grounds into terrifying battlegrounds. One spring Saturday night in 1979, fifteen thousand youngsters made an Ontario resort town the scene of fights, drunkenness, and drag racing that went on until rain finally cooled it off at dawn. A police corporal said, "We expected it to be pretty bad, but not as wild as it was." Three hundred youngsters were arrested. At Mosport Park, police were reported to have said they did not dare enter the auto race track and camp ground, where every outhouse was burned one weekend: "Things have gone too far. We can't police the interior of the track. If we went in we'd never come out, our car would get burned. It's completely out of control in there." The trouble was attributed to gangs of youths with cans of gasoline.

Suicide is the strongest expression of human misery. Suicide rates rise very rapidly at the onset of adolescence and would, it appears, go on rising throughout life, though at a slower and slower rate, were it not for some countervailing factor – perhaps resignation – that begins to reduce them after about age fifty-five. In the 1970s, however, the suicide rates for people under thirty rose sharply and are now close to the highest rates for any age group.

For Canada as a whole, accidental deaths, mainly traffic accidents, are the chief cause of death for people in the fifteen-to-twenty-four age group, but suicide is now the second highest cause, having overtaken cancer and heart disease, which were the second and third highest causes of death a quarter of a century ago. In big cities, suicide has replaced accidents as the chief cause of death at that age.

Doctors, sociologists, and psychiatrists who have tried to understand those recent high suicide rates among members of the Big Generation are hampered by the obvious problem of being no longer able to ask direct questions. By carefully reconstructing victims' lives and by talking to young people who have failed in attempts to kill themselves, the professionals have come up with some answers. They tell a lot about what is happening to the generation:

> "The individual most likely to attempt suicide is one with extremely low self-esteem and a hopeless attitude about what he/she can accomplish in life." – a marriage and family therapist.

> "With young people who commit suicide, we're talking about the losers, the ones who aren't making it. They have a sense of impermanence, especially in the family. Many parents are reluctant to impose their values on their kids so the kids are almost in a vacuum – they're treading water emotionally, their direction is negative." – the director of a hospital crisis intervention unit.

> "Adolescents are so seriously depressed that they consider suicide as the only viable alternative available. Up to a few years ago I would say it was rare to see this fully developed depression under the age of fourteen. We're now seeing it under the age of ten, in occasional cases. A feeling of hopelessness about the present and future. Living in a grey world. There's nothing to enjoy, nothing to look forward to. They feel in some way responsible for what has happened, but they can't see anything they can to do alleviate it." – the psychiatrist-in-chief at a large hospital.

While the rising suicide rate of adolescents and young adults has been widely remarked, no one as far as I know has calculated the influence of peer pressures on these rates. But over the post-war period there is a clear relation between the suicide rate and the size of the fifteen-to-twenty-four age group in relation to the whole population. In 1955, for instance, only fourteen per cent of the population was that age, and there were fewer than five suicides for each thousand people in the age group. By 1976, the group was nearly twenty per cent of the population and there were over fourteen suicides for each thousand of that age. Taking the relative size and suicide rate of the group for several years in the period, it is possible to plot points on a graph and put a line through them. In this case, the line statistically "explains" ninety-three per cent of the variation in the suicide rates, which means the relation between the two is fairly convincing and suggests that the size of the Big Generation is a major cause of its suicidal tendencies.

The official suicide death rates for children under fifteen are very low. The real rates are not known: most coroners will not call their deaths suicide because they feel children are too young to have made a conscious decision to kill themselves. But all over Canada child-guidance workers are finding evidence of increasing depression in the youngest of the Big Generation, and even in children as young as ten. Between seven and ten per cent of students in secondary school are going through a serious depression, one counsellor estimated. "They feel they are worthless. . . . They feel they are living with an absence of values. . . . There's a lot of futility in the language they use." Similar phrases turn up everywhere.

The Salvation Army's suicide prevention centre in Toronto reports that teenagers born in "the permissive 1960s" are more likely to commit suicide than any other age group they deal with. They are having the most difficulty coping with problems of drugs, unemployment, debt, alcohol, and family breakdown; they face more threats and pressures at a time when often both parents are working and they have no one else to discuss problems with. One seven-year study of five hundred children under fifteen who tried to kill themselves found that the typical child had an unemployed or runaway father, a working mother, and was having problems at school and suffering from stress-induced depression or hostility. Another study of over 150 would-be suicides found that family stress and loneliness were the chief causes, and that as youngsters nearly half had lost at least one parent by death, divorce, or abandonment.

The Big Generation's potential for hostility and violence is enormous, whether its members direct it against themselves or against parents, teachers or anyone they feel has cheated or hurt them. The kind of people they are, and the circumstances more and more members of the generation find themselves in, have combined to produce a deeply threatening situation. They have a sympathetic, impulsive, emotional response to the world they live in, a response that is less disciplined than in previous generations. They are aware of their own individuality and interested in their own development. Many are alienated from the organized social life going on around them and are deeply involved in their own unique culture.

Canada now finds itself a polarized society, split between those born before the Second World War and those born after it. The direction of our path into the future depends increasingly on how well the Big Generation copes with its transition into adult life, and how well the society can assimilate the generation.

PART III

THE
IMPACT
OF
THE BIG
GENERATION

On the first day of 1980 the oldest member of the Big Generation was still only twenty-eight years old. His history recorded more of what life had done to him than what he had done. That is true of this book, too, up to this point. It has dealt more with what has shaped and influenced the members of the Big Generation than with how the generation has affected the rest of society.

From here on, however, the impact of the Big Generation is going to be the main concern. Until now its presence has been felt to a great extent only in the school system, and to a smaller extent in the job market. Within a few decades, every part of the society will be profoundly and irreversibly changed as the Big Generation matures, moves to centre stage, and takes over.

CHAPTER 6

A HUGE NEW MARKET

"My friends and I made the Bee Gees famous . . ."

Many people have already made fortunes out of the Big Generation: the Rolling Stones, McDonald's, the producers of *Star Wars*, Levi Strauss, Adidas, the author of *The Joy of Sex*, Panasonic, CHUM, the Granola people, the estate of J.R.R. Tolkien, the Frisbee company, Honda, and mirror makers everywhere, to name some. But there is good reason to think that the impact of the generation in the market place to date has been small by comparison with what it is going to be. So far the generation has been a rather limited, specialized market. What lies ahead is far larger.

The Big Generation will create a new market by combining three factors. Each by itself would increase sales; in combination their effect will be powerful and innovative.

The first factor is the size of the Big Generation, an unprecedented concentration of people very much of an age: successively a market for diapers, peanut butter, school books, jeans, rock records, marijuana, take-out food, used cars, somewhere to live, and for diapers again.

The second factor is the fact that young people like to try new things. "The young people have always been a step ahead of the rest of us," an advertiser wrote in the mid-1970s. "And that goes for everything from music to civil rights, from Vietnam to TM. . . . Not only do they get there first, they're faster to try new things. Whether it's a new product, or a whole new life-style." The advance of the generation into the teenage and young adult markets provoked more rapid and, in many cases, more surprising changes in the goods and services available in the market place than had ever been seen before.

The third factor is money. No teenagers ever had as much

money to spend as these. The general level of affluence has meant that much more money has filtered down to youngsters. A teenager's letter to a newspaper in 1979 told the whole story:

> I bought four $15 Bee Gees tickets from BASS [ticket agency]. When I went to pick up my tickets, my mother's Chargex bill was marked with the time 5.24. Officially, ticket sales started at 5.30. Although I was six minutes early and was told I was getting the best tickets available, the seats are at the opposite end of the arena from the stage.... I'm 13 years old. My friends and I made the Bee Gees famous by buying their records. I think that we should have been able to purchase the best seats, close to the stage for that much money.

This child, the last of the Big Generation, is not only part of an economic phenomenon, but she knows it.

Older teenagers have benefited not only from the rise in their parents' disposable income, but from the raising of the minimum wage and the opening of hundreds of thousands of part-time jobs. A recent survey of guidance counsellors in Toronto suggested that about seven per cent of students in the senior grades of high schools had part-time jobs. "If a student begins to fall behind," one counsellor said, "we often discover the problem is that he's got a job that's taking up too much time." Turning sixteen is often when the hand-outs and pocket money from parents begin to dry up and the job-hunting starts in earnest. "Getting a part-time job is the only way to maintain the flow of life's basic necessities – records, new clothes, movies, travel," as one student put it.

I have not seen any recent Canadian estimates of the teenage market, but as long as twenty years ago there were American estimates that the average adolescent's pocket money was ten dollars a week, and that teenagers bought fifty per cent of all the records sold, forty-five per cent of the soft drinks, and more than a quarter of the cosmetics. The proportions are likely to have been higher, perhaps much higher, through the 1970s.

The older members of the generation, now at work, independent, and married or the equivalent, are increasingly living off more than one income. One couple, born in 1951 and 1953, say, "We couldn't keep up our style of living without two salaries." Another, born in 1950 and 1955, say that where the previous generation waited for retirement to have fun, "We want to travel and enjoy life before we get tied down." They both have jobs, and they have a house with a swimming pool, which they paid for while they were in their twenties, go south for two weeks in the winter, go camping in the summer, drive two cars, and have no children.

Most people catering to the generation have still not recognized it as the hundred-year phenomenon that it is. They are like people standing on a bridge who watch the water level in the river rise and fall, and think of it as being like the tide; they are unlike those who note the spring thaw and follow the flood all the way down from the distant mountains, past the bridge, and on to the sea. Thus people will tell you that the teenage market has been growing for the past quarter century, without seeing that it is the passage of the generation through its adolescence that has caused this growth.

The proportion of teens in the population was at an all-time low in 1953, less than eleven per cent, reflecting all the children who were not born during the Depression. The rising number of births after 1939 started the increase, and the big numbers began to show up in the 1960s when the first members of the generation reached the age of thirteen. From two million teenagers in 1960, the number increased to three and a third million in 1976 and 1977 – the highest number of people aged thirteen to nineteen in Canada's history. Now the number of teenagers is dropping. The generation is in passage: the first member of the Big Generation turned twenty in the summer of 1971, the last became a teenager in 1978.

The continuous interaction of these three forces – the Big Generation, novelty, and affluence – has led marketing people to identify various markets at different times; but most of these were really the Big Generation entering or dominating a particular age. In 1977, the owner of a rock-music radio station laid claim to "the youth audience," which he described as people aged fifteen to thirty-five, that is, born between 1942 and 1962. Sixty per cent of these people were members of the Big Generation and the proportion is still growing. In fact, by 1983, the whole generation will be neatly centred in that age bracket, after which the size of the market will start to go down. Rock radio has not many years left, if that owner assessed his audience correctly.

In 1976, the magazine *Oui* identified its readers as "the faster crowd," people aged eighteen to thirty-four. Nearly half of them at that time were members of the generation; by 1984, the Big Generation will be situated slap in the middle of that age group, leaving the magazine's long-term future in doubt if it does not shift with the generation.

In 1977, McDonald's described its main market as people aged twenty to thirty-four; nearly half were then Big Generation people. In 1986, the generation will be the whole of the main hamburger market, after which, of course, the main market will begin to decline.

I do not suggest that the Big Generation is a single, enormous market with homogeneous taste. It has a left wing and a right wing, or perhaps it is an advance guard and a rearguard, or an older component and a younger. But to an unusual extent, the generation's tastes spread throughout the whole seven million, making it at the same time more uniform than other groups and less like them. Its sheer size, naturally enough, has an enormous attraction for marketing people. The mechanics of product design, advertising, promotion, and retail presentation make it worthwhile to try to aim very precisely at a homogeneous group. But because their rapidly growing market must just as rapidly decline after about ten years, it is a game that has to be played with speed and assurance as well as precision. Alternatively, the product must be transformed into something else just as the generation is transforming itself into something else – and that is an even harder trick. Highly stylized eating places might find it very difficult, as would companies making sports equipment, guitars, specialized publications, and the like.

But a number of businesses have already been successful in shifting from teenage to young adult tastes. The music business is notable among them. The Big Generation was the first teenage group to spend big money on phonograph records. Veterans remember when most records were bought by the twelve-to-eighteen age group. But instead of building around adolescent taste, the music industry seems to have quite deliberately concentrated on the Big Generation. A music promoter, Richard Flohil, says record buyers at the start of the 1980s are predominantly eighteen to thirty years old, and to a remarkable extent they still buy the records of musicians they have been buying all along: Bob Dylan, Barbra Streisand, Fleetwood Mac, Led Zeppelin. "Their audience is growing up with them. There is a more rapid turn-over of groups and artists, which means that people get a quick reputation in their mid-twenties, but the big reputations belong to people who are now in their thirties."

The Globe and Mail's rock critic, Paul McGrath, himself a member of the Big Generation, commented several years ago with every evidence of regret that the music industry was trying to accommodate "what they assume to be maturing tastes," promoting artists and records that appealed to adult sensibilities. "There's no full-tilt boogie, no 'I want to hold your hand' and very little hoarse screaming. It's clever music with all the roughness honed away and all the implicit revolution co-opted."

Perhaps needless to say, it was for the Big Generation that so many staid dining rooms were turned into discos.

Clothes manufacturers have also started to make the shift. Take Levi Strauss, for instance. They sold huge volumes of the blue jeans that were the uniform of the Big Generation, a million dollars a week in Canada at the peak in the mid-1970s; but in 1978, for the first time, sales were lower than they had been the year before, and now Levi Strauss is making cotton dresses, tweed jackets, shoes – a variety of clothes for the young adult.

Another industry that is growing up with the generation is the games business, though here new manufacturers are making much of the progress. Many of the games – computer games, board games, dice games, war games, electronic games, fantasy role-playing games – look as though they were designed with only the Big Generation in mind. They exploit technology, they call on fantasy and imagination, they are non-physical, and in many of them the player can pit his wits against the machine. Gammaworld, Dungeons & Dragons, Head to Head Football, Simon, Merlin, and Chess Challenger are going where Scrabble and Monopoly never ventured, and at far higher prices.

The last time family income categorized by the age of the head of the household was widely surveyed, it was found that people spent most when they were age thirty-five to fifty-four. That may reflect the age distribution of the population at the time of the survey (the mid-1970s); the relative shortage of people born in the 1920s and 1930s may have won them a larger proportion of well-paying jobs than would otherwise have been the case. But it is unlikely to have accounted for more than a small part of the age group's eminence as consumers. In a similar survey carried out ten years earlier, while average household expenditures were only half as much, the ratios of the amounts spent by the various categories of household were very similar.

The main difference was that in the later survey, the gap between the spending of people over fifty-five and under fifty-five had widened; the older households' expenditure had dropped from about three-quarters of the younger households' to about two-thirds. For a long time, the years from thirty-five to fifty-four have been thought of as the period when earning and spending are at a peak, and it is probably going to remain true.

That means that the Big Generation's spending should be rising throughout the rest of this century and on into the next, until it dominates the economy. The generation is now spending about a fifth of the money spent by all households, but in ten years this should approach forty per cent and from then through most of the first decade of the twenty-first century the generation should account for between forty and fifty per cent of all consumer spending. Yet the members of the generation, who will then be in their forties and fifties, will constitute only about a quarter of the total population. Age dictates the choice of goods and services that people buy to a considerable extent, but as in everything else the particular qualities of the cohort are also important, and the Big Generation's unique tastes will lead the market for at least the next three decades.

The generation is different in so many ways that it is really a new kind of market. Because of their level of education, members of the generation are much more interested in experiences than their predecessors. Their independence, the openness of their feelings, their egoism, their experience of growing up in a time of great change and amazing technological innovation: all have influenced the kind of things and services they buy, and even where they buy them. The small specialized store or boutique returned after years in which big chain stores and department stores dominated retailing, just as the generation started to spend big money.

Take their frequently emotional, sensual approach to life. It has predisposed them to works of fantasy and imagination, to science fiction, Tolkien and his innumerable imitators, to horror movies, and stories of the occult. The newest element is science fiction, which was probably stimulated by the pace of change and innovation during the generation's childhood. At any rate, there is a noticeable difference between the approaches of Stanley Kubrick, who made the cool, cerebral *2001* in the mid-1960s and captured an audience born during the Second World War or before, and of George Lucas's *Star Wars*, Steven Spielberg's *Close Encounters of the Third Kind*, and Richard Donner's *Superman*. All of these were more fantastic as well as more spectacular, warmer, even sentimental, and deftly aimed right at the Big Generation.

Compare *Alien* with *2001*. Both take place in space and in the future, both show earthlings directed or diverted by computer, both send their human beings on long voyages, both concern earthlings' encounters with unearthly forces. But the alien in *2001* is an abstraction clothed in geometry; in *Alien* it is a ferociously predatory monster. No one would call *Alien* sentimental, but what chiefly distinguishes it from *2001* and most other science-fiction movies of the 1960s or earlier is the powerful feelings it arouses.

The life of feeling has made members of the generation into music addicts, and their music is almost wholly without intellectual content, almost wholly sensed. Feelings have a great deal to do with the generation's taste for natural materials, the open air, bicycling, country living, and natural foods, all of which are more strongly sensual, often tactile, than the conventional alternatives, packaged food, automobiles, plastics, and so on. Many members of the generation do not specially like these things, but those who do are the largest part of the market for them. Along with long hair for men, and rough hardy clothes, they are the trappings of a new and separate culture. (Punk rockers now have to wear short hair and shiny plastic to rebel against established style.)

The more open and cheerful attitude toward sex is another instance of the generation's devotion to its feelings. A fairly widespread interest in demystifying the orgasm, enjoying sexual relations more communally, and exploring pornography has produced a huge market for magazines like *Penthouse, Hustler, Playgirl*, and probably thousands of others, and for general and specialized books on every aspect of sex. I am not saying that previous generations were not sexy, but that they felt compelled to interiorize most of their interest and to confine what they could not contain to a few well-tested, conventional public forms of expression, the locker-room joke, absurd romantic novels and movies, and so on. As a result there was very little sale for vibrators, dildoes, pornographic magazines, flavoured douches, illustrated manuals, topless waitresses, blue movies, and all the rest of what is now an avalanche of sex material pouring into bookstores, drugstores, cigar stores, milk stores, variety stores, movie theatres, restaurants, bars, and hotels.

Education has made the Big Generation more independent and more interested in experiences, and these qualities overlap with its sensuality. Riding a bicycle or motorcycle is obviously a more intense experience than driving a sedan or riding a bus. Living in a rural commune is more physically stimulating than living in an apartment building, and devotees say it is more spiritually stimulating, too. The huge rock concerts are emotionally powerful social experiences.

The generation is addicted to travel almost as obsessively as to music. A year in Europe is not only a common ambition for youngsters coming out of high school or breaking their time at university or college, it is surprisingly often achieved. The lure of skiing in the Rockies, swimming in the Caribbean, or surfing in the Pacific has turned the generation into an impoverished imitation of the jet set. You cannot shine up a rock concert and hang it over the fireplace; you cannot trade in a two-year-old trip to Rome on this year's model; you cannot raise a mortgage on life in a commune, or get daily interest on it. What assets there are in experience build up in a different way.

The independence comes through in the generation's willingness to go against the rest of the world's conventions and institutions: not, however, against the conventions and institutions of its own youth culture. Blue jeans were a strong expression of independence. Charles Reich thought jeans were "a deliberate rejection of the neon colors and plastic, artificial look of the affluent society." Wearing jeans, you did not have to be cautious, constrained; you could sleep in them, roll down a hill in them, repair a car in them. And they made the claim that all life was one: "there is not one set of clothes for the office, another for social life, a third for play. The same clothes can be used for every imaginable activity, and so they say: it is the same person doing each of these things." Reich found the clothes of the new generation expressed "profoundly democratic values," and added, "There are no distinctions of wealth or status, no elitism." Just what Dewey's disciples preached.

Since Reich wrote *The Greening of America*, the Big Generation has added work boots to the uniform, and all the same things could be said of them, too. They reject the polished, socialized, conformist world of the adult. So do rural communes. So do vandalism and crime. So does the health food or natural food movement. So does rock music. So, for that matter, does women's lib, which surprised older men and women but swept through the generation like a prairie fire.

Cynics have sometimes objected that in revolting against established values and styles the generation has built an even narrower conformity of its own. Well, first, the variation within the uniformity of the generation's dress really is greater than the variation within the uniformity of men's three-piece business suits, and that goes equally for hair styles, tastes in reading (what, another Toronto *Star* reader?), eating (what, another T-bone steak?), and transportation (what, another Thunderbird?). And second, in running its revolution or independence movement, the generation has had to develop its own internal solidarity, its own strength: like the Red Guard in China. Remember how circumstances simultaneously conferred independence and membership in the "barbaric" youth culture on the generation! It needed to find ways to express both its separateness from other generations and its shared interests with its peers, preferably at one and the same time; for adolescents, clothing was one of the available tokens.

Egoism is contained in most of the Big Generation's actions and choices. It comes out in the passion for jogging, the most solitary and self-centred exercise. "Look at the face of a jogger," said Mary McCarthy. "It's not like the face of a pedestrian, who is in contact with the ground, or a cyclist, who is in contact with his machine. The jogger is in contact with some idea, some abstraction." In what it eats and how it exercises, this generation is devoted to its own health and well-being, its own muscles and skin tone, as no earlier generation was. The generation is probably more given to masturbation – without doubt the women are – and it certainly is much readier to discuss what a more euphemistic age called auto-eroticism and even read novels and how-to books about it. Self-love: the epitome of narcissism. Music, too, is often a self-engrossed pleasure, when the listener engulfs himself in world-obliterating sound. Drugs turn the user inward, shut out reality, transform perceptions of the environment with personal memories, fears, and desires.

The easy gratification of wants in childhood taught the generation that its adolescent and adult wants would be as readily met. This self-indulgence leads to some of the paradoxes in the generation's tastes. Smoking, for instance, is common, even though the Big Generation knows far more about the health risks than did previous generations and despite the frank desire to be healthy: smoking and jogging! Or in the same day taking care to avoid bread with chemical additives, high cholesterol fats, white sugar, and so on – following the natural food regime – and then gobbling down a late-night snack of hamburgers, french fries, and milk shakes from the fast-food chains. Can the crunchy granola chocolate bar be far behind?

Simple circumstance has given the Big Generation other attributes that make them a special market. For instance, they were largely responsible for reviving movies after television had nearly killed them. The parents of the generation were once dedicated moviegoers. Television arrived with the Big Generation. As children they watched it for hours, but as adolescents they wanted to go out when their parents stayed home, which was increasingly often as more and better and later movies showed up on TV. So while their parents treated TV as movies-at-home, the generation treated movies as TV-away-from-home. A recent survey found that sixty per cent of the people under twenty-five had been to at least one movie in the previous seven weeks, while only thirteen per cent of people over forty-four had. This is not just the result of older people's wanting to stay at home: less than fifty per cent of the under-twenty-fives had attended a sports event in the same seven weeks, for instance, but nearly thirty per cent of the over-forty-fours had. There is no firm evidence yet whether members of the generation will remain moviegoers as they get older. A good part of the marketing flurry over big-screen TV, video recorders, video-discs, and other enhancements of TV is an attempt to capture the Big Generation as it enters adult life and gets a home and set of its own.

Marketing experts think people switch from soft drinks to beer to wine to liquor as they get older, and there are even theories about what kind of liquor, clear (e.g., gin) or coloured (e.g., rye), people favour at different ages. Most are agreed that alcohol consumption increases up to middle age and then goes down again, thirty-five to forty-four being the prime drinking age. From all this, the soft-drink and beer companies are now drawing gloomy conclusions about their markets for the next several decades, while the liquor companies are noticeably brightening.

If the "prime drinking age" theory is right, the liquor companies are going to strike it richest around the end of the century, when some five million members of the Big Generation will be that age. The trouble is that it is by no means clear they will dutifully switch to hard liquor and lots of it as their parents did. Wine, marijuana, or some new intoxicant is at least as likely to attract them. There are tiny flickers in the consumption of scotch whisky that suggest to some distillers that the leading edge of the Big Generation is reaching the whisky age and performing as predicted, but the numbers are not solid enough to convince outsiders.

The same kind of switch from radio to television to newspaper has been postulated by media experts. Certainly radio has been the Big Generation's medium in adolescence, certainly TV is the pre-eminent adult medium today, and certainly old people spend more time with newspapers than young people. But the chain of transition seems even weaker here than in the case of drinking.

It seems improbable that the Big Generation will ever take to newspapers or any other kind of intent reading the way their parents did, and there is already evidence of that. If newspaper reading was entrenched, the increase in educational level would push newspapers sales upward faster than the population is growing; that is, the sale of newspapers per person would increase. In fact per-person sales have been static for some years, despite the production of several new tabloids aimed at younger readers – the "bosom and bullets" formula, as it is called.

The greater importance of radio than TV to teenagers is shown by two sets of statistics. Radio advertising is charged according to a station's rating with particular audiences. For each rating point for teenage audiences the cost is $141; for adult men, $336; for adult women $293. But the proportions are reversed in television, where it is harder to reach teenagers. Television advertising is sold on the basis of the cost to reach a thousand people. For teenagers, the cost is $24.69; for adult men, $9.10; for adult women, $8.09.

Awareness of these data no doubt helps to persuade marketing people that teenagers will inevitably progress to the viewing/listening habits of today's adults. So they may, giving up their radios and movies and turning into replicas of their parents. But a lot in their upbringing and character suggests they will not. Education is the most persuasive factor. It is well understood in the ratings game that the more highly educated a person is, the less likely she is to watch TV.

A Statistics Canada study of culture statistics used the attendance rates for people of various age groups and education levels to project the growth of various activities. It concluded that in the rest of this century, attendance at theatres, classical music, dance, and opera performances would grow two or three times as fast as television watching and attendance at sports events and movies. In other words, the Big Generation is a new kind of market, not a replay of previous generations.

Obviously all such statistics reflect the past quality of the media as well as the characteristics of their past audiences, and there is every reason to suppose that in the future all the media will try to move with the Big Generation from adolescence to maturity, just as beer companies buy wineries and wine companies buy distilleries and all of them ponder the market for marijuana. But here again, I would not be surprised to see the generation stick with radio and movies, or at least to a much greater extent than older generations do now.

Another circumstance that makes the oldest members of the Big Generation special right now is the fact that many couples have two salaried jobs and are both away from home all day, so that they have become huge consumers of restaurant meals, fast-food snacks, and meals at home that require little preparation, such as TV dinners, sliced vegetables, canned puddings, and ready-made gravy. This is also the diet of many young people who have left home and remain single. They are all prime customers for commercial household services of all kinds, from day nurseries, baby sitters, and diaper services to cleaning women, dog walkers, plant waterers, and repairmen of all kinds. It is for them that banks, trust companies, and credit unions stay open evenings and Saturdays; that twenty-four-hours-a-day automated banking services are springing up; that launderettes stay open all night; that all kinds of stores are open late two or three evenings a week. Much of this is probably going to persist at least throughout this century, and there will be large opportunities to extend all these services, and more.

CHAPTER 7

ON THE MOVE

*"Youth is the time to go flashing
from one end of the world to the other."*

By 1986, more than two-thirds of the Big Generation will live at an address different from the one they had in 1981 – in another country, another province, another town, at the very least another house. That means well over four and a half million people will have moved. By contrast, little more than a third of the rest of the population will move house.

The late teens, twenties, and early thirties are commonly the time people choose to move. Young people do not want to move before they finish their schooling, and as they get older they again become less willing to move. But in between, it is time to fly; always has been. "Youth is the time to go flashing from one end of the world to the other both in mind and body," Robert Louis Stevenson wrote a hundred years ago; "to try the manners of different nations; to hear the chimes at midnight; to see sunrise in town and country." In the first half of the 1980s the whole of the Big Generation will be in its migrant age, its vagabondage, and the impact will be large.

A lot of that impact depends on where the generation manages to alight. The obvious prediction is that it will be in the cities, the bigger the better. Ever since the Second World War young adults have moved up the urban ladder from wherever fate put them as children. One very telling statistic that can be computed from the census every five years is how people of any age group are distributed among places of various sizes. A good way to get the broad picture is to imagine all the people of one age group, fifteen to nineteen, for instance, arranged in a line according to the population of the place where they live – those from places with the largest population at one end, those from the smallest at the other – and then note where the one in the middle lives. This is the median size of place for the age group. At the 1976 census, the median location of people in their late teens was a place of about 85,000 population, somewhere like Brantford, Ontario, or Sydney, Nova Scotia. But the median location of people in their twenties was a city of well over 200,000, a metropolis the size of Victoria or Windsor. In fact, there are only fifteen cities that size or bigger in all Canada, and half the people in their twenties lived in them.

The 1976 median location for people in their twenties was two and a half times the size of the teens' median location, and that has held true ever since the census of 1951. The break between teens and twenties, far and away the biggest between any age groups, shows dramatically where youngsters go when they leave home.

The jump is intensified by the fact that immigrants from abroad characteristically come to a few big places – Toronto, Montreal and Vancouver take half of all immigrants to this country – and a third of all immigrants are in their twenties. Half a million more people in their twenties must have come into the cities in the past ten years.

But in the 1970s a counter-movement out of the cities has been discernible. In the 1950s and 1960s people in their twenties, thirties, and forties had the largest median locations; but at the 1971 census, for the first time, people over thirty began to move down the urban ladder to smaller places. These were people born in the 1940s; in other words, the first people born after the long lull through the 1920s and 1930s who could have begun to feel the pressure of living in a larger cohort. In 1976, for the first time, people in their late twenties and early thirties began to show up in larger numbers than expected in the rural areas, often in places just beyond the edge of a metropolitan area but within an hour's drive of it. Not back on the farm, though. In the first half of the 1970s the rural but non-farm population increased by nearly a million people, that is, by nearly a quarter. Proportionate to their numbers, the largest increase was in people born between 1941 and 1956 – the early baby boom and those who just preceded it; people who were in their twenties in 1971 and in their late twenties and early thirties by 1976. The number of them in rural non-farm areas increased by nearly forty per cent.

In the same period, half a million people aged twenty to thirty-

128

four moved into the metropolises, but almost exactly the same number moved out. The reason for all these moves was not hard to find. Jobs, which were probably the main reason for going to the cities in the first place, were becoming scarce for young people. They were as scarce outside the cities as in, but outside at least it was possible for young adults to find housing they could afford.

In its migratory flight, the Big Generation will find that these housing and employment conditions have become worse, and will in itself make them worse. The well-established movement of young people to the country's metropolises and big towns will almost certainly be slowed and could, with a few exceptions, be halted. There is little doubt the generation will move: the desire to leave home and become independent is almost irresistible. But where its members will go is much less certain. The only certainty seems to be that they will not move back to the suburbs, which grew in the post-war years largely to accommodate them as children. Even if they wanted to, the cost of suburban housing and apartments is out of reach of most of them.

The suburbs will have to become ghost towns before the Big Generation decides to move back in. But, by the 1990s, that might just happen. David Lewis Stein said recently:

> Now the subdivisions are filling up with lonely old people, with angry teenagers who can't find jobs, with bewildered new immigrants who can't even find out what's going on around them, and with single parents desperately trying to raise children alone.

As in so much of what it does, the Big Generation is setting new trends in migration. Not, in this case, purely from choice, but because the pressure of its numbers, coinciding with economic slowdown, forces its members to find new ways of doing things.

The impact of the generation can only be guessed at, but three cities – Calgary, Ottawa-Hull, and Quebec – got a small foretaste of it in the first half of the 1970s. What drew the migrants in each case was a spate of new jobs: the new oil boom, the growth of the federal government, and the growth of the Quebec government, respectively. The effects were quite similar; they ranged from rapidly rising house prices and apartment rents to pressures on police and welfare agencies, from traffic problems to demoralizingly quick changes in once stable neighbourhoods, from strains on city budgets to startling political shifts. Immigration from abroad was comparatively small in all three cities. The influx consisted almost wholly of people moving from other parts of Canada.

Vancouver, which combined a fairly large invasion from all parts of Canada with substantial immigration, got a slightly different preview of what the arrival of the Big Generation might be like. Young people virtually took over whole neighbourhoods, and there was a sharp increase in racial antagonism and violence, as well as significantly higher employment problems, high rents, and soaring house prices.

In the central cities – the original cities around which the metropolises congealed – the concentration of people in their twenties is even more marked. To take examples at random, one in five people living in the City of Toronto is in his twenties; in Edmonton and Halifax it is one in four. These large bulges in the population pyramids are responsible for the election of mayors in blue jeans, mayors who are unsympathetic to real-estate developers, mayors who support gay rights, mayors who openly live with their girl friends – young, unconventional, and even rather radical mayors who could hardly get a seat on the board of education a decade ago.

As these cities found out, a dominant cohort becomes a clear target for people selling goods and services. They find it profitable to concentrate on a narrower age group if it is large enough, because its tastes are more homogeneous. It becomes harder to find family movies among all the movies exploiting sex and violence, harder to find a quiet, dull bar among all the discos and places with topless entertainers. And this is even more noticeable in places smaller than Vancouver or Ottawa; the big cities still have sizable populations of every age group, even if they are comparatively smaller, and can still support their tastes. The opening of farmland and tar-sands plants in northern Alberta drew large numbers in their twenties and thirties, and some communities experienced near-riot conditions.

The ugliness of racism is an uncomfortably good parallel to the response of older people to an increase of younger people. A "reasonable" number of people who are different is easy to accommodate, but at some point – five per cent? ten per cent? – the number begins to look "unreasonable" to a growing number of citizens, and a kind of social paranoia develops. The newcomers are thought to be grabbing all the jobs, to be rude and pushy, to be making the stores stock too much "foreign" stuff and not enough "Canadian" stuff, to have unpleasant personal habits, to smell bad. It should be easy to show that, on the contrary, the newcomers are largely beneficial, and that their differences are enriching. But experience in Toronto and Vancouver proves that a rapid build-up of immigrants brings heavy strains and makes for bad feelings that persist. And this is the reaction the Big Generation will induce.

No solid information about the plans of the majority of the generation can emerge before the 1981 census, however; and even it will not do much more than hint at what will happen in the following five years when the biggest movement of all will take place. It is a fair guess that emigration will rise, though by how much is hard to guess. Canadians are much like people from other countries: the time of life for emigrating is predominantly in the twenties and early thirties. When the Gallup Poll asked Canadians if they could think of any other country they would rather be citizens of, thirteen per cent aged eighteen to twenty-nine said they could, but only half as many older people could. These statistics reflect young people's desire to break away from home as well as the fact that the great majority in their twenties are native-born Canadians, while a substantial portion of older people are immigrants, have made the decision to become citizens of another country once in their lives, and are already living in it.

All things being equal, the 1980s should see a sharp rise in emigration, perhaps by a third or even a half over what it was in the early 1970s. But what may not be equal is the appeal of the United States, particularly if the economy weakens or if it reinstitutes the draft for young residents. The Vietnam war chopped Canadian emigration to the US dramatically, and it was slow to pick up after the draft ended. And most other countries either refuse entry, except to people who will do the most unpleasant kind of work, or limit it severely.

People in the moving business, telephone companies, apartment owners, employment agencies, and others who deal with transients may like to note that the figure of four and a half million Big Generation migrants in the first half of the 1980s considerably understates the uprooting that is going to take place in Canada. For a lot of people will move more than once between 1981 and 1986. Some will go west (or east), find they do not like it, and move back home. Some will transfer to another city and then move on to a third.

Two independent estimates of migration between provinces, both made by Statistics Canada between 1971 and 1976, showed how much of this kind of movement must be taking place. One, the census, found that in 1976 about 400,000 people aged twenty to thirty-four were living in another province than the one they lived in in 1971. From the other, a set of annual estimates based on family allowance changes of address, driving licences, and other information, it appears that more like 700,000 people of that age changed provinces during the five years. So it took seven inter-provincial moves, on average, to end up with four people living in another province.

Is the same pattern likely to hold good for moves within a province, or within a city? Because distances are shorter and leaving home just to move across town is less dramatic, it is likely that even more moves are involved in proportion to the final number of changes. But to be conservative, applying the inter-provincial rates to all moves, in the first half of the 1980s there will be well over eight million moves by the Big Generation.

Immigration is a major threat to the Big Generation. Immigrants from other countries have already increased the generation's size substantially, even though it is obvious that excess of people is the generation's biggest problem. In the fifteen years of the baby boom, 1951 to 1966, there were more than a quarter of a million immigrants of the same age as the generation. From 1966 to 1979 there were another 600,000, and the total number added to their ranks since 1951 will pass a million by the end of 1983.

The age distribution of immigrants does not change much over the years. Most are young adults. A third are in their twenties; half are aged eighteen to thirty-three. The Big Generation, on the other hand, is inexorably aging. Since 1976, at least a third of the immigrants each year have been the same age as the generation, and the proportion has been getting larger. The worst year will be 1984, when half the immigrants will be the generation's age. As late as 1990, at least a third will be the generation's age.

Canada has received close to 150,000 immigrants a year on

average since the Second World War. If there were that many each year from 1976 to 1990, that would add a million more to the ranks of the Big Generation, an increase they could only regard as an extremely unfriendly act. If Canada had been acting in the interests of the generation, it would have reduced immigration sharply from the early 1970s, would bring it down to a very low figure in the mid 1980s, and would not allow it to start rising again until the 1990s. But government immigration policy is dictated by the unemployment rate. In the first years of the 1970s, when unemployment was low, immigration averaged around 200,000 people a year. It has dropped since the mid 1970s, but not until 1978 were there fewer than 100,000 immigrants in a year.

Of course, to the extent that the Big Generation contributes to high unemployment, its interest in low immigration will likely be met. But it is safe to predict that the government will be pressed to increase immigration long before its capacity to harm the generation has passed. People in many poor countries and many Commonwealth countries look to Canada as their future home. The pressures of over-population are still growing in most parts of the world.

A more difficult option would be for the government to let in very young immigrants and old immigrants while keeping out people in their twenties and thirties. But since young and old are typically the families of those in the middle, it would be difficult. The very young and the old are also much more likely to be a burden on government services, particularly education and health care, and less likely to support themselves, so this choice is not going to be high on any government's priority list.

CHAPTER 8

LABOUR PAINS

*"I'd just like to have enough money
so that if I wanted to sit around, I could;
if I wanted to work hard, I could."*

For the best part of a decade now, members of the Big Generation have left school or college with the same insistent question: "Will I get a job?" From one end of the country to the other, the unemployment rates for people in their late teens and early twenties have been nowhere less than miserable, and for some of the generation – teenage school dropouts in Newfoundland being the worst example – they have been disastrous.

The facts began to appear in front-page newspaper stories in the mid-1970s and are still there, years later: "He has 2 degrees – but no job," "The unwanted graduate: who's to blame?", "Youth squeezed out in search for jobs," "The fading dream: children of Baby Boom try to keep job hopes alive." These were the youngsters who had been lured into college by the human-capital theory that was so popular in the years when they were growing up – the premise, as a federal government briefing paper described it, that public investment in educational systems and educated manpower would ultimately lead to economic benefits for both society and individuals. The theory was repeatedly stressed by economists, who were indeed able to show right through the 1950s and into the mid-1960s that a degree brought its holder a higher salary, direct enough proof of one part of the theory.

What the Big Generation had not heard was that the theory was much more tentative than it was represented, and that a whole generation of students had been made the victims of an academic con job. In the words of *The Globe and Mail*'s business columnist, Ronald Anderson, "The argument was put forward principally to encourage greater public support of the educational system." No one had thought through the implications of a rapid rise in highly educated workers. "One flaw in this reasoning," Anderson wrote, "was that it assumed that the economy automatically would be capable of absorbing the university graduates in employment appropriate to their training."

Of course, that assumption did not pan out. As the federal government brief commented:

> If, indeed, a post-secondary education ever guaranteed these economic benefits in the past, it is clear with the recent change in the economic environment that it no longer continues to do so. The legacy of those times is a condition of exaggerated individual expectations coincident with a continuing surplus of post-secondary graduates.

An Ontario Economic Council study estimated that during the period from 1974 to 1982, "at least ten per cent of the new entrants to the labour market from Ontario colleges and university will not get jobs of the sort traditionally reserved for persons with post-secondary education." The forecasts showed forty to seventy thousand people surplus to demand in Ontario, most of whom would then displace high-school graduates from their traditional jobs.

Since the mid-1970s it has scarcely been possible to open a newspaper without running into evidence of the misery this confidence trick has brought to the Big Generation:

Robert Cook, born in 1955, graduated with a BA from the University of Western Ontario, could not find work, took a Canada Manpower creative job-seeking course, and then failed to get taken on as a dishwasher in an Ottawa restaurant: "I was overqualified. They were hiring Vietnamese boat people."

Vera Mykolajiw, born in 1951, has an MA in Slavic languages and was an A student at the Ontario College of Education. She scored "excellent" in every practice-teaching session. She registered for employment as a clerk, recognizing that she stood a better chance of getting work than if she had been listed as a teacher.

Wolf Ballman, born in 1951, specialized in Italian and German literature at the University of Toronto, finishing up with a degree and a job maintaining paint machines. He recently enrolled in a community college course in business administration.

The plight of the graduate is one of those ironies that have plagued the Big Generation at every turn. In the early 1970s a third or more of all employees with degrees in Canada were working in schools or universities, by far the largest fraction in any single profession or industry. They were there in large part to educate the generation. But it was they and not the Big Generation who benefited from the human-capital theory. When it was the generation's turn to go to work, not only did they need higher degrees to qualify for teaching posts, not only did they find that their predecessors had locked up all the jobs and were grimly fighting to hang on to them, but the number of students who needed teaching was falling to levels not seen since before the generation went to school in the 1950s.

The feeling among the generation and many of the people who have anything to do with their efforts to find work is that the situation has been extraordinarily mishandled. "The Canadian economy has been seriously out of joint with the Canadian educational system," University of Manitoba economist Ruben Bellan wrote. Stephen Threlkeld, a McMaster University biologist, looked at the employment problems of doctoral graduates, and concluded, "We're going to destroy a whole generation of these bright young people." The most renowned comment of all, because it was the bluntest, was Pierre Elliott Trudeau's: "If they don't like it here, let them find another country where they can use university graduates, and if they can't use them anywhere else it's because there are too many university graduates, that's all."

Is that true? Are there too many graduates? Yes, clearly, in the case of Ph.Ds. The doctorate is the culmination of up to twenty years of education, which is more than enough for any line of work but university teaching and a few research posts. But a Science Council study estimated that, by 1985, anywhere from seventy to ninety per cent of Ph.D. graduates in the previous ten years would be surplus to the needs of the universities, depending on the field of specialization. And yes, equally clearly, there are too many graduates in the whole field of education: teacher-training college graduates intended for public schools, bachelors of arts heading for secondary schools, and graduates with higher degrees hoping to teach in universities. And yes again, if the measure of "enough" is the number of jobs formerly done only by graduates.

But there are not necessarily too many if highly educated people start to move into jobs formerly performed by less educated workers, with the result that these jobs are carried out more skil-fully, more sensitively, or more efficiently. Some of the dis-satisfaction the Big Generation graduates feel arises from expecta-tions that can now be seen as unrealistic or outdated. A Carleton University journalism graduate was bitter that she had to search for six months for a job, and felt underemployed in the one she finally landed as a reporter for a country weekly. Yet countless older journalists without degrees started work on country weeklies or their equivalent. Should the degree replace experience?

Thousands of students have graduated with the expectation that they will never have to work outside their chosen field. Janet King, born in 1955, decided to take a year off in Europe after graduating with a political science degree from Queen's University, "because I can't see too many jobs that interest me, particularly ones that are a function of political science." Is that a reasonable expecta-tion?

The attitudes of the Big Generation toward work differ mar-kedly from those of previous generations, which is not surprising considering the influences that formed them. It is therefore point-less to make unflattering comparisons between them and the solid, loyal, oh-so-reliable workers of earlier generations. Educa-tion has done the most to make them different, pushing them beyond a simple concern for the ways of the community and the needs of the enterprise to a dominant interest in their own capacities.

"A youth who accepts the importance of 'self-actualization' is not likely to adjust to the assembly line at General Motors or to any regimented corporate institutions," Jack Quarter observed. "His strivings require creative outlets, and he is likely to rebel or withhold a commitment to any institution that is incompatible with his outlook." Managers have been baffled by this lack of commit-ment, which was almost routinely demanded when the manager and his colleagues started work. After all, as late as 1953, the US Supreme Court ruled, "There is no more important cause for dis-charge of an employee than disloyalty to the employer." But what employers are being met with is not an unqualified refusal to pitch in. The American poll-taker Daniel Yankelovich wrote in a study of modern work values:

The New Breed [of workers] often start a job willing to work

137

hard and be productive. But if the job fails to meet their expectations – if it doesn't give them the incentives they are looking for – then they lose interest. . . . The preoccupation with self that is the hallmark of New Breed values places the burden of providing incentives more squarely on the employer than under the old value system.

Two things are indicated by the Big Generation's demands that work help the younger worker develop his own potential, that it be interesting and meaningful. One is that the employer's and employee's priorities are no longer going to be entirely dictated by who wields the pay packet. The other is that, while employer and employee should both be capable of judging whether the work is worthwhile in itself, and both be interested in doing so, realistically speaking it is only the employer who can make it so.

Richard Sennett, a sociologist at New York University, commented: "The demand of employees that work be made worthwhile if they are going to work hard confuses many employers. They ask, aren't security and money enough? Evidently not." That one's life and activity should have meaning, that one is responsible for one's work, that putting bread on one's table is not in itself a sufficient reason for doing certain kinds of work: these ideas arise from a variety of sources – Marx, Keynes, Galbraith, Marcuse, and all their disciples – that even today are hardly accessible to the conscious minds of the poorly educated. Yet they do operate throughout the Big Generation.

The young, we are left to observe, act like the old rich elites: discriminating, qualifying, denying, with a freedom of action that all the events of the post-war world have granted them *en masse*, and that employment problems have not softened. "Young people from comfortable homes increasingly look for intrinsic satisfaction in their work, while the poorer and less educated attach more importance to its indirect benefits," a Swedish professor wrote of the young people of North America and Western Europe. "But the gap between the two groups is narrowing, which suggests that the new values are no longer restricted to the privileged articulate groups."

Although they are still unrefined, the ideals of the Big Generation can be seen as clearly in their attitude to work as anywhere – not just in their job and professional preferences, but in their broad expectations throughout the workplace. As Dr. Max Clarkson, the dean of management studies at the University of Toronto, said recently:

> There are some key psychological requirements for making work satisfying. You need a chance to learn, and to continue learning, so there's a sense of making progress. The work has to give you a sense that you're making a contribution, that it is valuable, and worth doing. Your work has to lead to a desirable future, in terms of personal growth; it can't be a dead-end.

Many of the ideals are common to the young of many countries. Torsten Husén, the University of Stockholm professor quoted above, listed some of them. He noted in particular that the young believe that education is intended to develop the whole personality, not just vocational skills; that jobs should allow the worker freedom and initiative; that workers should have their say about the conditions and organization of the work; and that they have rejected the notion of a continuous career with a series of selection points at which one passes or fails. Many of these ideas arise directly from the progressive education that Dewey shaped, and from the liberating and individualizing experience of high school and, in many cases, post-secondary education.

The sense of being an independent individual, so strong in the Big Generation, really marks the end of the old Protestant work ethic that Max Weber first revealed. The Big Generation does not, as far as anyone can see, feel that "in building the tremendous cosmos of the modern economic order" it is "labouring for the glory of God." The idea that work is a religious duty has completely disappeared with this generation. "For most of history, men have *been* what they *did*; a man's work provided him with an identity that was recognized both by others and by himself," Stanley Parker wrote in *The Future of Work and Leisure*. But members of the generation do not yearn to discover themselves in honest toil.

Educated people are more interested in figuring out new things to do and new ways of doing them than in trying to get by with what exists; it is the old military distinction between those who give orders and those who take them. Probably no other quality of the Big Generation's has caused more friction. "It's a generation that won't accept a Prussian authoritarianism at work," an American sociologist remarked. A poll by Daniel Yankelovich found that over fifty per cent of American workers believed they had a right to share in decisions affecting their job. "They want to participate in job-related decisions," the president of the Work in America Institute, Jerome Rosow, said, "but our managers are technocrats who don't think in terms of the individual." This management reaction is continent wide. A London, Ontario, city controller warned the city against hiring over-qualified job applicants because, he said, "they might look for ways to subvert the supervisory process." A survey of Canadians in 1975 found that the youngest, born in the second half of the 1950s, had a strong sense of frustration about their jobs. They were notably more ambitious to have a career, whether or not they felt their present jobs were leading them in that direction: only five percent denied the ambition, whereas more than a quarter of those over the age of thirty-five said they did not want a career. Yet eighty per cent of the young ones felt their jobs demanded less than their full ability.

The Big Generation questions the basic technological-economic thrust of industry. Ian Wilson, a senior corporate planner at the General Electric Company, has suggested that what he calls the "New Reformation" is a shift of emphasis in the generation:

> From considerations of quantity, toward considerations of quality; from mastery over nature, toward living in harmony with it; from the primacy of technical efficiency, toward considerations of social justice and equity; from the dictates of organizational convenience, toward aspirations for self-development in an organization's membership; from authoritarianism and dogmatism, toward participation.

The protesting students of the late 1960s and early 1970s are becoming the career professionals of the 1980s, and in Wilson's view they have abandoned violence not for apathy, but for legal and political strategies, which will lead to equally traumatic confrontations.

Many of these concerns focus on the industrial ideal of efficiency. "The oncoming generation have new doubts about the ideals of efficiency," the authors of a study of work and society wrote. "They are unwilling to pay the crushing price of loss of pride, mind-killing monotony, dehumanization, and stress diseases in return for the highest wages in history."

A major problem for the Big Generation is its attitude to commerce and industry. The generation's heroes are almost exclusively in what has been called the New Class, the class of professionals, civil servants, workers in the media, artists, and the like who, long denied power, now sense that it is within reach: they are sometimes represented as the semi-official opposition to Big Business. The campus poll already cited on page 100 pinpointed where students put their trust and where their doubt; ninety per cent had confidence in television news, ninety per cent had no confidence in business executives and major corporations. Yet there must be twenty or a hundred job opportunities in the business sector for each opening in the New Class. "A message of estrangement from the principal economic and political institutions that shape society," the man who conducted the survey, Richard Finlay, called it.

To comments that these ideas are not new, that they are typical of the callow idealism of youth, that they will be burned away by the hard struggle for existence, that a good depression will soon straighten them out, I must answer, wait and see. So far, the values of the post-war generation have survived a rough passage. They have survived in the oldest up to the important turning point of age thirty; and they have survived without bravado or apparent obstinacy, but rather as the only imaginable attitudes. Perhaps most significant of all, they are values held by millions of young people, not just a tiny privileged elite or radical minority. (It might be remarked that the federal government could hardly have picked a worse time to loosen the unemployment insurance regulations than 1971, when the first members of the Big Generation were just beginning to flood the job market. The new rules gave out more generous support for longer periods and allowed workers to qualify for benefits after a shorter period at work. They made possible a whole new way of life: short runs at a job, any job that could be held for the qualifying period, then a lazy sojourn under the UIC's auspices until the payments ran out. The famous UIC ski team at Banff was just one of hundreds of abuses that the generation managed to operate. Some cynics think the government introduced the new rules in a deliberate play for the generation's votes; some think that it was just another case in which authority simply failed to see the generation coming. Whichever it

141

was, it had the effect of drawing thousands of youngsters out of school and college into the labour force as well as encouraging tens of thousands already at work to get out of their jobs, thus raising the youth unemployment rates by several percentage points. It was seven years before Ottawa started to correct the mistake.)

Some of the generation's job-hopping, certainly, is characteristic of the generation's age rather than of any new values. "It is natural to expect considerable employment experimentation by young persons," Arthur Donner and Fred Lazar observed when the generation's flighty record first came under attack. "Indeed, only in this way can they achieve, in the long run, the most satisfactory employment opportunity."

Talking to a sympathetic reporter recently, a high-school dropout, Amy Bearg, born in 1962, offered one of those half-exculpatory, half-confessional observations so characteristic of adolescents: "I can't find a job because I'm inexperienced and it costs money to train me and the reason employers don't want to put money into training me is because they think I won't stay with the job or I will be constantly late." Right: the employer who would have put up with a few inexperienced young workers in other times can pick among older and more reliable applicants today.

There is no doubt that the alienated Big Generation has a more critical and more egotistical view of work, which encourages them to hop from job to job more often and more easily than earlier generations did. Youth unemployment was high not because young people could not find jobs, a Statistics Canada study of 1975 observed, but because they shed them quickly if the jobs were disappointing. The Economic Council of Canada pointed out in its 1979 annual review that "More people can regard employment as one among several options." A youth co-ordinator with Canada Manpower in Ontario said, "There are jobs, it's just that some of them don't match the students' expectations. They don't have exams, they don't compete in sports much, then when they graduate they get a hell of a shock to find that they're going to have to compete to get a job and compete on the job."

No generation has been so cajoled with promises of a bright future. None has been so ill prepared by education for the realities of adult life. None has come out of school with such high ambitions and expectations. Few have encountered so unwelcoming an economy. Throughout all the personal encounters, media interviews, and accounts of employment counsellors rings one persistent note: the generation feels deeply shocked and wounded by its rejection. Listen to some of the unemployed:

Barry Switzer: "Society has misled us ever since the first day of nursery school. For years we gullibly accepted the propaganda that education was a valid substitute for the 'working one's way up from the bottom' route to success. But now that we have graduated there are no middle-level jobs. The fault is not with us, but with a society that can't deliver on its promises."

Topaz Amber Dawn: "Mick Jagger says if you lose your dreams you lose your life, and it's really true."

Anthony Iamundo: "I'm not really interested in a house in the suburbs, or anything like that. I'd just like to have enough money so that if I wanted to sit around, I could; if I wanted to work hard, I could. I really don't expect too much."

Doug Skelton, who has been unemployed four years, ever since he left school at seventeen: "Like one time I asked the man about training and he just looked blank. He didn't care. So at that point I asked myself, 'If they don't care, why should I care?' ... You get into figuring that you're not needed. If you're not needed, what's the sense? What's life all about?"

These are the voices of the unemployed. No doubt there are thousands who have had less trouble getting work, and thousands who face the problems with optimism and even enthusiasm; but the dominant tone is disappointment, frustration, bitterness, hurt, and anger.

A Canadian study published in 1978 found that more than forty per cent of those who tried to commit suicide were unemployed. In recent years attempted suicide has become "a mental health problem of epidemic proportion," in the words of a Toronto social worker. A Johns Hopkins University study also published in 1978 found that sustained rises in unemployment raised the number of suicides, imprisonments, homicides, and mental-hospital admissions.

Do the Big Generation's problems come from an absurdly exaggerated sense of its own importance? Are these kids waiting for the world to serve up prime jobs on a silver platter? Are there lots of jobs out there if only they would go and look for them? Or is this in truth an encounter between a uniquely swollen cohort of young workers and an uncommonly depressed economy? Are the problems of the generation's own making or are they real?

With few exceptions, press coverage has concentrated on the personal histories of the generation and the world's indifference to their ambitions. Perhaps because it is harder to do, perhaps because they have assumed it is impossible, the media have made little effort to answer the generation's anguished question. But in fact quite a lot can be said about the generation's job prospects.

CHAPTER 9

CAN THE ECONOMY COPE?

"In information economies, the home has become a source of isolation, insecurity, and boredom."

At a point in the fairly near future, some futurists and economists believe, about three-quarters of the population between the ages of twenty-five and forty-five will be in the labour force, either working or looking for work. Over five million members of the Big Generation are likely to be among them. Is it possible that the Canadian economy will be able to find jobs for them? To such a technical question there can be no simple answer. But to such a vital question, it would be wrong to offer less than a serious answer.

Although it is still the conventional view that economies can be made to grow at almost any desired rate if only you set the levers right, it is becoming more widely believed that the economy went through a unique stage after the Second World War. This was true not just in Canada, but in many industrial countries. Why did the economy grow so rapidly just then? Furniture, clothes, factories, and cars that had worn out or been destroyed during the war needed replacing; many families had the whole of the 1930s to compensate for; some remarkable war-time inventions and methods started to filter out into civilian industry; people felt they had broken through to a new era – peace and maybe prosperity, too. A lot of attitudes and opportunities merged to produce the growth.

What do people mean when they call the post-war economy a boom? If you are prepared to accept a single measure for the strength of the economy, the best one is the gross national product, the grand total of all goods and services produced in the country. The size of the GNP is significant if you have something else to compare it with, but with a single measure the thing to look at is its rate of growth. Some of the growth is due merely to price increases, to inflation; growth can be recalculated so as to remove inflationary increase. What is left is often called "real GNP." Some is due merely to population growth; it too can be removed. What then remains is "real GNP per person."

From the middle of the nineteenth century to the end of the Second World War, real GNP per person grew an average of 1.5 per cent a year. During the post-war economic boom, growth was about three per cent a year. In the first stage, 1949 through 1956, it was three per cent, which among other things helped stimulate the baby boom. In the second stage of the boom, 1961 through 1973, real GNP per person grew at four per cent a year. A late-1950s recession brought the average down to three per cent. But since 1974 it has dropped back almost to the historic long-term growth rate, about two per cent a year. Compared to what came before and after it, the twenty-five years of three per cent growth of real GNP per person has to be viewed as exceptional.

Over the next quarter century, it might be thought too pessimistic to expect real GNP per capita to grow at no better than the historic, pre-boom rate. But there are some economists, and many futurists, who think just that. Among them is one who is commonly reckoned among the optimists, Herman Kahn of the Hudson Institute. Kahn expects the economies of the world's rich nations to grow at a steadily declining rate, dropping to two per cent by the end of the century. The rich nations include several with higher growth rates than North America's and, in Kahn's forecast, the growth rate drops as real GNP per capita rises; on both scores the Canadian growth rate could be expected to be lower than the average of the rich nations.

It would certainly be absurdly optimistic to expect the economic boom rates to return. There are so many other things working against fast growth in the next decades. Energy, for a start. The petroleum-exporting countries can simply dictate how much oil will be available, to whom, and at what price; and this will probably be the case well into the 1990s. The limiting effect of an energy shortage is the most obvious constraint, since so much economic growth in this century has resulted from replacing human or animal energy with fuel energy.

In the years of cheap energy, for instance, the French automobile industry was able to double its output in about ten years. To do this it needed to increase its labour force by only about thirty per cent; but the amount of energy it used went up nearly seven hundred per cent. In other words, large increases in energy consumption made it possible, not only to produce more automobiles, but to reduce the amount of labour that went into the manufacture of each automobile. Now that oil costs twenty times what it did before 1973, that route to increased output is impossible.

The long, slow slide away from the peak of industrialism in North America is another factor working against high growth. Looking around the world and back in history, it now seems clear that economic growth is fastest when the greatest portion of the economy comes from industrial production, rather than from agriculture, which is the condition of pre-industrial economies, or from services, which is the condition of post-industrial economies.

Another factor is North America's decline from world economic leadership, which has seen other countries take over the production of crucial raw materials, the main industrial products, and increasing amounts of the world's consumer goods. Inflation may well be another. But the biggest factor of all is affluence, which has produced an apparently new phenomenon in economics, the backward curve.

Until now, people have always been prepared to work harder for higher rewards, and it was possible to plot the relation between rewards and work on an ever-rising curve. But today an increase in rewards often leads to a reduction in work: people who were getting enough money before, now respond to more by saying they will take some of it in time off.

At the turn of the century, Max Weber identified the backward curve as the normal response of what he called the traditional worker – the pre-industrial, pre-Reformation, probably Catholic rather than Protestant peasant. Even in his time, agricultural employers sought to speed up the harvest by raising the piece-work rates:

> But a peculiar difficulty has been met with surprising frequency: raising the piece-rates has often had the result that not more but less has been accomplished in the same time, because the worker reacted to the increase not by increasing but by decreasing the amount of his work. . . . The opportunity of earning more was less attractive than that of working less. He did not ask: how much can I earn in a day if I do as

147

much work as possible? but: how much must I work in order to earn the wage, 2½ marks, which I earned before and which takes care of my traditional needs?

Weber used this to illustrate the traditional attitude to labour that was displaced by industrialization and modern capitalism. "A man does not 'by nature' wish to earn more and more money, but simply to live as he is accustomed to live and to earn as much as is necessary for that purpose," Weber remarked. The Big Generation has rejected the ethic of the Industrial Revolution and returned to this traditional "natural" attitude. This return to a pre-industrial attitude is one element in determining whether the economy will be able to provide enough jobs for the Big Generation.

Put in the plainest terms, the number of jobs depends on three other factors: how many consumers there are, how much each consumes, and how much each worker produces. These four factors – number of jobs, number of consumers, rate of consumption, rate of production – can be put together in an equation. If you can estimate any three of the numbers in the equation, the fourth will appear automatically. I will now estimate the future number of consumers, the future rate of consumption, and the future rate of production.

THE EQUATION: CONSUMERS

There have been times when the economy grew more because of an increase in population than an improvement in real GNP per person. During the years between the two stages of the post-war boom, for instance, when real GNP grew at three per cent a year, 2.5 per cent came from growth of the population, on average, and real GNP per capita grew hardly at all. Could population growth speed up the economy in the future? Not according to the federal government's demographers. The seven main population forecasts they published in 1979 show population growth in this century of between 1.25 per cent and 0.5 per cent. The high figure assumed, wrongly as we can now see, that the Big Generation would have a rather large baby boom of its own under way in the last half of the 1970s; the forecast that yields the low figure is by no means the lowest reasonable forecast that could be made, as I show in the next chapter. In short, the whole range of government forecasts is on the high side, and population growth has little to offer by way of economic stimulus.

One aspect of population growth that is specially significant to the economy is immigration. The difference between making a population grow by the birth rate and by immigration is that babies consume without producing, while immigrants consume and produce. A hundred thousand immigrants will typically include fifty thousand workers, all of whom will compete with the Big Generation for jobs to some extent. Almost half of them will be of exactly the same age and thus more directly competitive, and they could probably produce all that the hundred thousand immigrants will consume. A hundred thousand babies, on the other hand, will consume for fifteen years or more before they contribute a penny to the GNP. At that stage of their lives they are pure cost to someone, their parents or the community, and it all shows up as economic growth. Their arrival represents an unqualified increase in jobs. As a solution to the Big Generation's job problem, however, another baby boom is already late; and there is good reason to resist the alternative – trying to make the economy grow faster by raising the level of immigration – because that would also intensify the competition for jobs.

THE EQUATION: HOW MUCH CONSUMPTION?

The most promising prospect for increasing the demand for goods and services is something that already shows some signs of happening: increasing the number of households faster than the population. This could be done – is being done, in fact – by persuading young people to leave home and set up on their own sooner, and by increasing the number of people who live on their own: single, separated, divorced, or widowed. This is unglamorously called "undoubling." It goes against some of the old ideals of big happy families, togetherness, and sharing; but the statistics show there is a lot more of it about, only some of it involuntary, and many of the more independent members of the Big Generation would clearly like to live that way.

The economic benefit in this development is in duplication: two hundred households of one person need twice as many kitchen sinks, bath tubs, kettles and frying pans, refrigerators, newspaper and cable TV subscriptions, stereos, dieffenbachias, and probably even cars as one hundred households of two people. But this solution depends on the people who might live alone having enough money to do it in reasonable style. The people who make up most of the one-person households today are members of the Big Generation and pensioners. Neither category is notably wealthy. The prospect of getting the economy rolling again by undoubling is still more potential than actual.

If the economy does go well, and the generation starts to prosper, its impact is likely to be large at the turn of the century simply because of the way household-spending patterns change with age. Forecasts of the future number of households show that even with no increase in the "real spending" of the typical household at each age level – no increase except that caused by inflation, that is – undoubling would produce a measurable increase in household spending by 1996. Spending should grow at two per cent a year, one per cent coming from population increase and one per cent from undoubling. The generation will be spending close to half of all household expenditure by then. Of course there are risks in assuming that household-spending patterns from the 1970s will hold twenty years later: one risk is that smaller households may spend less rather than the same or more; another is that as in the past real spending per household may increase rather than stay the same. Perhaps it will even out.

THE EQUATION: HOW MUCH PRODUCTION?

The third element in the job equation is efficiency, or automation, to look at it from the other side. A highly efficient worker is worth two or three inefficient workers; in fact, he can replace them as far as the employer is concerned. What makes a worker efficient? Skill, education, training, commitment, yes, but also tools. One clerk with a typewriter can out-write three clerks with pens; one driver with a tractor-trailer can out-deliver a dozen horse-powered carters; one man with a bulldozer can out-dig twenty labourers with shovels; one operator with a computer can out-calculate a hundred with comptometers.

Mechanization and automation were the bugbear of the 1950s, when factory workers feared machines would take over their jobs.

But the economic boom of the 1960s absorbed all the automation that was going and still pushed up the demand for workers. It came to be believed that automation produced more jobs than it destroyed, since there was little unemployment and people could see that a lot of workers were directly employed in making, selling, and servicing automated machine tools, computers, powered construction equipment, and other such things.

Since 1973, however, we have been looking at a different picture. The economy slowed right down; growth was two per cent a year instead of four per cent. Did employers stop hiring? Yes, or at least they held back. But they did not cut their work forces to match the new level of production. They simply restrained their workers' efficiency by stopping automation. The argument must have gone like this: "I can always go out and buy that computer next year, but if I let Sybil go I may never get her back again." How long employers are prepared to persist in that attitude remains to be seen. But most are not noticeably sentimental, and if it looks to them as though it will be more profitable in the long run to fire Sybil, buy the computer, and let the remaining staff run it, Sybil will go and the unemployment rate will start to rise again.

There are people who think automation has the potential to devastate the labour force. Computer technology has suddenly moved into a lot of new fields. The Japanese are pioneering the use of industrial robots, in which the strength, accuracy, and tirelessness of a machine are controlled by a computer. Some ten thousand robots were at work in Japan at the end of the 1970s, and the forecasts for a decade ahead show huge numbers. Ford and General Motors are already using several hundred robots and, ominously, have found that over its eight-year life a robot costs less than five dollars an hour, a third the cost of a single auto worker. North America is pioneering word processing, the combination of office equipment and processes with computers. There are forecasts that all accounting will be done by machines within a decade. Typing, filing, scheduling, co-ordinating are clearly within reach of machines that are in use, in production, or in advanced development. A number of countries are making efforts to turn most retailing activities in stores over to computers: inventory-keeping, pricing, checking-out. One Montreal futurist, Kimon Valaskakis, said, "What with robotics and the office of the future and home terminals, there have been projections that between twenty per cent and fifty per cent of the labour force could be unemployed by 1990."

In the 1960s and early 1970s, the second stage of the economic boom, worker efficiency grew by 2.5 per cent a year on average. What this meant was that after ten years of growth it took only about eighty workers to produce as much as a hundred workers produced before. In other words, efficiency took away twenty per cent of the jobs. In those years, population growth and, particularly, growth of real demand per consumer were more than strong enough to compensate for efficiency: after ten years there were two million more people at work. But automation is a powerful dis-employing force.

Since wages started going up faster than prices, efficiency has been the main source of growth and profits for corporations. They have a strong incentive to reduce the number of workers for any given level of output, or get more output from the same number of workers. In the long recession years from 1974 onwards, however, efficiency has grown at less than one per cent a year on average. It has saved the country from appalling unemployment: if efficiency had continued to grow at boom rates, by 1979 there would have been almost a million fewer jobs and unemployment would have hit sixteen per cent. But how long will corporations be able to survive without an increase in efficiency? How long will Canada be able to survive, come to that, for it has to compete against other countries to sell its products? (The decline in value of the Canadian dollar is one answer to that question; it reflects the difference between our efficiency and that of other countries.) Somewhere between the recent one per cent and a more desirable 2.5 per cent growth of efficiency lies the future compromise between the needs of international trade, corporate profits, and employment.

Before we put the equation together, one other question has to be dealt with. The number of jobs that is "enough" depends not only on how many jobs there are but on how many people want them. Ninety jobs are more than enough for eighty people seeking work, but not enough for a hundred. So it is necessary to consider the prospective size of the labour force as well.

That would not be hard to predict if we knew that labour-force participation rates would not change in the future – that the same proportion of each age and sex group, the same proportion of thirty-year-old women or fifty-year-old men, would join the labour force, working or looking for work – because the number of people of working age for the next two or three decades can be forecast fairly accurately.

But doubts arise because of the still-rapid increase in the number of women in the labour force. In 1976, for instance, the Economic Council of Canada predicted that the numbers of women at work or looking would start to flatten off because "many of the women who want to work are now in the labour force." Instead, over the next three years, half a million more women got jobs. In 1978, the federal Department of Finance published a forecast of economic trends in the 1980s that assumed the participation rate for all women would rise more slowly, flattening off to just under fifty per cent by 1990. Instead, the participation rate reached fifty per cent in 1980 – after two years instead of twelve. And there is still no evidence of any slackening off in women's desire to get work outside the home.

My belief is that the Big Generation marks the transition between all the generations of women who knew that a woman's place was in the home, and all the coming generations who will see no difference between men and women in the workplace.

To doubt that women will continue to flock into the labour force is to doubt that several well-documented revolutions have taken place. It is now widely accepted that women should be treated as equals in the work place, though it has not yet happened everywhere. In the Big Generation very few doubt that women will have equal access to work and equal pay for doing it. Woman's role as baby-minder and house-keeper is under assault at many points. Perhaps most important of all, the post-war educational revolution irrevocably altered women's position in the outside work world. It is blindness to suppose that the movement of women into the labour force is now complete.

Every census brings clearer proof, in fact, that women's labour-force participation rates are strongly related to their level of education; the rates depend on their education, one could say. The 1976 census showed that among women who left school before Grade v, only about one in six were in the labour force; in the case of women with university degrees it was three quarters; and in between these extremes ran a kind of ladder: the longer women had stayed at school, the higher their rate of participation in the labour force. This was also generally true for women of different ages, though the rates for women over fifty-five were lower at each level of schooling.

In fact, all this had been broadly true for years; but until recently the numbers of women with a lot of education were much smaller, and their participation rates were slightly lower at the same age. In 1961, for instance, only one in seven women who left school before Grade v was in the labour force, while among women with a university degree the proportion was one in two. In both cases, the ladder was straight enough to encourage the forecast that, if you could raise the general level of education, you would also raise the participation rate. In 1961, when women of working age typically had no more than eight years of schooling, the educational revolution was already under way, and it would not have taken a very bold forecaster to anticipate that the average might soon rise to twelve years of schooling. From that alone he could have predicted a ten per cent rise in the number of women in the labour force. By 1976, as it turned out, the ladder had been raised higher up the wall, and the extra four years of schooling meant a fifteen per cent increase in the number of working women.

Even if there were no further raising of the ladder, the 1976 figures suggest that when the average number of years at school is raised from twelve to sixteen, enough to get a university degree or community college diploma, something like two-thirds of women will be in the labour force instead of the present fifty per cent.

The difference between the 1961 and 1976 figures is partly the result of the lower birth rate, which means that during their lifetimes women spend less time tied to the house by the needs of their young children. It is also partly the result of economic pressures. More women are running households on their own and need jobs to survive. According to Statistics Canada, the participation rate of divorced and separated women is higher than the rate of married women. There is the making of a vicious spiral in this: although the statistics to prove it are scarce, marriage counsellors and others have a good idea of what is happening. The sharp rise in the divorce rate "reflects, at least in part, the strains that working wives produce in marriage," according to an American source. Having a job tells women that they are valuable to someone other than their husbands; it tells them that they are capable of supporting themselves. It tells them, in short, that they are not permanently bound to their marriages. More jobs, more divorced women; more divorced women, more jobs.

Beneath these pressures is one even harder to document, but powerful nonetheless. Jeanne Binstock, the Ottawa sociologist, puts it this way:

> In industrial societies, home is still thought a privilege protecting women from a savage work world. In information economies the home has become a source of isolation, insecurity, and boredom. The "predatory jungle" has turned into a stimulating white-collar environment filled with opportunities for earning money, satisfaction, and growth.

Canada's transition from an industrial to a post-industrial or information economy coincides with women's invasion of the workplace.

More families need or want two incomes to live on. Even among the oldest members of the Big Generation, who found it easiest to get work and whose degrees earned them better-paying jobs, both members of a couple commonly have full-time jobs. Ed Buckley, born in 1951, and Annette, born a year later, are typical of many urban middle-class couples their age. He is an investment administrator, she is a steel products buyer; they have one five-year-old child, and an income big enough to let Ed spend four thousand dollars a year on his car-racing hobby and allow them three vacations a year. But there are hundreds of thousands of couples with less-well-paying jobs who both work simply to raise family income above the poverty line. So it would not be surprising to see the schooling-participation-rate ladder shoved higher up the wall in the coming years.

Many women looking for work want part-time jobs. A 1979 survey of Canadian women showed that the higher a woman's level of education, the more likely she was to want a full-time outside job and the less likely to want to be a full-time homemaker. At every level of education, however, more women wanted part-time than full-time work. This is likely to have significant consequences in future.

My guess is that by the end of the century, about a half of all women will act just as men do today, spending virtually all their adult lives in a job. Perhaps as many as a quarter, but not more, will be like their grandmothers, working for a few years, getting married in their twenties, retiring from outside work at least until their children have left home. The remaining quarter will fall between. This suggests an overall participation rate for women of about sixty-five per cent in the year 2000, the same figure forecast by an average of sixteen years at school.

Some Statistics Canada extrapolations show men's and women's participation rates gradually converging over the next half century, the men's rates dropping slowly toward the rising women's rates; in the age groups between twenty and retirement, the women's rates are projected as high as seventy-five to eighty-five per cent. But some of those women will be the grandchildren of the Big Generation.

Such high participation rates imply or assume (whether cause or result is not clear) a much lower fertility rate. As I will show, this too is related to the level of schooling. Education drives the wheel women's lives are turning on: higher education, higher labour force participation rates, and lower fertility all reinforce one another. It is absurd to think that women's role in the workplace has now been set.

A smaller but still important question is whether young people will continue to stay away from university and college and go job-hunting after high school, as they have in the last few years. Given the decline of births after 1960, it is a question that has less impact on the size of the labour force with every passing day, but it bears thinking about.

The reason the Big Generation abandoned post-secondary education was that they thought it gave them no advantage in the job wars. They were wrong: statistics persistently show the highest unemployment rates for those with the least education, and vice versa. But there are many more unemployed and underemployed degree holders than anyone expected. The generation saw that a degree did not include the cast-iron guarantee of large economic benefits and the unconditional choice of a job, and in their disappointment many gave up their schooling too quickly. Cooler reactions are now returning, and it is likely that before the last of the generation has graduated from high school, enrolment rates in universities and colleges will be back to their peak or close to it.

The next generation, born in the late 1960s and the 1970s, is significantly smaller; it is going to be in demand when it reaches employment age, and will know this by the time it reaches high school. With reasonably astute counselling it is likely to continue the upward trend of enrolment rates established during the post-war educational revolution. This in turn will mean lower participation rates for people under twenty-five. The problems the Big Generation is going to have in getting satisfactory work will go on long enough that the following generation is not likely to be attracted prematurely into the labour force.

Immigration is the other factor of any significance. Here the question is how certain kinds of work will get done without immigrants. It seems to have been fairly firmly established that native-born Canadians will not take low-paying jobs in hotels and restaurants – as chambermaids, waiters, busboys, and so on; they will not run late-night milk stores in big cities, and they are increasingly unwilling to take on any dirty, dangerous, and uncomfortable work. They are also increasingly unable to take on many kinds of skilled technical work such as toolmaking and instrument-making. If Canada continues to need these kinds of work, immigrants will continue to be needed, though the Big Generation will have to lobby against it. The result is already becoming evident in Ontario, the most industrial province, where more than one worker in four is an immigrant, although in Canada as a whole immigrants are only a seventh of the population.

THE EQUATION: THE FOUR PARTS

Will there be jobs for the Big Generation? The four elements in the economic equation – the population, the average consumption of goods and services per person, the workers, and the average production of goods and services per worker – must balance. Any growth in the first two has to be balanced by growth in the second two. If the population goes up, the work force or efficiency or both have to go up. It works in the other direction, too, and it must also work if any of the four go down. If efficiency goes down, the population or average consumption has to go down.

When you use the equation to predict jobs, it works like this:

> If demand for goods and services grows and everything else stays the same, there will be more jobs.

If population grows and everything else stays the same, there will be more jobs.

If the labour force grows and everything else stays the same, there will be more unemployment.

If worker efficiency grows and everything else stays the same, there will be more unemployment.

In the rest of this century, assume that population will grow at one per cent a year, on average. Assume that real demand per consumer will grow at two per cent a year. Assume that worker efficiency will grow at two per cent a year. It is then apparent that employment can only grow at one per cent a year. The two terms on one side of the equation have to balance the two on the other side.

In 1979, 10,300,000 people had jobs. If employment grows at one per cent a year until 1996, there will then be 12,200,000 jobs. Will that be enough?

Although the answer has to be slightly qualified, it is no. The qualification is this: what effect would severe unemployment have on the millions of couples in which both wanted work? On young people who were wondering whether to go on to university or get into the job market? On immigration? On older workers unsure whether to retire? If the past is a guide, it would discourage a lot of people from even looking for work; as statisticians put it, it would reduce the participation rates.

Two estimates should make this clearer.

We have a good idea of how many people of each age group over fifteen will be around in 1996, because nearly all of them have already been born. So the questions mainly concern their participation rates. If these rates remained the same as they were in 1979, there would be 13,700,000 people looking for work in 1996. Eleven per cent of them would be out of work.

If the participation rates change, men's rates dropping slightly and women's rates rising fairly steeply in the direction already described, 14,400,000 people would be in the labour force, and fifteen per cent of them would be unemployed.

In practice, those unemployment rates might be lower, because of the discouragement factor. In 1979, the unemployment rate in Newfoundland stood at over fifteen per cent and the overall participation rate was fifty-three per cent. In Alberta unemployment was only four per cent and the participation rate was sixty-nine per cent. The difference between those two rates nationwide today would be the difference between fifteen per cent unemployment and ten per cent labour shortage. They are also the difference between people wasting their lives in frustration and idleness, and people finding some reward in the outside world.

The assumptions in the equation could prove different. Real demand might be higher, efficiency might grow more slowly; but there is not much leeway in the numbers. The most optimistic case that looks feasible produces a million more jobs, still not enough to satisfy the labour force that I think is likely to develop. But there is just as reasonable a pessimistic projection, with lower population growth and higher growth of efficiency. This would create a million fewer jobs and produce unemployment rates of over twenty per cent, higher than during the worst year of the Depression.

Since the Second World War we have become used to seeing governments take responsibility for employment. It started when politicians found out that high enough unemployment could quite easily turn the government into the opposition at the next election. Governments became obsessed with creating jobs. That they increasingly did so by ignoring other economic problems did not stop them. In the past quarter century, the backbone of government policy has been to manage the economy so as to produce the largest number of jobs.

The private sector's policy has been to manage corporations so as to produce the most efficient work force. At their worst, which has been often, these two policies have been at complete loggerheads: more jobs as the objective on one side, fewer employees on the other. For at least a century, employers have been very skilful at pursuing their policy. With the growing skill of governments in pursuing the opposite policy, the direct confrontation was bound to produce tensions, distortions, and, in the end, some kind of economic collapse. Since most of the battle took place in the brilliant glare of the economic boom, attempting to assess the damage was like trying to count the stars at noon. But the stagnation of the economy since 1974 is the direct result of the havoc caused by this continuous and increasingly frantic pulling in opposite directions by two powerful forces. As an International Monetary Fund historian put it in a retrospective of the 1970s, after 1973 "stimulating the economy only produced more inflation, not more employment; depressing the economy produced more unemployment, not less inflation.''

For this reason, I think it is useless to look to government to create the jobs the Big Generation is going to need. Governments cannot create jobs directly, except in government departments, and their attempts to do so indirectly are largely responsible for the present economic mess.

The unhappy answer to the generation's question, then, is that there are not going to be enough jobs; certainly not on the scale and of the variety that members of the generation grew up to expect. In some industries and professions, particularly those that have recently grown fast, there will be persistent job shortages for decades. Teaching is the glaring example: faculties of tenured professors aging in place, desperate public-school teachers terrified to make a move for fear of losing their toeholds. Another is medicine. The profession built up very quickly when Medicare swept through Canada. More than half the physicians now in practice graduated since 1960, and there will be little chance for newcomers to break in for a long time.

The persistence of a cohort bulge in a profession is seen clearly in the federal civil service, which built up during and immediately after the war, and developed an extremely lop-sided age profile: although the largest age-group of employees was born after 1950, the next largest was born in the 1920s, with a real gap in between. This not only meant a surplus of people looking for senior management positions in the recent past, but now leaves an awkward shortage of experienced people to promote. This sector has hired and over-hired in a hurry, starting another bulge. Therefore the federal government is not likely to employ many of the Big Generation: in 1978 it hired just five per cent of the thirty thousand college and university graduates who applied for jobs.

What, if anything, can be done about this gloomy employment prospect?

CHAPTER 10

NEW ANSWERS IN THE JOB MARKET

"The opportunity of earning more
was less attractive than
that of working less."

The belief that Canada is on the verge of a new manpower shortage like the one we experienced in the mid-1960s is common among economists, but it is wrong. It fails to take sufficient account of women's still rising participation rates, of couples' persistent desire for two incomes, and of the long-term slowdown in the economy.

What will appear is a manpower shortage in certain industries and occupations. There will be a dearth of people under twenty-five. A quarter of the labour force is now under twenty-five, but by my estimate, at the end of the century that will be down to fifteen per cent. Sectors now heavy with young people will feel the pinch. The most obvious is retail trade: a third of its employees are under twenty-five. Bureaucratic services, such as insurance companies, governments, and banks, have an above-average number of women in their early twenties on staff. Obviously it would be costly to replace young employees with older ones, and the shortages will turn managers' thoughts to automation sooner.

Shortages of skilled technicians have already begun to surface. In 1977, the Department of Manpower noted the lack of sewing-machine operators, motor-vehicle mechanics, and hairdressers. In 1978, Ontario employers started crying out for mechanics and toolmakers. In 1979, about half the manufacturers in Ontario who answered a provincial government survey were having trouble finding skilled tradesmen. In 1980, General Motors of Canada sent recruiters to Europe for a hundred journeymen for a new transmission plant. Alberta had trouble finding welders. The aerospace industry faced a severe shortage of skilled technicians.

Everywhere millwrights, machinists, and tool- and die-makers were in short supply.

These shortages took years to develop, and will take years to cure. Apprenticeship programs are the only effective way to train skilled workers; but they have fallen far short of supplying Canada's needs for a number of reasons: not enough money was put into them; unions were not anxious to have their ranks increased too fast; employers resisted the expense of training apprentices when it was easier to recruit trained immigrants; and few of the Big Generation wanted to be apprentices. That last failure can be traced back to the attitude of the schools in the educational revolution, which pushed hard for a more academic curriculum and gave little support to the youngsters who might have headed for the skilled trades.

While Canada may have to worry about manpower shortages in particular industries, occupations, and age groups, it is not a problem that is ever going to concern the Big Generation, at least not directly. Work tends to be related quite closely to age. There is a shortage of managers today, but the generation is too young to fill it. If shortages of twenty-year-olds develop in the future, it will not be easy and probably not even possible to fill them with members of the generation, who by then will be in their thirties or forties. There will be some leeway in spreading the generation a little above and below its age group, but basically it is going to go right through life oversize. If the economy does run into unemployment of fifteen or twenty per cent, the rates for members of the generation will be higher, and some significantly different ways of working the economy will have to be found.

Part-time work may be the generation's salvation. Its attitude to work is less committed than that of earlier generations, anyway. Many members of the generation have already shown that they would rather earn less if it meant they could do work they enjoyed more. Many have combined a part-time job of little interest with a vocation that cannot support them. Actors wait on tables, mothers work two days a week as bank tellers, photographers sell shoes on Saturdays, and dancers are cocktail waitresses in the evenings. The personnel commissioner at Ottawa City Hall reports "a lot of applications from people who want to keep in touch with the work force but don't want to make a full-time career out of it. They have creative interests to pursue and prefer a permanent part-time job."

Workers look for jobs that will let them stay at home long enough to get children off to school and be back home when the school day ends. Libraries, doctors' offices, and real-estate companies have proven receptive. Students look for jobs they can hold down after school hours: supermarkets and fast-food outlets have obliged. At the end of the 1970s, about one Canadian worker in eight was part time, and the trend suggests it might be one in five by the end of the century.

Part-time work is the easiest way to give a lot more people work without disturbing the whole economic system. It is usually reckoned that a full-time job takes forty hours a week and a part-time job about fifteen hours a week, which means that forty people working part time put in as many hours as fifteen people working full time.

Job-sharing is another way of spreading the work that looks increasingly appealing to the generation, and for the same reasons. Two dentists find that they can comfortably share one surgery and office; they split the day at the lunch hour, and each earns enough to live on. A growing number of teachers have been able to negotiate job-sharing arrangements. The spate of firings made it easier, of course; even people who would not otherwise have been keen about sharing a job would rather share than have none. Sixteen social workers and psychologists employed by the Toronto Board of Education in 1979-1980 filled the equivalent of eight full-time positions.

A third way of splitting the available work is reducing everybody's hours. There are strong arguments against cutting the full-time work week much below its present level. One is that it is inefficient to leave expensive machinery unused. This objection could be met by reducing the hours from, say, forty to thirty, compressing them into three or four days, and then running two shifts, one in the first half and the other in the second half of the week. Another objection is that people are unfulfilled by jobs that offer much less than forty hours; no doubt similar concerns were heard at the turn of the century when radicals were agitating to get the work week reduced from sixty-six hours to sixty. A large drop in hours would require a significant shift in public opinion, something like the spirit that reigned during the Depression; twenty per cent unemployment certainly would help to create it.

What impact would these three methods of spreading work during a time of high unemployment have on the economy? Assume a labour force of ten million, of whom twenty per cent are unemployed; assume that twenty per cent of those who do have work are on part time. Assume no increase in the total number of hours of work done by the labour force.

The *reduced hours* solution would cut the existing eight million workers' hours and pay by a sixth. Full-time workers' pay packets would decline from, say, three hundred dollars a week to two hundred and fifty. Workers on part time would be down to twelve and a half hours a week. But a million and a half unemployed people would get work.

The *job-sharing* solution, applied here only to full-time jobs, would cut the number of workers on full time by a million and a half and create a job-sharing sector of over three million.

The *part-time* solution would increase the number of part-time workers by two and a half million and reduce the full-time workers by about a million.

In practice, some mixture of these solutions is more likely than the exclusive application of one. In its total effect, reducing everyone's hours to increase jobs is the most radical solution, and increasing the number of part-time jobs the least radical. All involve a fairly substantial rejigging of the labour force – another indication of the Big Generation's likely impact on the economy and society as the end of the century comes closer.

We and the Big Generation should not ignore some less obvious options:

We could abandon the notion of efficiency and return to a much simpler and more rural society. "Back to the old-fashioned farm!" is not a worthless cry. It is honest, healthy work. It can make a family self-sufficient. Bring back the horse and save energy. Many industries could be made less efficient, so that they would employ more people for the same volume of production. They would not be able to pay the same wages, but they would restore some lost jobs. Failing that, we could encourage large numbers of people to go into work where there is no prospect of increasing the level of efficiency. Government work is the obvious choice, but a large increase in the monastic orders would be very helpful, too.

We could conduct a campaign to turn child-raising and housework into a satisfying and well-paid occupation. It could be addressed to men as well as women; but if it slowed down

164

women's rising rates of participation, in the conventional labour force, it would have a doubly beneficial effect on unemployment.

We could encourage large-scale emigration. It would take some research to find out where emigrants could go: the United States and Europe both have employment problems for people of the same age as the generation, and the poorest countries of the Third World are also suffering chronic unemployment. The middle-income nations now industrializing – Mexico, Brazil, South Korea, Singapore, South Africa, some of the oil countries of the Middle East – are probably the best bet.

In many respects the Big Generation looks like a cohort raised and educated for the future. What can be done to bring the future nearer? Futurists use the term "post-industrial" to describe an economy that has passed the industrial stage. By some definitions, Canada and the United States already qualify as post-industrial economies. Less than a third of Canada's workers are now employed in industry – in mining, manufacturing, and construction. A much smaller fraction are employed in agriculture and the other primary industries – fishing, trapping, and forestry. Two-thirds work in the service sector.

Services range from teaching to banking, from reading gas meters to playing the cello, from driving a bus to drafting an Act of Parliament, from selling shoes or insurance to serving martinis or hamburgers. It is the kind of work that an overwhelming proportion of the generation would prefer to do. Where that kind of work dominates, as in Ottawa, Quebec City, and Vancouver, the community takes on an atmosphere quite different from what is found in, say, a farming centre like Saskatoon, an oil town like Edmonton, a steel city like Hamilton, a mining town like Sudbury, a fishing port like St. John's, or an automobile city like Windsor.

Service work is significantly less disciplined. The physical conditions are softer, cleaner, less threatening. The level of education is higher and the cultural facilities larger and richer. Service industries are broadly homogeneous. They support each other at least as much as they support industry and agriculture. Note how rarely television, itself one of the most prominent of modern services, makes dramas, or comedies about people who work in industry or agriculture. Note the increasing interaction of the professions, the media, and the bureaucracy, the community of interests among members of the New Class. Note how large quantities of information are vital to many services; and so on.

An important difference between the goods and service sectors is that efficiency growth has been concentrated in agriculture and industry, where it has been possible to maintain a high output of goods despite declines in their share of the economy's workers. But it has been much harder to automate the service industries, with the result that efficiency has changed very little for years, and employment has kept pace with output.

Another difference is that service employment lends itself easily to part-time work, whereas agriculture and industry have so far resisted. That is one reason women have flocked into service jobs; another is that many jobs turning out goods require muscles and are therefore still dominated by men, whereas almost all service jobs require brains and are therefore equally open to women and men. As a result, many more women work in services than in goods-producing jobs. A quarter of all women employees work only part-time; the vast majority of these part-time jobs are in services, specially in retail trade, hotel and food service. Not coincidently, in the last three years of the 1970s, a third of all net new jobs were part-time.

Many services are performed by small companies, not the gigantic corporations that dominate the heavy manufacturing, mining, and resource industries. Even where there are large corporations, much of the work is effectively decentralized to small outlets, such as bank branches, movie houses, shoe stores, and fast-food outlets. Usually the effect is to keep employment higher than if the work were carried out centrally, which is saying in different words that it has not been easy to automate services and reduce the labour they require. Again not coincidentally, three quarters of all net new jobs in the 1970s – many of them part time – were in businesses employing fewer than twenty people.

Many services are much harder for governments to control or regulate, although there are obvious exceptions, such as broadcasting and the telephone industry. Most need less regulation, since they are less likely to be hazardous or threatening. Along with other attributes of the service sector, this has tended to make services more diverse, less predictable, more innovative.

Members of the Big Generation are large consumers as well as producers of services. That desire for new experiences – for travel, education, information, entertainment – is assuaged more by services than goods. But it can be almost as satisfying to work in a service corporation as to use its output. There are few apprenticeship training programs in Canada, but there are now at least eighty theatre schools, even though most actors earn only a few thousand dollars a year at their profession. As well as the most obviously glamorous jobs in entertainment, sports, the media, and so on, large numbers of sales people actively enjoy the goods they sell, the clothes or furniture, and the environment they work in, as few assembly-line or steel mill workers, for instance, could claim to do.

One way and another, the post-industrial world of services has a lot to offer the Big Generation. They like its output; they like that kind of work. The work promises to be harder to automate away, easier to do on a part-time basis, more congenial to small businesses, and thus more accessible to young entrepreneurs.

For years people have worried over the prospect of running an economy with little industry; the Victorians used to joke about a mythical land whose inhabitants made a living by taking in one another's laundry. But there does not seem to be any reason why an economy should not concentrate on services, provided enough money can be generated by exports to secure the import of whatever goods are needed. At any rate, the two thirds of gross national product and employment now derived from the service sector are no apparent threat to economic stability, and the likelihood that services will rise to three quarters of total employment by the end of the century seems hardly more problematic.

At one time it was supposed that the only way to add to the world's wealth was to dig gold out of the ground. Now we understand that any kind of work that adds value is a way of adding to wealth. If you turn virgin rock into an ounce of gold, new wealth has certainly been created. But if you turn a hundred dollars' worth of gold into a five-hundred-dollar necklace, new wealth has also been created. As it has if you turn a hundred dollars' worth of newsprint into five-hundred-dollars' worth of newspapers. There is no technical or economic limit to the spread of services. No finite reserve threatens to run out in the service sector, as it does in resources. And consumers have a much larger capacity for services than for goods. Once you have sold someone a car or TV set you cannot expect her back for several years. Yet millions absorb hours of services every day – transportation, information, education – without getting sated.

So this, if any, is the kind of work the Big Generation will be doing. It is a field that is only now beginning to attract the thousands of enterprising innovators who will soon be turning to it. The generation has appeared on the scene at the beginning of the post-industrial era, which will transform the economy and the society beyond recognition. During the next half century we will undergo as radical a change, probably, as in the 150 years of the Industrial Revolution.

Information services, at work and at home, are starting to proliferate: hundred-channel cable TV, communications satellites, computerized data banks, microprocessors in increasing profusion, electronic images and sounds everywhere – all virtually unlimited by the old physical constraints. Leisure services offering sports, travel, entertainment, and almost endless opportunities to take part or to watch are even less developed. These two alone seem likely to dominate the economy within fifty years: already information accounts for half of the gross national product and half the employment in North America, and in many states and provinces tourism is already the second or third largest industry. Unlimited kinds of new services remain to be explored.

The Big Generation's work prospects and patterns are going to be established in the next decade. The chances are that, for the first time, a generation of young people is going to do less well than its parents. The unique circumstances of their birth and their place in time will force them off course and break the chain of material progress. Already there are signs that they are going to reject the whole idea of that kind of progress and set their own rules. Once again, the Big Generation is getting ready to make history.

CHAPTER 11

BIG FAMILIES, LITTLE FAMILIES

*"We're reluctant to make a baby
with someone who, good sense tells us,
will not be there in five years."*

Unemployment is the spectre the Big Generation sees hanging over it, but for the rest of the country another question is almost as crucial: how many children will they have?

The answer will make a huge difference to Canada's future. On their fertility depends the size of the population and its rate of growth. That, in turn, will do a lot to determine how fast the economy grows – whether the housing industry prospers or collapses, for instance – and, in turn, whether unemployment rises or falls.

If the members of the generation decide to have many children – as many as their parents did, for instance – that would not only boost the economy but would reduce the number of women in the labour force, which might well generate full employment and even manpower shortages.

If, on the other hand, they decide to have far fewer children than their parents did on average, the economy would grow more slowly, more women would likely try to enter the labour force, and there might well be a tremendous struggle for jobs.

Official government attempts to forecast population have always stumbled on this question of fertility. The first shot at population forecasting made by Statistics Canada, in 1974, was out of date almost as soon as it was published. Within two years of the forecast's appearance, Canada's actual fertility rate had already fallen to the lowest level that the government demographers had foreseen for any year in this century. In two of the largest provinces, British Columbia and Ontario, the rates quickly fell below the lowest figures the forecasters had anticipated.

In its most recent forecasts, published in 1979, Statistics Canada has again chosen as its low forecast a figure that may well be undercut within a few years of publication; and this time its high forecast has been sharply reduced, so that the range of fertility forecasts is actually narrower than it was in the 1974 paper. The government forecasts now fall in so narrow a range, and are so close to the present fertility rate, that they are almost certainly going to be wrong. Several possible futures seem to me to be more likely than the scenarios implied in the Statistics Canada forecasts.

One real possibility that should be looked at is the Easterlin model mentioned at the beginning of this book. In that scenario, the baby boom was not a unique event triggered by the special circumstances of the Depression, the war, and victory, it was a rational response to an economic opportunity. The people born in the late 1920s and the 1930s were a small generation; they were in short supply and could therefore command good wages, which meant their wives had no need to go out to work, meant they could count on continuing prosperity, and therefore were justified in raising larger families. The theory goes on to point out that the cohort following the Big Generation, those born between 1966 and 1981, are going to be in very much the same circumstances as those born forty years earlier. They will be in demand, will be able to command higher wages and count on continuing good fortune. They will be the parents of the next baby boom, which should show up at the turn of the century.

The second scenario assumes a new pattern of family behaviour rather than a return to earlier patterns. It is compatible with the new pattern of women's work life outlined in the last chapter. It predicts that half of all women will come to think of themselves very much as men do: committed to a career and just as interested in doing well, in becoming president of the corporation or prime minister of the country, as men are. They will be no more likely to leave their careers and give birth than men are. Their fertility rate would be zero. Another quarter will see their role much as their grandmothers did: to bear and raise children, to be good wives, keep home and family together. Their fertility rate would be somewhere between two and three, perhaps closer to three, the long-term average in Canada in the sixty years that accurate records have been kept. And the remaining quarter will fall between, with a fertility rate under one and a half: say thirteen or fourteen children born to every ten couples. This averages out to a total fertility rate of one. One child per woman, one child per couple: half the rate at which the population would replace itself.

Either of these futures seems to me at least as defensible on the basis of the statistics, and more likely in human terms, than the government projections with their scarcely varying fertility rates. After all, childhood experiences are important, the state of the economy will have an impact, ideas about the family will change. It is possible that the population will become more polarized than any of these scenarios suggests, with two rather extreme camps of sharply differing fertility rates, which will cancel each other out and leave a total rate not much different from today's. It is possible, but not probable.

To judge what is likely to happen one needs to look at the underlying arguments about fertility. In favour of high fertility, the biggest argument is biology: the potent urge to procreate, the bodies so purposefully designed, and the glands that trigger deep instincts. All these combine into an irresistible life force that can no more be denied in the long run than the need to eat and sleep. Having children is natural, not having them is unnatural. The fashion of a decade or two is nothing compared with the power of an instinct humankind shares with every living thing, the impulse to maintain life on earth. Even some feminists who have hitherto treated having babies as the modern equivalent of being sold at slave auction are now treating biology with more respect. "We are all talking about making babies," Joanne Kates said. "We are loath to miss out on parenting." The American feminist Phyllis Chesler kept a diary of her experience as a mother, which was published under the title *With Child*. "To some extent, any woman who decides to have a child is succumbing to imprinting, but beyond that there's a desire to do something irrevocable and a longing for intimacy," she said recently. "Possibly it's a biological yearning, an urge to use all your organs out of a sense of feminine pride."

The social imprinting Chesler mentioned is in part simply a determination to see women, and men too, continue in their familiar roles. This desire is obviously a strong force for high fertility. Motherhood has been institutionalized as the dominant role for women, as the most important thing a woman can do. It is obviously a strong enough institution to resist many attacks. "A willingness to regard childlessness and the only child as desirable or even acceptable is still rare," an American demographer wrote as recently as 1974. "Psychological propensity for motherhood remains strong among North American women," a Canadian demographer agreed. Women's and society's ideas about childbearing have changed somewhat in the intervening half-dozen years, but many people still hold these views, and women who give up the idea of having a family to pursue a career are still criticized in some circles.

A whole complex of feelings surrounds Chesler's social imprinting. We remain a nation that likes children. Women see with what pleasure other women nurture and care for their children. Many people recognize that they need the experience of being a parent to complete them. The Big Generation needs love and human intimacy; this is already felt in the closeness between members of the generation. Their need as children for love, unless it was frustrated and embittered by circumstances, may well transform into an adult need to give love.

Another factor likely to raise fertility in the population over the long term, if Richard Easterlin is correct, is the arrival of the next cohort in the labour force. "Demographers should acknowledge that there will be at least one important factor working against a continuing decline in fertility [over the next decade or so]: the growing scarcity of young adults and the resulting rise in their relative affluence." Here Easterlin is specifically exempting the Big Generation from the pro-natalist influence of affluence. But even the smaller cohort following them could generate quite a large baby boom of its own: the 1966-1981 cohort will be larger than the cohort of the Big Generation's parents.

Several things support these arguments for higher fertility. Government policies have made it easier for people to have and keep children: welfare programs aid poor and single parents; government support of medical insurance and education lifts a large financial burden off families in the lower tax brackets; public support for day-care centres, nurseries, and kindergartens back up the working mother; and so on. The only thing a politician would find harder to do than increase unemployment would be to attack motherhood. Presumably government policy on maintaining or increasing the birth rate is far from what it was when family allowances were introduced in 1944, and it has been possible to reduce its importance by neglecting to keep payments up with inflation, but it would take a bold government to stop the allowance.

The suburbs are just made for families, and when the parents of the Big Generation move out, which is likely to be soon, those three-bedroom houses close to parks and schools will become vacant in large numbers. That might become an inducement. Or, if the generation persists in moving out beyond the limits of the metropolises, as it has begun to do, that might work in very much the same way the suburbs did for the earlier generation. The mental picture raised by the idea that fertility is higher in the country than in the town is amusing and perhaps misleading. It is not that a particular location physically induces babies, but that people who want larger families look for the best place to have them. There may be some small inducement effect as well. Modern housing and facilities will spring up to meet the needs of the couples planning large families, their very newness will attract other young people, and the environment of enthusiastic parents and family-oriented stores and services may encourage their desire to be parents. But mainly these shifts are useful as indicators: any large-scale move of people in their twenties to the suburbs or the rural non-farm areas would presage a rise in fertility.

The generally more relaxed attitude toward sexual activity is likely to have done something to raise the fertility rate. Despite fairly easy access to the Pill, unwanted pregnancies among teenagers continue to increase, according to Professor Edward Herold of the University of Guelph. Teenagers are readier for sexual intercourse but not yet skilled in contraception. All things taken into account, however, the sexual revolution is probably the least of the influences pushing fertility higher.

What factors are pushing it lower? Something exceptionally powerful, obviously, since the fertility rate has dropped from about ten children per woman to below two in the past 400 years. Although we do not have reliable Canadian records before 1921, there are good American records for a hundred years before that, and Canadian and American rates have been close for the sixty years both have kept good data. There is also good anecdotal evidence of fertility rates at occasional moments in Canadian history and sporadic information about the birth rates in the mother countries of France and Britain over the years. The earliest Canadians, certainly, were not aiming merely at replacement, they were actively colonizing the new world. While it is clear that birth rates were higher in the past to compensate for high infant mortality rates, the difference between birth and death rates was larger than it is today. So people then had big families. Now we do not. Something has reduced the family steadily over the centuries, and that something is not explained by arguments about economic opportunity, biological imperatives, government policies, or the rise of the suburbs.

What is changing, it appears, is parents' attitudes about children, the family, family size, parenting, and their own lives. The number of children thought to be ideal has undergone extraordinary change. Until about 1960, a majority of Canadians thought four or more children was the ideal family. (The highest proportion to say that to Gallup poll takers was sixty per cent: that was in 1945, when Gallup started asking the question.) Since 1974 the majority have said two or less, and fully two-thirds of the people under the age of thirty answered two or less. There are still very few who think – or are ready to confess it to poll-takers – that one child or none is ideal, but there is evidence to suggest the number is larger than these polls show and growing rather fast. One straw in the wind was a 1978 poll on class structure in Canada in which people were asked among other things which social class they expected their children to belong to. Astonishingly, a quarter said that they had no children and would have none. And the number of people who think "it is perfectly all right to be married and to choose not to have children" rose to over eighty per cent in 1976.

The question of family size is inextricably tied up with the general attitude toward children. It has been suggested that one motive parents have for keeping their families small is so that they can give each child more attention, and this may well be so for some parents. But much of what is going on all round us suggests that many people's attitude to children borders on dislike. A new phenomenon has emerged in recent years: divorces in which neither mother nor father wants to take the children. "Do we fear and loathe the unknown in kids?" one newspaper heading asked. Yes, the article said, paraphrasing Edgar Friedenberg, head of the education department at Dalhousie University, "our society loathes and fears its kids. Kids today are an entire underclass of people who have no power, no rights, no income. They don't produce anything. No one *needs* a robust breed of kids to help plow the back forty any more."

For further evidence note the increase in movies about

monstrous children: *The Exorcist, Rosemary's Baby, The Little Girl Down the Lane, The Changeling*, and many others. Note the resentment at school taxes. Note the rapidly increasing number of cases of child abuse in major cities, the teenagers thrown out to fend for themselves. Note the "visible anger against children," to use the words of a Toronto child welfare consultant, building up all over North America. Note the new organizations campaigning for no-child families, promoting the idea that the good life is the childless life: "None is fun" is the slogan one of them uses.

Michele Landsberg wrote not long ago,

> The parent's only reward today is love. What a lot of loving a kid has to do to make it all up to us. How cheated and angry some parents must feel, now that kids grow out of uncritical devotion so fast. Almost before we store the tricycle away for good, the kids are turning into precocious rebels, dyslexic dropouts, sexy disco dancers. Kids are somehow dependent and out of control at the same time, demanding everything of us, but living a mysterious inner life fed by the dark streams of television, rock music, and the automotive subculture.

Note what cool young couples say when asked why they have no families. "We analyzed it from the point of view of what was best for us," Brian Emmons of Calgary said. "I realized children would gain nothing personally nor particularly add anything to my life. I didn't need the ego trip to procreate and my relationship with my wife would probably be better off. I like kids as much as anybody else but I don't want the twenty-four-hour responsibility." No, no one needs children any more for farm work, no one hands down the family business to the eldest son, no one wants to rely on children's charity in old age, no one any longer seeks to increase the glory of God by obeying the command to "be fruitful, and multiply, and replenish the earth," for in this too the Protestant ethic has entirely disappeared with the Big Generation.

Today, there are not only adults-only apartments but whole communities of detached houses for adults only. One, near Ottawa, has residents in their early thirties as well as older people.

People with children have a growing awareness of what children cost to raise and educate and, it appears, a growing resentment about it. And people without children are often unwilling to make an increasingly costly commitment.

These attitudes, like the new attitudes to work, are rare among people over forty and much more common among the Big Generation. Daniel Yankelovich describes views held widely by two kinds of parents, the traditionalists and the New Breed of parents. The traditionalists put duty before pleasure, think people in authority know best, value the institution of marriage, and are oriented toward children. They are ready to sacrifice for their children, want the children to be outstanding, believe the children should do as they are told. (These are not Max Weber's traditionalists, but those brought up in the more modern tradition of the Protestant ethic.) "In contrast, the New Breed are self-orientated, not as ready to sacrifice all to their children. They have a laissez-faire attitude that says both they and their children should do as they like."

Behind the Big Generation's attitude toward children is a re-ordering of priorities. Older people looked for the consummation of their own lives in the lives of their children, the life of the community, and even the life of the company they worked for. These values are still drummed into children in primary school. The Big Generation is the first to include a majority of people whose education inclines them to put their own objectives first, ahead of the company they work for, their community, and even their children.

Education has always had a lot to do with fertility: highly educated people have few children (a factor that Easterlin ignores). To take an extreme example, the class of 1973 at the Harvard Business School was revisited five years later. Thirty-four women graduated. Their average age was thirty-two, half were married, and they had just six children between them. At the 1971 census it was found that married women in their most fertile years, fifteen to forty-four, who had only grade-school education had three children on average, while at the other end of the scale, wives with university degrees had an average of less than one and a half. The fertility ladder slopes downward as education rises; a rise in schooling forecasts a drop in fertility. The post-war rise from eight to twelve years of schooling forecasts a drop in fertility from three children to two, roughly.

The reason is obvious. It is not that education is a contraceptive but that education leads a woman to work outside the home and that in turn persuades her to have fewer children. An outside job is the contraceptive. In the case of women in their early twenties, for instance, their fertility rate in the 1950s was a little over one child in five years and their participation rate about fifty per cent. By the mid 1970s their participation rate was up to sixty-five per cent and they were typically having many fewer babies: their fertility rate was down to less than half what it had been. The relation between the two rates over a quarter of a century was so consistent that in statistical terms, changes in these young women's participation rate "explained" ninety-seven per cent of the changes in their fertility rate. That is not quite the same thing as saying that the one caused the other, but it is coming close. The mathematical relation between the two implies that if their participation rate rose to 78 per cent, they would have no children at all.

The same sort of correlations can be found between the participation rates and fertility rates of women of all ages. Combined with the growing pressures on women to take paying work, the need for income, for a more public kind of fulfilment, for access to the lively world outside the kitchen, it makes a strong case for expecting fertility rates to drop.

The growing financial independence of women is a consequence, and indeed one aim, of women's attempts to liberate themselves from the restrictions of their former narrow role. Women who bear fewer children or none find it easier to do what they must to achieve economic independence – "which in turn makes marriage and childbearing less of an automatic social response," as the Princeton University demographer Charles Westoff pointed out. "The future seems less and less compatible with long-term traditional marriage." Westoff argued after long study of trends in women's work, marriage, divorce, and fertility that "it is not difficult to visualize a society in which perhaps one-third of women never have any children." He concluded that fertility in the United States would probably stay below the replacement level.

Women's rising independence has surely had an enormous effect on their attitude to child-bearing and child-raising, even for those who do not go out to work. Feminism developed in a climate that linked marriage and maternity with everything that ailed women. Judith Finlayson recalled that early feminists commonly declared, "I'll never have children," though they now more often say, "I'm thinking of it," or "It depends on whether I meet a suitable man" – still a far cry from the desperately determined husband-hunting and baby-making of young women in the 1950s. "We watched our mothers get burned by being confined to the role of mothers," Joanne Kates wrote. "And we aren't having any of it."

There is increasing evidence for the belief that more and more women think of themselves as men do. The sexual behaviour of women, whether married or not, is now much more like men's. A survey at the University of Toronto a few years ago showed that female undergraduates had about as many sex partners before marriage as men did. Effective contraception freed them from fear of unwanted pregnancies. A University of Manitoba sociologist concluded after three years of studying couples who had chosen not to have children that there is no such thing as an instinctive urge to bear and raise children. The magazine *New Society* called Britain "a society in steady retreat from child-rearing" and attributed the change to women's campaigns for equal rights and equal pay: "The stereotype of the *hausfrau* had to be smashed if women generally were to obtain equal rights." Pornographic movies, once strictly segregated as stag films, are now standard fare at movie theatres looking for young adult audiences of both sexes.

The real impetus behind unisex styles, equal rights, and women's liberation is women's desire to share the world with men: share the work, share the babies, share the housekeeping, the money, the recognition, and even share the clothes and hair styles. A large number of women in the Big Generation are doing these things, and an increasing number of men, too. The changes have come very rapidly for older people, but for the generation, they have been happening all their lives, beginning with the way their mothers raised them and the way they were educated, and continuing in the wave of liberating revolution they saw sweep the whole world, from the European empires in Asia and Africa to the blacks of the United States, from the universities to the work place, literature, and the performing arts. To most old people, women's liberation is just a foolish idea. To the middle-aged it is a radical concept that is going to take a long time to catch on. To the Big Generation it is a reality, though not yet perfectly realized.

Jeanne Binstock wrote a much reprinted article, "Motherhood: An Occupation Facing Decline," in 1972. In it she said:

Many of the young women now liberating themselves are committed to avoiding the traps that their own mothers were caught in. Young men, over-identified with their seductive, nurturing mothers, want to release women from the restrictive roles that damage everyone. The young men wear their hair long, carry babies on their back, and oppose war. The young women wear pants, defiantly assert their independence and initiative, and spend less time making marriage traps for men.

Just as women's liberation has led to a general blurring of sex roles, a dissolving of limits and restrictions, it has been accompanied by an increase in overt homosexuality and wider acceptance of it. As women have moved more openly into what was formerly men's territory, some men have felt threatened, some released. Many of the hard-core feminists are also lesbian. Unisex has many meanings: in this case, more sex without pregnancy.

Members of the Big Generation are influenced by their uniquely wide experience of broken homes and divorce. Warner Troyer wrote in *Divorced Kids* that children from broken families were more cautious about getting married: "Many girls simply said they did not want families." He also interviewed adults who had suffered through divorces as children: all said the experience had reduced their chance of happy marital relations. "Many said they had determined in their youth that they would have no children of their own – had even made that a condition of marriage in later years."

The situation is a little reminiscent of the cohort born in the 1920s and 1930s, many of whom felt they had been brought up too strictly. What did they decide to do with their children? Bring them up less strictly. Now, in its turn, the Big Generation has a complaint to make of its parents' behaviour: the children feel their chances of married happiness have been spoiled by the breakdown of the parents' marriage. So what will the generation do? Be more careful whom they marry? Stick together no matter what until all the children have left home? Have no children? Not get married at all?

Girls are now physically able to give birth at a younger age than ever, though a higher proportion than ever are remaining "children" by continuing with their studies. An Ontario government study found that although teenagers are having fewer children, three times as many unmarried teenagers who do give births are now keeping their children rather than putting them up for adoption compared with ten years ago. Phyllis Marles, born in 1961, came from a broken home and helped to bring up three younger children in the family. At thirteen she got pregnant and decided to keep the child, and at fifteen she became a mother again. What she craved was love, to give and to receive. But if that suggests that Big Generation teenagers are turning the tables and planning to have more children, it is surely wrong. The only certain figures so far are that the fertility rates for the Big Generation are still dropping, as they have been ever since the first member of the generation matured.

At least a third of marriages are now likely to end in divorce, and sooner rather than later: the highest divorce rate is for people in their late twenties. That influences fertility too. People do not look at divorce statistics when they are thinking about getting married, but they watch TV and read books and go to the movies, all of which show in increasingly devastating detail the collapse of marriages under the pressures of ambition, self-doubt, egoism, and richly nurtured tastes for all varieties of experience. This is the country Woody Allen has harvested perhaps better than anyone, but *Kramer vs. Kramer* was another recent good example: the wife of an advertising man and mother of a seven-year-old walks out because she feels stifled by their demands, miserable in her feelings of inadequacy, driven by the desire for liberation. "Her story is a seventies archetype," one critic said. Joan Barfoot's novel *Abra* covers similar ground. People thinking about marriage see what happens to their parents, their friends, and their parents' friends. Everywhere there is a growing awareness that modern marriage is at risk, and a feeling that if it no longer delivers happiness it is a failure and should be ended. As Joanne Kates noted, "We've seen marriage lose its durability; we've lost our childhood confidence in the longevity of the knight on a white charger and we're reluctant to make a baby with someone who, good sense tells us, will not be there in five years."

Every year since 1972 there have been more divorces and fewer marriages. The figures do not match up yet, but they are getting closer. In 1950 marriages outnumbered divorces about twenty-five to one; in 1965, fifteen to one; in 1970, six to one; in 1977, there were only three marriages for every divorce.

What makes the latest statistic more striking is that by any reckoning the number of marriages ought to be at a record high level and rising. The median age of brides in 1977 was twenty-two: half were older, half younger. That means the median bride in Canada was born in 1955, the same year as over two hundred thousand other girl children. There should be an increasing number of brides each year until 1981, but instead the numbers have been falling throughout the last five years for which we have data. The cause of the drop is a very sharp decline in the marriage rates for women under twenty-five, the women of the Big Generation, a quarter to a third lower than any marriage rates on record. Older women's rates have dropped too, but only slightly. Various explanations have been advanced for the decline of marriage among the young. One is that marriages are not in decline, they are simply being postponed. Another is that more couples are living together without marrying, heterosexual as well as homosexual. A third is that more people simply prefer to retain their independence and live alone.

People may indeed be delaying marriage, but if so, there are going to have to be a larger number of marriages of people in their late twenties and thirties over the next decade to catch up; in fact, the generation would have to match the marriage rates of women right at the end of the Second World War to equal the same proportion of women who eventually marry. In previous cohorts, those born since 1925 at any rate, ninety-five per cent of women have eventually married. On present trends, it seems possible, even probable, that only seventy-five or eighty per cent of Big Generation women will marry.

Although demographers resist the idea that such large shifts can take place so fast, the change in the life-style of many women of the generation – no children, full-time careers, financial independence – would certainly be compatible with a drop of that magnitude. There is good reason to say that, like justice, marriage delayed is marriage denied. The longer people put off getting married, the less likely they are to do it. For as long as we have records, marriage rates for women have been highest when they were in their early twenties, and the rates for women over twenty-five have always been quite a bit lower. So far, ninety per cent of women who were going to get married have done so by the time they reached thirty. Perhaps needless to say, if a fifth or more of women do remain single, the generation will have many fewer children.

An unexpected reason for marriages to go on dropping lies in the special circumstances surrounding the people born just after the peak of the baby boom, 1959. Women typically marry men two or three years older than themselves: the age difference has been decreasing, but only slowly. Each year about five per cent more boys than girls are born, and the disparity holds until well into middle age, when the lower death rate for women allows them to catch up and in the end overtake the men. And from 1939 to 1959, the number of births each year was rising.

What all this means is that ever since about 1960, when the first of the rising tide of youngsters reached marriageable age, there have been almost exactly as many men of marriageable age as women: typically, women aged twenty-two and men aged twenty-four. Starting around 1980, however, there will be an excess of men, which will continue for the rest of the century. The worst case is for men born in 1964, who exceed by twenty per cent the number of women born in 1962. Over the whole of the next twenty years there will be an unmarriageable surplus of 300,000 men, or one in twelve. Marrying slightly older women would help them somewhat to alter the odds, but all men would have to marry women older than themselves to have the same chance of getting married as men have had for the past twenty years.

So this quirk of fate is likely to produce hundreds of thousands of unwilling bachelors or three-way sharing arrangements. Not coincidentally, these phenomena are showing up in small but growing numbers among members of the generation. Conditions like this do not happen as neatly or in such a clear-cut way as in my analysis. They are already affecting some men of the Big Generation, they will never affect many others.

The bright side of the picture is that every woman who wants a man to live with, whether she marries him or not, should have a noticeably larger selection to choose from, or, to put it another way, she should find more men competing for her and therefore a distinctly better chance of getting paired. ("Competition over women probably is the single most important cause of violence"—Donald Symons, *The Evolution of Human Sexuality*.)

Between 1971 and 1976 there was an enormous increase in the

number of young people living alone or in some more or less untraditional arrangement, perhaps as a single parent or with other single or divorced people. The total number of people aged fifteen to twenty-four increased by twelve per cent; the number of young families increased twenty-two per cent; the number of non-family household groups increased forty per cent; the number of young people living alone increased a hundred per cent.

The glamour of the single's life must have won tens of thousands of followers, at least for a while. The independent streak in the Big Generation encourages them to leave home, partly, no doubt, because they have larger families to get away from. Many of those who set up on their own are probably first-born children, who are still more independent than their siblings. Not all of them want to be singles but the generation is full of people who find it hard to get on with others. The YMCA, social counselling groups, and community colleges now offer dozens of survival courses for singles. "How to deal with loneliness is a big issue in their minds," a Catholic family service worker said. "So is how to deal with rejection and depression." Another social worker observed, "They say they want to talk about where and how to meet people, but what they really mean is they want to discuss their problems with intimacy, how to get close emotionally to other people. They're mostly attractive, intelligent people. Most are university-trained. What they need most of all is self-sufficiency, and secondly they need friends."

But as Herbert Passin, a Columbia University anthropologist, said, "For the first time in human history, the single condition is being recognized as an acceptable adult life style for anyone. It is finally becoming possible to be both single and whole." Frank Furstenberg, a sociologist at the University of Pennsylvania, thinks Americans are becoming "separate economic and psychological modules" who move in and out of relationships rapidly. Soon, he has suggested, "family living will be relegated to a certain short part of the life span, the middle years, and outside of that segment people will spend time living alone or in transitory arrangements." The Big Generation is the first in history that has been trained for this life.

Many singles live in the metropolises. In 1976 the city of Vancouver, for instance, had more single households than any other kind, in fact a third of all households were single.

The current decline in births is being explained as either a plain desire to have fewer children or, like the decline in marriages, as a delay. Demographers are much more insistent that it is delay in the case of births than they are about marriage, but again, while the long tradition of preserving the human race or at least replacing oneself seems immensely strong, the arguments against delay really need to be looked at critically. Over the decades child-bearing has ceased to be a middle-aged person's occupation and has become the prerogative of the young. Women who were born in the first decade of this century had twenty-five per cent of their children after they were thirty-five but women born twenty years later had had ninety per cent of their children by that age. Child-bearing has been concentrated into a shorter span of time, and for a number of good reasons: women no longer want to go on mothering children into middle age; they know more about the risks of bearing children when they are older; in general they want more of their lives to themselves. It is hard to imagine how women of the Big Generation could revert to earlier patterns.

Newspapers come out with occasional enthusiastic headlines like "A baby boom begins for couples over 30," but the figures show that the birth rates for women over thirty are close to their all-time low. There is a two- or three-year lag before fertility rates are published, but a calculation made from information on age distribution and the number of births in 1979 suggests that the over-thirties' fertility rate could not have shifted much by the end of the 1970s, and may have dropped. Women who put off having children until their late twenties or early thirties are guaranteed (statistically) to have fewer children than women who start earlier. In fact, the relation between the mother's age at her first child and the number of children she has is one of the strongest correlations there is. Starting early is the surest way of all to have a big family; delaying is a powerful contraceptive. As a London, Ontario, woman put it when she discovered at the age of thirty-five that she was pregnant, "I suspected also, in all probability, that this would be my one and only chance to enjoy all the facets of pregnancy and motherhood." Or, to quote a noted Ottawa population expert, "Fertility delayed is fertility denied," an axiom fully borne out by the research of Jean Veevers, a University of Western Ontario sociologist, who interviewed more than a hundred married couples with no children for her book *Childless by Choice*. An almost identical pattern appeared in the lives of two-thirds of them: at first they put off having children until they had reached a specified goal (graduation, the down-payment on a house, a trip to Europe): then they became vaguer about the timing of the first child; then they began to debate whether they really wanted to be parents at all; and at last they agreed they did not.

Add to this, that the Big Generation is the first to be exposed when young to the idea of the population explosion – "the population bomb" as Paul Ehrlich so dramatically called it – and the persuasive campaigns of the Zero Population Growth movement. Add that they were the first to know from childhood about the Pill and the IUD, the first to be able to get an abortion legally and fairly easily (a third of all teenage pregnancies were ended by abortion in 1979), and perhaps most significant of all, the first to have simple sterilization available to them. I have no Canadian figures on sterilization, but in the United States fully half of all white couples who had been married ten to twenty-four years told survey takers that at least one of them had been permanently sterilized. Even among couples married only five to ten years, a fifth had been sterilized.

For all these reasons I conclude that Canada can expect a continuing decline in fertility. And what will the results of this decline be? Certainly, any level of fertility much lower than the recent figures, which have been around or above the replacement level of two children per woman, will have extraordinary effects on the population's size and growth.

If the fertility rate were to drop steadily to one child per woman by the end of the century, for instance, even with 100,000 or so immigrants a year, the population would actually start to shrink by the middle of the 1990s. By the end of the century it would be down below twenty-five million, or only about a million more than it is today. By the year 2026, assuming that fertility stayed at one after the turn of the century, the population would have dropped below the level of 1976, and some time in the 2040s it would fall below twenty million.

The proportion of people under twenty would decline from the present figure of thirty-three per cent to about twenty per cent at the end of this century and to fifteen per cent by 2026. By that time people over sixty – that is, the surviving members of the Big Generation and any tenacious hangers-on who are older than they are–would once more represent a third of the total population. Low fertility, in other words, would severely distort the distribution of the population as well as limit its size. It would guarantee the dominance of the Big Generation throughout its life, with all the problems for advancement, social security, communal support, and so on that that implies. Low fertility would do a great deal to create the kind of future that the Big Generation now only has nightmares about.

The housing industry is the most likely to suffer from the Big Generation's low fertility, because it will mean that more and more couples in their thirties are going to want one-bedroom or two-bedroom apartments rather than three-bedroom houses. The generation's passage into adult life and early middle age in the 1980s is going to bring the end of the high construction figures that started in the early 1970s (one could say started again, after the housing boom of the years right after the war which heralded the arrival of the generation). Central Mortgage and Housing Corporation, the federal government's housing agency, estimated that nearly a million and a quarter housing units would be needed in the last half of the 1970s and that the number needed every five years after that would drop steadily until it reached about 800,000 in the last five years of the century.

Not only will there be fewer housing units, then, but, if fertility drops, there will also be a good chance that many more of those housing units will be apartments rather than houses, built at a lower cost and requiring fewer construction workers. All this with a labour force that will continue to rise. "The picnic in the housing industry is over," a Royal Bank mortgage manager said in 1979. "If builders carry on as they have in the past and ignore the future realities of the market, there could be a lot of bankruptcies in the industry."

Already the housing industry has been urging the federal government to increase immigration. Michael Walker of the Fraser Institute suggested that rising labour rates were delaying large building and engineering projects and that as a result the government would be under pressure to loosen immigration standards and bring in more workers–and that would be the major factor in increasing the number of housing starts and saving the construction industry. This idea is not one likely to appeal to the job-hungry Big Generation.

Others have suggested that builders with an eye to the future will become more involved in renovation and modernization – the sort of thing that has been happening in Atlanta, Philadelphia, and New York – to provide housing for people who want to live closer to the centre of the city and avoid the cost of commuting. "It seems clear that when the new generation of families look for a home, many will focus on the mid-town section of the urban area – not the downtown area, but the area between the suburbs and downtown," as one expert put it.

One other development that could help the housing industry is the shift from housing as shelter to housing as investment. In recent years, housing has been one of the few investments to beat inflation consistently. "This desperate feeling that 'I've got to have something real,'" two Rutgers University professors called it. "For the middle class in America, there is nothing more real than a house." For the Big Generation, they might have added, it is particularly real because so many grew up in a solid, protecting, free-standing, three-bedroom, two-car-garage, picture-window house big enough for the whole family. Clearly they see it as the ultimate security, and the bigger and more expensive the better. Nine out of ten people in their late teens and early twenties hope to buy a house, although at current prices it looks as though less than half the population will actually be able to. Any government program making it easier for people to start buying a house is popular. The British Columbia scheme that reduced mortgage rates in 1980 brought floods of applicants. "A pent-up demand for housing," a credit union official called it.

Investing in a house is probably the biggest single reason that both husbands and wives in so many families go out to work, and therefore the cause of the rising participation of women in the labour force, the high unemployment level, the rise in the cost of houses in the metropolises, and, probably, a fair chunk of the inflation everyone wants to beat. Therefore, in return for the security of that big house they and their brothers and sisters once lived in, the Big Generation will pay an ironic price: their own families will be the smallest on record. Once more, a squeeze the generation is going to find itself in will, as in so many other cases, produce unexpected and long-lasting consequences for the whole country.

CHAPTER 12

TOO MANY CHIEFS

"They're going to have to find other life-styles
that don't include executive positions."

Those who have thought about the future of the Big Generation look toward the end of the 1980s with trepidation. By then the oldest of these children of the baby boom will be approaching forty and the youngest will be in her mid-twenties. Virtually all will have had some taste of how the world is going to treat them, and the majority, those in their thirties, will have begun to understand the pattern the rest of their lives are going to follow.

Although that pattern cannot yet be foreseen with certainty, here are two scenarios for the 1990s that bracket the most reasonable prospects:

The economy becomes less urgent, somewhat more informal, with more women in the labour force, and many more people employed in part-time work with peculiar arrangements of working hours, working months (say, summer and fall only), and working years (say, five years at work, one at college, one at leisure). The economy has migrated to post-industrial kinds of work: information and leisure services particularly, combined with small-scale and medium-scale pre-industrial work centred on renewable resources, notably various kinds of energy programs, gasohol, sun and wind and tide, but also on food and lumber. At the fringe this is little more than subsistence farming, at the centre it is business. Post-industrial work and pre-industrial work both lend themselves more easily to working at home (or living at work) than industry does, and so more people live in rural areas and on farms, and there is less commuting. A successful elite of New Class professionals thrives in the metropolises. But most people live wherever it is cheapest, in cities, suburbs, or villages, with much renovation and some startling conversions of abandoned factories and office buildings in some cities. Efficiency drops and the gross national product grows sluggishly, but barter increases (a haircut for two chickens, a brake job for pulling two teeth). The professions suffer the loss of middle-income clients and are pushed in both directions, to more specialized work for corporations, work through the pervasive electronic networks, and more storefront work for ordinary citizens. Prospects for skilled technicians are good but the shift away from industry has eased the demand somewhat. Overall, real personal income per household is about the same as it was in the 1970s. Immigration is lower than it was in the quarter century after the Second World War, and emigration drops off, too. Fertility and family size are down, one and a half children per woman or less.

The other scenario goes like this.

The economy continues to concentrate on resources, nonrenewable energy and minerals as well as renewable food and forestry, but the industrial sector grows by making several more North American common market arrangements along the lines of the pioneering automobile pact. Efficiency rises, thanks to the renaissance of industry after rationalization. The service sector continues to develop, though not as strongly as was once expected. Immigration rises to 1950s levels, spurred by the demand for industrial workers. There is less part-time work because of the increase of industrial work in the economic mixture, and many people speak cheerfully of a return to the good old days. Fertility rises; families of two or three children become the norm. There is much construction work in renovating, extending, and densifying the suburbs. Over all, real personal income per household is higher than it was in the 1970s.

The problem with the second scenario is that it suits everybody but the Big Generation. For older people, it would be comfortably familiar; youngsters now in school could be redirected so they could take advantage of it; and people who want to immigrate to Canada could be more easily accommodated. But the Big Generation grew up with different expectations.

Sometimes it is hard to envisage precisely the kind of world they were prepared for: a world in which thirty to fifty per cent of the work force would be researching, teaching, writing, practising law, medicine, architecture, counselling, and advising. Who their clients would be, who would employ and pay them, who would take away their garbage, keep their sewers running, make their shirts, build their apartments, and empty their hospital bedpans is not so clear. The dream of the future that inspired the post-war educators was certainly not the world they then lived in. The hopes and ambitions of the generation's parents were almost as vague: the world they envisaged for their children was something like what they then lived in, but enlarged and exaggerated at many points. No more hospitals, perhaps, but more doctors; no more construction workers, but more highways; no larger government, but more lawyers; more schools with more teachers; more supervisors and managers but fewer workers; many more machines to do the dirty work; many labour-saving products, imported from the United States.

The Big Generation gained unique capacities while it was picking up the qualities its parents and teachers wished on it. Big Generation people are on the whole more sensitive to the world they live in, more adaptable, ingenious, and innovative. Many are also deeply uncomfortable in any kind of structured situation, or following a planned system, or taking orders. It is hard to get members of the generation to work in big hotels or restaurants, though they delight in running small cafés on their own. Many find assembly line work unpalatable to the point of nausea but would stay up all night to get a radio program ready for broadcast. In general, though, their attitude to work is "Catholic" rather than "Protestant" (in quotation marks because the words concern only the work attitudes Weber identified), pre-industrial; many of them see work as a means to an end, not as an end in itself. If they must work, then post-industrial work is preferred: work in the professions, the media, government, teaching, computers, any kind of information processing, selling food and clothing, social work, meeting and talking to people. These would be the choices of the majority, but a sizable minority are drawn to the real pre-industrial world of nature and growing things, fresh air, camaraderie, preferably somewhat

190

softened and glamorized by modern comfort and convenience (cars, radios, air travel, waterproof clothing). At a push, both kinds would likely choose pre-industrial work or post-industrial work over straight industrial work or the arid reaches of the great civil bureaucracies.

The Big Generation therefore makes the first scenario the more likely, simply because by the 1990s they will make up close to half of the labour force. Work has a tendency to fit the desires of the people who are there to do it – as we have seen in the past ten years or more, when unemployment has been high but vacancies in certain kinds of work have also remained high.

Strong forces are pushing for the second scenario, however, and it has just as reasonable a chance of coming about. It would not necessarily even produce enormously high unemployment rates: unemployment rising through the 1980s would reduce the participation rates, in effect sending women back to the kitchen and the nursery and restoring many of the conditions that existed in the 1950s.

What will tip the scale? The most important factor is likely to be the continuing frustration of the Big Generation, particularly of its most educated members. A number of college graduates have been unable to find work of any kind; most of those who have jobs feel disappointingly under-employed. The stories of Ph.D.s driving taxis because they are over-qualified for clerical positions may have been told too often but they are a reality. The proportion of young people who say they are capable of doing more than their jobs demand is much too high.

Each new generation should be able to refresh society and the economy. "If this process of renewal is seriously interrupted, future growth will suffer," the Organization for Economic Co-operation and Development said. "In effect, there will be a 'lost generation' for whom educational investment in 'human capital' will be partially depleted, and skills, productive work experience, and even the will to work itself will be substantially eroded."

The potential waste of a generation is a prospect that has troubled all kinds of people. Pressing for a rapid solution to unemployment and under-employment, a Toronto stock broker said, "Otherwise, five years from now, say, Canada will have too many people under the age of twenty-five who have had only intermittent employment or who will never have worked in the

191

trades and professions for which they were trained. This would be a major political embarrassment and danger, to say nothing of the economic and human misery." A Newfoundland priest said, "We may be witnessing the creation of a generation that is not only unemployed but unemployable." A Montreal economist said, "A certain amount of bumming around never hurt anyone, but if they spend the next five years locked out of the system, there will not be much left that is of use to society in the 1980s, when we may be very glad of their talents."

The next two decades are vital for the generation. The vast majority of scientific discoveries are made by scientists before they reach the age of forty. The young are creative and energetic, not yet locked into prejudice, not yet afraid to ask impossible questions. The work that has won Nobel prizes in physics was done, typically, when the scientist was thirty-six; in the case of theoretical work, at thirty-three. For Nobel-prize-winning work in chemistry, the average age was thirty-eight; for medicine and physiology, forty-one. The first members of the generation will reach thirty-three in 1984. They are unlikely to achieve any theoretical breakthroughs while selling encyclopedias.

They are always going to be denied their full share of the acclaim that now comes with age and achievement. Fully half the well-known people in my profession, futurism, at the end of the 1970s were born in the period 1918-1933. Less than a quarter of the adult population was born in that period. Renown, in short, is age related; people reach their peak in late middle age. When the Big Generation reaches that point, in 2011, there will only be three pedestals for every four who would have been famous if they had been born in 1918-1933.

The same thing is happening in the ranks of business. There is a widespread feeling that if you are not climbing the promotion ladder by the time you reach thirty-five, prospects are bleak. And more is being heard of the promotion squeeze. "Large numbers of low-level employees will vie for the few middle management jobs being vacated as the small group born before 1947 moves up to the top," an American writer noted. "As a consequence, people expecting to climb the career ladder rapidly are more likely to be disappointed—especially the highly educated, who traditionally move up quickly." A Harvard University demographer, Roger Revelle, said, "A lot of people are going to be frozen out. They're going to have to find other life-styles that don't include executive positions."

The Big Generation's prospects of getting into management are measurably smaller than those of anyone alive today. Promotability depends on how many people of your own age there are in relation to the number of workers to be managed. If the worker group is large and the potential management group small, chances of promotion are good; the other way round, chances are poor. On this theory, promotion prospects do increase with age, but variably because of differences in the population pyramid.

Using two separate measures of the workers, I calculated the promotability of each five-year age group in the work force every ten years from 1976 to 2026, and the Big Generation's chances stand out as abysmally poor, ten to twenty-five per cent lower than those of people a little older or younger, and fully a third lower than the notoriously lucky cohort born in the 1930s. Given their life-long expectation that they would rise high, succeed, and achieve greatness, one can anticipate a growing frustration, resentment, and bitterness, which must turn to apathy or to anger. Of course, it will always be possible to inflate the number of management jobs. A corporation could simply reduce what is called the span of command – the typical number of subordinates each manager oversees – and create the desired number of chiefs despite the lack of Indians.

The trouble with this, as with other kinds of inflation, is that it reduces the rewards. A company in the late 1970s wanted to increase management positions so as to hold on to bright people who it feared were looking elsewhere for advancement. When its president retired, his duties were shared among five new group presidents. None, however, drew presidential pay or had the satisfaction of wielding full presidential responsibilities.

It can be safely assumed that managers in the Big Generation will draw significantly smaller pay cheques than their predecessors in equivalent jobs. It is equally certain that a majority of the generation's members are condemned to spend the better part of their lives working below their potential level of achievement, and for many of them that will cause just as much frustration and unhappiness.

CHAPTER 13

CASTING VOTE

"Nobody owns me, so nobody rules me,
so I ought to be able to do what I want."

The countries of the European community are very nervous about their youth employment problems. Already there have been violent demonstrations reminiscent of the campus battles of 1968 but coming, this time, from the next generation. In Paris seventy policemen were injured in fights with young people after a march of seventy thousand unemployed in 1979. In Italy the brutal Red Brigades and other radical left groups have begun to attract followers from the hundreds of thousands of unemployed university graduates. Country after country is experiencing major political and social problems.

Some Canadian commentators have wondered whether the same sort of thing could happen here. "In all my years as a social worker, I've never heard people, particularly the young, talking so much about social injustice," said the head of a union-backed group lobbying for full employment. "There is so much talk about violence it amazes me. I wouldn't be surprised if this winter Canadians see problems of social disruption they've never seen before. It won't be like the Dirty Thirties when people stood patiently in food lines or sold apples on the streets. We want jobs and we're going to get them."

"One thing common to all unemployed youth is low esteem," Dr. Saul Levine, the University of Toronto psychiatrist, said. "They deteriorate personally. They feel humiliated, ashamed, and angry. Hundreds of alienated kids turn to destructive acts such as vandalism, drug abuse, and crime." Others think that the high unemployment and under-employment have been received with surprising passivity and resignation, and they fear the apathy could be even more damaging to the country's morale than an outburst of protest.

Behind the concern lies the realization that the generation is fast approaching its political years. The first federal general election any member of the generation voted in was 1972, after the voting age had been reduced to eighteen. By 1983 the whole of the generation will be able to vote. In a mere dozen years, nearly seven million new voters will have arrived on the scene; and suddenly, in 1983, they will be forty per cent of the electorate.

At first, the generation's impact is likely to be less than the numbers alone suggest. It is thought that young people are less serious about politics than their elders, either less informed and less concerned about the world outside their own immediate circle and interests, or more cynical. The 1980 referendum on sovereignty-association in Quebec, which attracted the interest of young voters, was an exception, probably because it was a one-issue poll on a matter they considered significant. Certainly Richard Finlay's campus survey revealed deep scepticism about political institutions in general. Ninety per cent had no confidence in politicians and thought they did more harm than good, ranking them even lower than economists, military generals, and lawyers. A majority thought political parties and, more remarkably, the democratic process itself needed fundamental reform. "While only twenty-two per cent say they have become more involved in changing society in the past two years, ninety-three per cent say they have become more interested in their own personal lives in the same period," Finlay wrote.

The Chief Electoral Officer does not record the number of voters by age, and I have found no Canadian figures on the number of young voters. The US government found that a smaller proportion of the voting population under thirty-five cast ballots in recent presidential elections than in older age groups; on average, about twenty per cent smaller. A smaller survey done for the Committee for the Study of the American Electorate suggested that the turn-out of people under thirty-five in the 1972 presidential election was thirty per cent lower than the turn-out of older people, and called the young voters a "lost generation" who "never really joined the system" and who by their own evidence will probably never vote. If, as the surveys suggest, people are more likely to vote as they get older, this last prediction may be no more than hyperbole, but it has uncomfortable echoes of the alienation and apathy discernible in some of the Big Generation.

From the generation's point of view, employment is the chief political issue and will remain so for years. A British cabinet minister, commenting on a political demonstration that turned into a riot in which more than a hundred people were injured in 1977, said he believed unemployment was at the root of the trouble: "Never let it be forgotten that Hitler came to power as a result of unemployment and not as a result of inflation." The Depression in Canada was deeply politicizing; it drove tens of thousands of people to what were then unfamiliar political ideas, communism, socialism, fascism, social credit, raising them to new and in most cases lasting importance. The main impetus was despair at the sight of wasted lives, work that needed to be done, and a system that could not bring the work and the workers together. There is reason to suppose that much of the support for the Parti Québécois has been a protest against the weakness of the province's economy, given direction by the belief that outsiders were responsible. Forty per cent of voters under thirty-five supported the PQ while only twelve per cent of people aged around fifty backed it. As in all provinces, youth unemployment in Quebec has been several percentage points higher than the rate over all. In France, where half the unemployed are under twenty-five, politicians say that voting by jobless youths played a big role in the unexpected victories of left-wing candidates in municipal elections.

Although the Big Generation's political future is not plainly apparent, the tendencies are clear. The generation is antipathetic to political parties, especially the established parties, the Conservatives and Liberals, mostly on the grounds that as big institutions they are untrustworthy. Its sense of the importance of individual decisions and personal worth makes it leery of all kinds of leaders.

So far the politicians have taken very little interest in the generation, considering its size and potential for damage or triumph. By 1983, to look at just one aspect, the Big Generation will be a larger bloc in the electorate than all men older than the generation or even all the older women. It will be larger than the entire Ontario electorate (though in that reckoning the Ontario members of the generation are included on both sides); larger than the Quebec electorate even if you take the Big Generation Quebeckers out of the generation bloc and count them in with the province; larger than the combined electorate of the prairie provinces, British Columbia, the Yukon, and the Northwest Territories; much larger than the electorate of the Maritimes. It will, in short, be larger than virtually any imaginable bloc, and yet it is almost virgin territory for politicians. True, in the metropolises where there are highly visible concentrations of generation members, young, swinging, post-war mayors have been elected. But in the 1979 and 1980 elections, nothing like the right proportion of candidates seems to have been drawn from the generation. Did you see a party policy or even a single candidate's campaign that paid any attention to the Big Generation, let alone gave them top priority? I recall a Toronto campaign in which the wealthy, middle-aged candidate was presented as tieless, shaggy-haired, somewhat uncombed on posters; with cheerful, colourful, game-like graphics. His platform included no national issues or party policies, just the candidate's assertion that "I don't know anything about Tory policy, I just know what's best for the riding, I'm my own man." The style was Big Generation, all right, but the lack of content was definitely not, and it did not get him elected.

If the American data apply in Canada, the Big Generation will represent an increasingly important bloc of votes as more of its members pass the age of thirty. By the 1990s it will be – or could be – the dominant voice at the polls. What will happen then? A decline in all political activity? A big swing to one of the existing parties? A new political party? A new kind of political action? A terrorist guerrilla movement?

All of these look possible. Apathy is a particularly deadly threat to democracy, and the students' doubts about the democratic process as it now stands show that they could easily give up on politics. Democracy without popular support can only turn into the rule of a minority, spreading dissatisfaction, collapse, and change. The Greeks said that a period of democracy inevitably leads into a period of anarchy, followed by a period of dictatorship. Hints of this are present today.

One of the existing parties could attract a considerable portion of the Big Generation's vote if it effectively represented itself as anti-establishment, anti-elitist, against bigness – Big Business, Big Government, Big Labour – deeply concerned with the problems of unemployment and under-employment, a champion of independence, a fighter for individual initiative, and in favour of at least some of the generation's *lares* and *penates*, which it would demonstrate perhaps by decriminalizing marijuana, reducing stand-by air fares, and cutting mortgage rates. But for a few details, that sounds remarkably like the New Democratic Party. Given the inertia of all parties, the NDP could easily be the official opposition in Ottawa toward the end of the 1980s and could form the government some time in this century.

While the generation's self-awareness and independent-mindedness stands out, the strength and conviviality of the youth culture is a powerful phenomenon. The movie *Tommy* was one attempt to follow this idea to its political end: a rock singer as the leader of a socio-religious cult. The novel *Ecotopia* built on the same idea of a cult-like social movement with obvious Big Generation attributes. A potential leader would have many keys to play on: pride, resentment, ambition, frustration, superior education, energy. A member of the generation, Jonathan Mills, wrote angrily to a newspaper about the way insurance companies discriminated against young male drivers and the announcement of an increase in premiums: "The matter can be seen in its true light if one considers whether higher premiums for 'high risk' ethnic groups would be tolerated, presuming such exist. Can you wonder that we young males might be disillusioned with 'democratic' politics? Just wait till we are forty-five and you want adequate old age pensions."

Dr. Saul Levine of the University of Toronto, who made a study of the social and psychological effects of unemployment on young people, said: "They form a fertile ground for leaders who claim to have easy answers for troubled kids. It's no mere coincidence that Italy has one of the highest unemployment rates in the Western world plus the fiercest terrorism led by the elders of the youth population." In Levine's view, a revolutionary movement is but one potential destructive choice for unemployed youth; fanatical religious cults like the one developed by the Reverend Jim Jones that ended in nine hundred deaths in Guyana are another.

The basis of terrorism has been analysed by a political scientist at the University of California at Los Angeles, Dr. Jeanne Knutson. She thinks three life-experiences are necessary pre-conditions for turning to terrorism: socialization to shared cultural beliefs, such as hearing dramatic stories about the community's heroes and villains while a child; intense psychological pressures, such as an urgent need to establish one's values as an individual; and major disappointments in life, such as failure to reach an educational or vocational goal. Dr. Knutson found these pre-conditions in the life of Zvonko Busic, a Croatian nationalist who planted a bomb in a railroad station, killed a policeman, and hijacked a domestic jet. Busic grew up hearing repeated stories about the hardships suffered by Croatians at the hands of their neighbours and admiring an heroic Croatian nationalist. He was continually urged by his parents to get a good education and better himself, but although he attended three different universities he left each for lack of funds and never earned a degree. There are obvious parallels with the Big Generation, including, in several regions of Canada, a fully developed sense of injustice and oppression.

The Big Generation's predecessors, the wartime and immediate post-war children, were responsible for the student unrest of the 1960s. Robert Spencer was among the most militant of them. "We thought an actual political revolution was possible and we would cause it," he said recently. There was no rallying at the barricades, however, and many of the militants felt they had failed. But had they? "I'm surprised now that we got as far as we did," the one-time president of the Canadian Union of Students, Peter Warrian, said. "The student movement was part of a process that got people to think more critically about society," a third militant, Steven Langdon, once University of Toronto student president, added. Many of Knutson's pre-conditions for terrorism were absent among those early offspring of the baby boom; few failed to achieve their educational goals, most were outstandingly successful in the business or professional world after graduation. Their militance as students may be seen now more as a kind of rehearsal or preparation for a revolution that the second phase of the post-war economic boom smothered. "Of the primary leadership group, a large, somewhat embarrassing number are now academics and have the embarrassment of tenure, the kind of thing we were fighting," Warrian remarked. Some of the others, however, are working in the New Democratic Party and labour unions.

The maturing of the Big Generation will increase the median age of the electorate. In 1983, half the voters will still be under thirty-nine, but then the median age will start to climb until, by about 2025 or 2030, it reaches fifty.

It is always assumed that people get more conservative as they get older, and in fact there are reasonably good studies to demonstrate it. So it has been supposed that the aging of the Big Generation would rapidly lead to a much more conservative electorate. The numbers do not support this. Even in the year 2001 the electorate will be slightly younger than the electorate in 1961 and much younger than the electorate of Britain or Sweden, neither of which is noted for conservative policies. There are many years still for some tumultous political upsets.

The enfranchisement of the generation will trigger a new kind of platform and government. Even older generations have found most government policy too dominated by farm interests, by rural interests generally, and in recent years – now that industry has gone into decline – by industrial interests. The Big Generation is unlikely to accept this kind of lag in policy with patience. It will remain a highly identifiable bloc of votes as long as it lives; when the first member of the generation reaches the age of sixty, in 2011, the cohort will still be thirty per cent of the electorate, a larger bloc vote than Quebec has today. It is safe to assume that even then the generation will be at least as demanding as Quebec ever was, and with as fully ripened a sense of injustice.

CHAPTER 14

THE END OF THE HUNDRED-YEAR ODYSSEY

*"Every man desires to live long;
but no man would be old."*

It would be nice to be able to say something cheerful and comforting about the Big Generation's old age. "As they enter their sunset years, these lovable and dignified old folks will be increasingly sought out for their remarkable understanding and knowledge. The country they have served so faithfully will spare no effort to ensure their comfort and security" – that sort of thing.

Unhappily, it is not going to be like that. More likely, they will be a problem and a source of acrimony from the time the first of them approaches retirement, about a decade after the turn of the century, until the majority have been buried, which will be about the middle of the century (the last member of the generation, it is safe to assume, will survive at least until 2075). On the other hand, the generation will be better equipped to protect itself and get its way than any previous generation of old people.

As in so much else, the Big Generation has been the first to get the full benefit of a remarkable modern development: the eradication of many of the most virulent causes of premature death. As a result it is going to cause a revolutionary change in society. Just as the radical notion of extending education from elementary school to high school came at the very moment the generation was passing through school, so the raising of life expectancy is about to combine with the generation's age, and with a probable drop in the size of the following generations, to give Canada an unprecedentedly old society.

People have already started to talk about this as an aging society, the greying of Canada, and so on, but they are premature. There are several ways to measure the age of a society. It will probably not be until 1996 that half the population will be over thirty-five, for instance (the median age in 1980 was about twenty-nine), and not until the next century that half will be over forty. It will not be until after 2006 that the proportion of pensioners, people aged sixty-five and over, in the population starts to go up. Pensioners were five per cent of the population in 1931, will pass ten per cent in the 1980s, will still not reach twelve per cent by 2006. But then within twenty years the proportion of pensioners will soar to about twenty per cent.

In short, not until the Big Generation is aging will it be appropriate to talk of Canada as aging, but when that day comes the aging process will be sudden and strong. By 2026, in one fairly conservative forecast, the median age will be forty-three, half the electorate will be over fifty, a fifth of the population will be over sixty-five, and the size of the population will have passed its peak and started to shrink.

There is no country in the world that has such figures today. In fact numbers like this can only be temporary. Several demographers have worked out what a country would be like if it achieved and maintained a stationary population, the objective sought by proponents of zero population growth. According to one, the median age would be thirty-seven, half the electorate would be over forty-five, fifteen per cent of the population would be over sixty-five. Before it is finished the generation is likely to take us well past this point of equilibrium. Certainly, not until the generation has passed through will it be possible for the population to settle down.

But it is not really surprising that people are talking about this aging society in advance of its arrival, because the impending change casts a shadow on our time. We know that some kind of miracle has been worked to let us live longer. "The reason why old age was venerated in the past was because it was extraordinary," the British author Ronald Blythe reflects in *The View in Winter*. "To be old today is to be contemptible. Why? Because to be old is to be part of a huge and ordinary multitude." It is one of the most radical changes in modern life that, as Marion Levy of Princeton has put it, "We take it for granted that practically everyone will survive into senility." But for the survivors and for the society, it is not an obvious improvement except in the sense of the old joke, that it is better than the alternative.

"Every man desires to live long; but no man would be old,"

Jonathan Swift said. Current efforts to increase longevity and improve life-expectancy follow two main lines: one is an attempt to cure more diseases and allow more people to live to old age, although without increasing the maximum lifespan by very much; and the other is an effort to increase the lifespan. Success in either would have an effect on the survival curve, which plots how many survivors there are at each age out of an initial population, but the effects would not be the same.

The present survival curve shows that about ninety people out of every hundred born survive into their fifties; half survive into their early seventies; twenty per cent survive to their mid-eighties. The first kind of research, which the Futures Group in a detailed study has called "curve-squaring," tries to get nearly everybody, say ninety-eight per cent, to survive into their eighties; then there would be a precipitate drop down to the present age limit of about a hundred, after which virtually no one would survive. The second kind of research, which the Futures Group called "lifespan-extending," aims to increase the maximum age from 100 to, say, 150 or 250, without necessarily altering the shape of the survival curve. With success in extending lifespan to 200 years, for instance, half the population might survive to the age of 130 and 20 per cent to 160.

Theodore Gordon, president of the Futures Group, said after his study, "Since the lifespan-extending technologies probably will be most effective if used from the time of childhood, the effects of these technologies will not be felt for many years." If Gordon is correct, they would have little effect on the Big Generation. Curve-squaring techniques, on the other hand, would be effective as soon as developed. They would increase life-expectancy at middle age and once more throw the population out of balance, almost as if the generation had been born again as a cohort of people disproportionately large in its social context. If substantial improvement in curve-squaring medical treatment were developed during the next few decades, it would be yet another of the ironies that has characteristically surrounded the Big Generation at every step through life.

The idea behind curve-squaring is that particular diseases and accidents prevent people from reaching the end of their potential lifespan. Penicillin and other products of wartime development allowed large numbers of people to survive infectious diseases that used to be fatal. The results of that research seem to have been exhausted, however, particularly as they benefit men. Death rates for men between the ages of fifteen and fifty have scarcely changed since the beginning of the 1960s, and for older men they have improved by only 0.5 per cent a year on average, though women's rates have gone on dropping. But there has been a considerable change in what kills. Today, out of every hundred deaths, thirty-five are due to heart disease, twenty-one to cancer, ten to strokes, and nine to accidents and suicide. These four killers together account for three-quarters of all deaths, so the potential for curve-squaring is quite concentrated. A medical breakthrough in the treatment of heart disease or cancer, particularly, would have dramatic effects on the survival of people in middle age. Even at mortality rates not much different from the present, the Big Generation will still be the largest fifteen-year cohort in the year 2021, but after that its dominance will start to fade. Any real success in curve-squaring in the next forty years could extend the generation's reign another quarter of a century.

Curve-squaring treatments would have a great effect on social security. An ingenious government might discover an answer to the extended demands of the pensioners in the unexpected good fortune that would befall the life-insurance companies. Since the insurance companies would be taking in premiums longer and paying out death benefits later, they should become richer; perhaps, if the curve-squaring breakthroughs were sufficiently dramatic, embarrassingly richer. Given that a militant consumer society would otherwise have them hanged, drawn, and quartered for profiteering, they might be glad to make a deal with the over-strained government social security programs.

Retirement is likely to be a thorny problem. It has already started to cause difficulties, and the pressures are only a tiny fraction of what they are going to become. Retirement is now general at sixty-five because for at least the past thirty years public and private pension plans have been designed to start paying at that age. It is enshrined in the Canada and Quebec Pension Plan laws, it is written into innumerable union contracts. Why should it be changed?

Arguments in favour of later retirement have the upper hand at present. There are four main strings to the reasoning:

First, improvements in health and life-expectancy have made

the eighty-year-old of today the equivalent of a sixty-five-year-old a century ago, when the retirement age was first set. Clearly the original idea was to retire workers only when they were unemployable, and that is no longer at sixty-five.

Second, inflation, which has been described as "a method by which the able-bodied rob the aged," means that fixed pensions are whittled away, leaving the pensioner with less and less to spend each year. No one wants to make the irrevocable step onto that slide. In many cases pensions are based on the worker's best earning years, which with inflation would start off much higher if he were allowed to stay on at work even five years longer.

"It is impossible to scratch very far beneath the surface these days without turning up the dominant worry in the late 1970s: deep concern over the continuing high rate of inflation," Lou Harris, the American poll-taker, said after completing a study of retirement. Harris found that a majority of Americans wanted to work on after reaching normal retirement age, most of them only part-time, however. Professor J.E. Pesando of the University of Toronto said that Canadian workers who want to keep on working after retirement age are also mainly motivated by fear of inflation: "Under private pension plans, retirement is most likely to be postponed because pension benefits are not indexed." A Canadian poll found that more than half would like a part-time job after retiring.

The Japanese steelworkers' union recently negotiated a new contract that allowed workers to stay on the job until they reached sixty instead of retiring at fifty-five. The explanation appears to be not that they are gluttons for work but that they too fear retirement; although they retired on a company pension before and after the new contract, it was not sufficiently generous. "Our government pensions don't begin until we're sixty-five," a worker in another Japanese industry complained, "but many of us leave work at fifty-five, so we have ten years of scrambling about trying to make ends meet."

Besides, by the end of the century some people will have to keep on working past retirement just to support their parents.

A third argument in favour of later retirement is that it is discriminatory and an infringement of a worker's civil rights to fire him for no other cause but age. There may be a few jobs where maximum strength, virility, and alertness are essential. Airplane pilots, miners, surgeons, firefighters, fishermen, it might be argued, are cases in point. But in general a post-industrial society can not only accommodate old workers but actually benefit from their experience.

The fourth argument is that forcing people to retire endangers their health, puts their lives at risk, and condemns them to a life of "poverty, aimlessness, and loneliness," in the words of Senator David Croll's committee on pensions. The sudden end of productive work "often leads to physical and emotional deterioration and premature death," a study by the American Medical Association concluded. One person in four who was retired from a British government agency died within six months. A British researcher commented: "When people feel that they are no longer needed they simply lose the urge to go on living." Dr. Jack Adamowitz of the University of Victoria said, "People who work past sixty-five are happier. There's an immense psychological boost for an individual to be able to decide when he can step down." As Oscar Wilde probably said, "Retirement is wasted on the elderly."

In the United States since the start of 1979 it has been illegal to make anyone retire before seventy, and many people expect a similar law in Canada.

The arguments for earlier retirement are less popular, but economically they are considerably stronger. First, it can be argued that earlier retirement, say at sixty or even fifty-five, would make a big dent in the unemployment figures. Sears Roebuck has calculated that the later retirement legislation will hold back promotions all the way down the line and reduce hiring. If a third of those who would normally retire at sixty-five decided to stay on until seventy, the company said, twenty thousand people would not be promoted and five thousand would not be hired over the next five years. France now pays workers to retire at sixty and urges their former employers to replace them with people under twenty-five. Such a plan would help the hundreds of thousands of Big Generation people who are out of work, under-employed, striving vainly for promotion, or facing years of driving with someone else's foot on the brake. It would remove a large source of conflict between old and young. Making it possible for people to retire at fifty-five would probably release a million jobs – just the number of unemployed in Canada in the winter of 1979-1980.

Another point in favour of early retirement is that workers want to retire earlier. A survey found that people of all ages, of all levels of education, and in all kinds of jobs typically thought sixty-one would be the ideal age to retire – although there seems to be a split between a smallish group of poor, poorly educated, older, English-speaking, Protestant workers who want to stay later and the rest who want to go at sixty or sooner. The youngest and the most highly educated showed a markedly higher preference for early retirement. A third in each category favoured retirement before sixty.

Employers also want to be able to retire employees early. Some want to get rid of deadwood and dread the thought of having to retain workers who have effectively retired though they still show up at the office. In some goods industries, automation is pushing hard against the labour force. Most employers have agreed to let automation reduce the work force by attrition rather than firing, but they would welcome faster attrition. Auto manufacturers, for example, like the idea of retirement at fifty-five now that they have powerful industrial robots on the job.

The situation in twenty years' time is likely to be just the reverse, however. The cost of the Big Generation's pensions, particularly if they are indexed to the cost of living, will be enormous. There may be a shortage of workers; certainly there will not be enough to support the army of old people who will then be requiring pensions. People will be healthier, live longer, be more alert. All in all, they will be better suited to stay on the job.

The discussion about retirement reflects two views that are present in the work force today. As a consultant put it, "With such a large percentage of the population involved, it is inconceivable that one correct age for retirement for all can be set." So why not simply drop compulsory retirement altogether and let everyone make whatever arrangements suits him and his boss? Because there has to be an age when pensions are started, and it has to be known in advance so that premiums and costs can be calculated in advance. Governments need to know, private pension plan managers need to know, union contracts need to specify the age. So, difficult though it is, one age of retirement for all has to be set.

If the age of retirement is kept low, the number of idle old dependants will suddenly start to climb like a rocket at the turn of the century. If retirement was set at sixty, for instance, one reasonable forecast shows that the number of elderly dependants would rise from twenty-five per hundred workers in the year 2001 to fifty per hundred in 2026. Along with even a small number of children, that would represent a heavy burden on the workers.

What would be in the country's best interests? It would take a Solomon to answer that. But the Big Generation's interests are easier to assess. I believe they would best be served by reducing the age of retirement now to fifty-five, followed then by a slow increase to about sixty by the end of the century and seventy by the year 2031. That would ease unemployment now, when it is at its worst, and would later simultaneously increase the labour force and reduce the pension burden, when both steps would be needed.

My guess is that the Big Generation would like the improvement in employment prospects offered by this plan but would prefer to keep the early retirement permanently, though in most cases that might mean retirement into a life of part-time work. The only thing that would make them agree to raise the retirement age in the twenty-first century would be the hope of avoiding the impending pension crisis.

The Big Generation in retirement is going to be an awesome sight. Old people used to be extraordinary and have become ordinary, but the generation is likely to make them extraordinary again, not for rarity but for forcefulness. They will have learned how to use their political power. They will probably be stronger and healthier. They will certainly be less inhibited, less conformist, less patient. Alex Comfort, the gerontologist, has described the social convention that, at a given age, people "cease to be people and become unintelligent, asexual, unemployable, and crazy." Most old people tacitly accept the role written for them and play it out. The Big Generation will surely topple that convention if it persists that long.

In the 1950s, when the cult of youth was fresh and potent, it was easy to patronize the old. "No matter how much we pride ourselves on how much we have done for the aging in recent years, one fact remains: no one has yet found for them a significant role in our society," a magazine declared at the end of the decade. In the 1970s the spirit of revolt is already stronger in the elderly. "The aging population, with its increasing political power, will not tolerate indefinitely a life of poverty in retirement," Senator Croll said in his committee's report on pensions. Croll himself is an example of an unbowed veteran, as old as the century. By the 1990s, and even more by the 2010s, old people will be as demanding as adolescents, very unlikely to subside discreetly into the guise of slightly mobile furniture, as they have earlier in this century.

Assume for the moment that the generation goes into its retirement and old age with head, morale, and pulse high, and imagine what it will do with the rest of its life. "Old age is not an emancipation of desire for most of us," Ronald Blythe cried in *The View in Winter.* "The old want (but their sensible refusal to put such want into words suggests to us that they have given up wanting) their professional status back, or their looks, or their circle which is now a lot of crossed-off names in an address-book, or sex, or just a normal future-orientated existence."

Can we see, afar-off but getting closer, that mighty throng of Big Generation widows and pensioners, spry, blue-rinsed, sharp-elbowed, hurrying from hotel to hotel on week-long coach tours, terrorizing the resorts, making the corridors ring with their insomniac shouts and perambulations, eating all the breakfast before anyone else is up, crotchety, demanding, unshamable, with nothing to lose but their aches? Can we guess who will fill the seats of every legislature on the continent? Who will put the weight behind the consumer and environment protection organizations? Who will attend all the shareholders' meetings and ask the nasty questions? Can we imagine how many college and university places will be taken by these education-besotted ancients, these degree junkies, as they go back to school for just one more fix of academe? Yes, we can, and if you look carefully you can see them preparing for the day already.

Here we shall not have the "continent of aged misfits" that some Europeans have begun to anticipate with fear, but a still-powerful lobby of knowledgeable, experienced, and lively human beings. They will face problems, but will have the means to solve most of them. A century-long trend, if it continues, will give couples twenty years of life together after their last child has left home, compared with five years or less before the turn of the century. Those who want to keep their houses may do so by new financing methods, like the reverse mortgage, that will allow them to sell without moving out, just as the original mortgage allowed them to move in without paying the full price. Some will move into old people's palaces or retirement hotels. An indication of where and what those might be is given by the transformation of a Toronto building: Rochdale College and co-operative residence, the haven of the radical student in the 1960s, called "the ultimate in Student Power" when it opened, "a place of intellectual ferment and an origin of social revolution," as one early collegian hoped. It has lately been turned into a senior citizen's home. In the twenty-first century, many of the Big Generation may find themselves recycling the institutions of their youth, by then too large for their original use.

The trend of death rates suggests that in the next century there will be a worsening imbalance between old men and old women: fifty years from now there will be a million more women than men over sixty-five. "The life-styles of older people are going to change," population expert Roger Revelle has predicted. "You're going to have some kind of communal living so the few men can be shared by the women." Since we are told that we shall soon see the emergence of the sensuous grandmother, free-spirited and self-directed, it is likely to be a big change in style.

Another big change will be in society's attitude to health. Since the end of the Second World War a new concern with personal fitness has arisen. It reflects the increased absorption in self and, it goes almost without saying, is concentrated in the members of the Big Generation, who are most of the joggers, tennis buffs, skiers, and health-food addicts. They started out with the advantage of good diet and sunshine. They also eat a lot of junk food, the women smoke more, and men and women drink more like their grandparents than their parents. But all in all, as these health buffs become the majority of the population and lead its reform, and given the continuing efforts of medical researchers, there seems to be a good chance that the generation will live longer and be healthier in old age.

The federal government has started to worry about the impact of the growing population of old people on medical services and hospitals. Some forecasts have foreseen towering increases in the demand for hospital beds and service, given the great increase in old people. But if the generation is going to be so much healthier at any given age, is that justified? The answer is, probably. The generation will be healthier, but it will also live longer. Past experience of the health problems of people over eighty, for instance, is sparse; the hospitalization rates we know about are for the current mixture of people over sixty-five. In future a group of people over sixty-five will include a higher proportion of very old people. Mark Abrams, a British researcher who looked into care for the aged, noted the very high incidence of chronic illness in people over eighty in some European countries (where populations are already notably older), and estimated that health costs for very old people might be twice what they were for newly retired people. When that kind of calculation is made across all age groups over sixty-five, the future cost of looking after the aged population in Canada would come out considerably higher. A recent Statistics Canada study of the demand for hospital space said, "By 2031, patient-days for the Canadian population as a whole are expected almost to double, from the present forty-three million to eighty-four million. But in the same period, those for persons of sixty-five or over will multiply by over three times." As a result, instead of being responsible for about a third of all the patient-days (ten patients spending a week in hospital account for seventy patient-days), old people would take up two-thirds of all the patient-days. The rapidly rising cost of construction, nursing, equipment, and drugs suggests a horrendous bill in the offing.

The solutions now being considered include more use of nursing homes which can look after five old patients for the cost of one in hospital. Another solution suggests that, given the Big Generation's present concern with its own health, it will produce an aged population less susceptible to sickness, more able to maintain good health by a sensible regime, and less likely to require institutional care. And a third line of inquiry looks at the factors that have led to growth in the health-care industry. A Stanford University economist, Victor Fuchs, said, "The subsidization of health care by government clearly induces additional demand. . . . A reduction in the price of medical care (at the time of utilization) through public (or private) insurance increases the quantity demanded." Some provincial governments are already considering fees for seeing the doctor or going to hospital.

Most of the concern about the aging of Canada revolves around health costs and pension costs. As it now stands, the Canada Pension Plan, which so many members of the Big Generation think will look after them in their old age, is a fraud. It is not, as so many believe, a funded plan; that is, the amount you and your employer pay in will not cover the amount you expect to get out in retirement, and was never expected to. It is instead a pay-as-you-go plan. Like many social security programs of the high old liberal days of the economic boom, it was designed on the assumption that the population would go on growing forever, that there would always be more people coming in at the bottom than leaving at the top, and that everyone was going to get richer and richer and richer.

For years the CPP has taken in more than it has paid out. The surplus money, which might have been invested to produce some of the extra money that would be needed, has instead been loaned to the provinces at low rates of interest to keep them from going outside the country for capital. They in turn have put the money into roads, schools, hospitals, and the like, none of which pay dividends. In 1985, however, expenditure will catch up with income. The flow of cash to the provinces will end. The next year expenditure will exceed income, and the federal government will have to ask the provinces to start paying back the loans. The provinces will not be able to mortgage their roads and schools and will have to raise the money by taxation: either direct taxation of their citizens and corporations or, more likely, by negotiating an extra share of the federal government's tax income. From 1986 onwards, then, a part – a growing part – of CPP benefits will be paid for out of current taxes. But all that will stop around the end of the century, because by then the provinces will have repaid all the money they borrowed. The plan will then be bankrupt.

In other words, in a third of a century the CPP will have been transformed from something that was thought suitable to replace many funded private pension plans into a tax-supported security payment system. The Economic Council of Canada has remarked that the CPP has implicitly become a kind of welfare scheme, a political agreement that income should be transferred from rich young workers to poor old pensioners. As the council said in its pension study, "This position can be defended on various grounds – for example, it may be seen as compensation to the older groups for their net transfers to the young for education; but, ultimately, it will be the subsequent generations who will decide whether it is appropriate and whether the 'pension promise' will be honoured." ("Just wait till we are forty-five and you want adequate old age pensions.")

The obvious question is, how will the CPP serve the Big Generation in the twenty-first century? The obvious answer is that it will not. Today there are a hundred workers for every fifteen pensioners. If the age of retirement stays at sixty-five, by 2026 a hundred workers will have to support nearly thirty pensioners, a much different prospect. If retirement were to come at sixty, a hundred workers would be supporting fifty pensioners: and that would be through taxes, remember. In the United States, where social security programs are already in trouble, forty per cent of workers in a recent poll said they had "hardly any confidence at all" that they would get the benefits they were entitled to on retirement.

What ways out are open? One would be to start funding the plan straight away, but inflation makes it impossible. No one is prepared to estimate what it will be necessary to pay a pensioner in 2035, and therefore no one can calculate what premium now would build up the necessary fund. Insurance companies get around it by asking the future pensioner, "What income would you like when you retire?", leaving it to the individual to guess what money will be worth when she retires. Governments have never taken this route.

Another way is to guess at the future rate of inflation and the average raises workers will get and calculate the premium from that. The federal Department of Insurance, which makes actuarial reports on the CPP, last went through this exercise in 1979. In its highest estimates, it assumed that inflation would average 3.5 per cent a year over the next half century, and salaries would rise at 5.5 per cent. Even on these conservative assumptions, starting around 1990 the contribution rate would have to go up from 3.6 per cent of income until in 2030 it reached nine per cent of income. The Economic Council of Canada, making somewhat different estimates of future population growth, calculated that by the middle years of the next century contributions would have to rise to ten or even fifteen per cent of income, depending on what happens to the population.

In addition, there are the old age pension and guaranteed income supplement, which go to everyone whether he earns and contributes to a fund like the CPP or not. A worst-case forecast by the Economic Council – based on low population growth, retirement at sixty, and pensions equal to last salary – shows retirement payments rising to one-third of gross national product in 2031.

One of the most interesting ideas that has been noised about is that all retirement pay to old people should be dropped and replaced by one single payment – a disability pension. As long as you have your health and your marbles, you work. Only sick people would get government support. A radical idea, stimulated by a radical situation.

The prospect for the Big Generation, in short, is that it will be on its own in its old age, like all the generations before the Depression. By the next century, the miracle years of the post-war economic boom – the economic boom that triggered the baby boom in the first place – will be well and truly over, and in a sense it will be as if all the years between the Second World War and the retirement of the generation had disappeared in thin air.

But only in the very limited matter of retirement income. For the echoes of the big bang will ricochet on through the generations from peak to valley, from valley to peak; and when at last they disappear in silence, Canada will have been completely transformed, and the hundred-year odyssey of the Big Generation will go into the history books.

2063

MAGDALENA ANNA KADAR
BORN 1961 DIED 2063
IN HER SLEEP
NO SURVIVING FRIENDS OR RELATIVES
REST IN PEACE

NOTES

Chapter 1

page
19 Numbering the Big Generation. The years 1952 through 1965 are the only ones in which more than 400,000 births were recorded. For convenience in using existing statistics and in making forecasts, this period was extended seven months back, to June 1, 1951, the date of a census, and five months on, to May 31, 1966, the eve of another. The actual numbers by year are:

1951	221,034 (from June 1)	1959	479,275
1952	403,559	1960	478,551
1953	417,884	1961	475,700
1954	436,198	1962	469,693
1955	442,937	1963	465,767
1956	450,739	1964	452,915
1957	469,093	1965	418,595
1958	470,118	1966	164,497 (to May 31)

The basic data for the numbering of the Big Generation on June 1, 1966, are in various volumes and editions of *Vital Statistics* (Ottawa: Statistics Canada). Births were recorded monthly at that time. Deaths are recorded for five-year age groups, and single-year data – e.g., the number of two-year-olds who died in 1954 – were estimated as a fifth of the five-year age group they fell in. Immigrants' ages are recorded by five-year age groups; but, for simplicity, an average distribution by single years of age based on the total count for 1956-1966, published in K.S. Gnanasekaran, *Migration*

215

Projections for Canada 1969-1984, Analytical and Technical Memorandum No. 6 (Ottawa: Dominion Bureau of Statistics, 1970), was applied to the annual totals. Emigrants, who are nowhere counted, were derived as the residual. An estimate of the size of the Big Generation in mid-1980 is 6,819,857.

20   Size of the preceding generation: M.C. Urquhart and K.A.H. Buckley, eds., *Historical Statistics of Canada* (Toronto: Macmillan, 1965). Size of the following generation: *Canadian Statistical Review*, May 1980, for births to the end of 1979, *Population Projections for Canada and the Provinces 1976-2001* (Ottawa: Statistics Canada, 1979), Projection 4, for the remaining 17 months.

20   The calculation creating a new demographic history was based on the average annual decline in the birth rate from 1851 through 1937, estimated from *Historical Statistics of Canada*. Birth rates for the years 1951 through 1966 were projected from this and applied successively to estimated annual populations through the period, starting with the actual population at the 1951 census. The number of births thus invented was totalled. This is roughly the procedure that would have been followed by a futurist of the year 1938. It is a forecast based on 86 years of observation, lacking only the knowledge of what was actually going to happen during the next 28 years.

21-2   The size and timing of baby booms in the various countries mentioned is based on Michael S. Teitelbaum, "International Experience with Fertility At or Near Replacement Level," in Charles F. Westoff and Robert Parke, Jr., eds., U.S. Commission on Population Growth and the American Future, *Research Reports, Volume 1, Demographic and Social Aspects of Population Growth* (Washington: Government Printing Office, 1972). Additional information about some countries' age distribution is found in various publications of the U.S. Bureau of the Census. For the U.S. white and black birth rates, see "Projections of the Population of the United States: 1975 to 2050" in *Population Estimates and Projections*, Current Population Reports, Series P-25, No. 601 (Washington: Government Printing Office, 1975): the white baby boom was mid-1950 to mid-1965, the black baby boom from mid-1953 to mid-1968. For the meliorating effect of aboriginal birth rates in New Zealand, see *1976 Census of Population and Dwellings* (Wellington: Department of Statistics, 1976).

23   Age distribution of the Toronto *Star* editorial staff and the CBC production staff is based on personal communications.

Chapter 2

28   Geoffrey Vickers, "Until two centuries . . . 19th century," in "The Weakness of Western Culture," *Futures*, December 1977, p. 470.

29   Noel Annan, "The strength of the consensus . . . to king and country," in " 'Our Age': Reflections on Three Generations in England," *Daedalus*, Fall 1978, pp. 83-85.

30-31 Robert Douglas Mead, "This was, after all . . . not the future," in *Reunion: Twenty-five Years Out of School* (New York: Saturday Review Press, 1973), pp. 48, 53, 74, 81, 108, 276.

31   Industrial production as a fraction of gross domestic product in Canada rose from 29% in 1926 to 40% in 1953, and since then has steadily declined. Annual data are in the CANSIM (Canadian Socio-Economic Information Management System) computerized data bank, Matrix 563. CAN-

SIM is the registered Trade Mark for Statistics Canada's machine-readable data base. See also *Executive*, February 1980, page 14.

33   Easterlin has numerous publications on this idea to his credit. The best known is *Population, Labor Force, and Long Swings in Economic Growth*, General Series 86 (New York: National Bureau of Economic Research, 1968); but see also Easterlin, Michael L. Wachter, and Susan M. Wachter, "Demographic Influences on Economic Stability: The United States Experience," *Population and Development Review*, March 1978.

34   William Butz and Michael Ward, "Other things being equal . . . the cost of children," in "Baby 'Boom and Baby Bust: A New View," *American Demographics*, September 1979.

35   George Masnick and Joseph McFalls, Jr., "The fertility rates . . . and settle down," in "Those Perplexing U.S. Fertility Swings," *PRB Report*, November 1978.

36   Charles Westoff, "There was a large . . . be called fashion," in "Marriage and Fertility in the Developed Countries," *Scientific American*, December 1978.

37   Rona Jaffe, "In the fifties . . . our identity," in "Rona Jaffe Scared of Class Reunion," *The Globe and Mail* (Reuter), November 21, 1979.

37   Marcos W. Bogan, Chief of the Planning and Evaluation Unit, the Costa Rican National Family Planning and Sexual Education Program, "With regard to the causes . . . who knows?", in "Rapid Fertility Decline in Costa Rica," *Intercom*, March 1978.

38   Kenneth Boulding proposed licences for child-bearing in *The Meaning of the Twentieth Century: The Great Transition* (New York: Harper & Row, 1964).

38   Margaret Mead, "There's something wrong . . . station wagon," in *Chatelaine*, 1958, quoted in *Chatelaine*, March 1978.

38   Ben J. Wattenburg, "If you've been reading . . . crowded parks," in "The Decline of the American Baby," *World*, August 29, 1972.

Chapter 3

44   The post-war growth of the Canadian economy was calculated by the manipulation of data in CANSIM Matrix 598. The growth of the economy in the years before the gathering of exact data was estimated and calculated from various series in *Historical Statistics of Canada*, cited.

46   Whittaker Chambers, "The change that ends . . . come much later," in *Cold Friday* (New York: Random House, 1964), pp. 296-97.

47   Jane Newitt, "in large numbers . . . childhood and adolescence," in *A Social Trends Handbook for Health Services* (Croton-on-Hudson, N.Y.: Hudson Institute, 1974), p. 42.

47-9   Dr. Benjamin Spock, *The Common Sense Book of Baby and Child Care* (New York: Duell, Sloan & Pearce, 1946). "When I was writing . . . if carried very far," in *Baby and Child Care* (New York: Pocket Books, 1957), pp. 1-2, 46, 324.

49   Bruno Bettelheim, "if, as modern middle-class . . . much morality," in *Surviving and Other Essays* (New York: Knopf, 1979), quoted in *The New York Review of Books*, April 19, 1979.

49   James Dobson, *Dare to Discipline* (Wheaton, Ill.: Tyndale House, 1970. New York: Bantam, 1977).

49   The relation between birth order and intelligence was discussed in Carol Tavris, "The End of the IQ Slump," *Psychology Today*, April 1976: the

article included references to work by Robert B. Zajonc, professor of psychology at the University of Michigan; a study of 800,000 U.S. students; another of 400,000 Netherlands students; and another of 100,000 French students. An article by Zajonc appeared in *Psychology Today* in January 1975. A study of the relation between birth order and personality is described in *Intercom*, November 1977.

50   Brigitte Berger, "the intensity of interaction . . . tribal, primitive, barbarian," in "A New Interpretation of the I.Q. Controversy," *The Public Interest*, Winter 1978, pp. 37-38.

51   The flood of divorces after the new divorce legislation of 1968, estimates of 60,000 children affected by divorce each year, and the estimate that a million Big Generation children were the victims of broken homes are all based on data in *Vital Statistics: Marriages and divorces*, Catalogue 84-205 (Ottawa: Statistics Canada, 1977).

51   Warner Troyer, *Divorced Kids* (Toronto: Clarke, Irwin, 1979), contains interviews with hundreds of children from broken homes, some now adults; for "two in five are victims," see p. 169.

51   Parents without Partners is mentioned in "Single Parents Outsiders at Christmas," *The Globe and Mail* (New York Times Service), December 18, 1979.

51   For the feelings of children of broken homes see, for example, Ellie Tesher, "Children of Divorce Tax the Schools," Toronto *Star*, January 27, 1979, or Warner Troyer, *Divorced Kids*, cited.

52   On exceptionally disturbed children, see Victor Malarek, "500 Children So Troubled that Helping them is 'Hair-raising'," *The Globe and Mail*, November 8, 1979.

52   Jeanne Binstock, "The emotional impact . . . rather than withdrawal," in "Issues of the Eighties: Dr. Spock's Babies Take Charge," *Planning Review*, September 1977.

52-3   Clifton Fadiman, "the alternate life . . . the chaos we observe?", quoted in Richard J. Needham, "A Writer's Notebook," *The Globe and Mail*, November 28, 1979.

54   Herman Kahn and Jane Newitt, "A forty-year period . . . from 7.7 to 0.02," in *Social Trends and Health Care*, Research Memorandum No. 19 (Croton-on-Hudson, N.Y.: Hudson Institute, 1975), p. 14.

Chapter 4

56   The rise and fall of enrolment in schools, colleges, and universities in the post-war years is discussed throughout this chapter. For convenience, full-time enrolment in the three main levels of public and private institutions is grouped here:

	Elementary	Secondary	Post-secondary
1945	1,824,300	340,900	80,600
1950	2,122,800	395,200	91,700
1955	2,681,200	507,400	106,000
1960	3,267,300	788,800	163,100
1965	3,679,800	1,250,000	273,600
1970	3,815,600	1,666,400	475,600
1975	3,481,100	1,710,700	592,100
1980	3,106,800	1,552,400	602,200

The source for the years 1955-1975 is *Historical Compendium of Educational Statistics*, Catalogue 81-568 (Ottawa: Statistics Canada, 1978). For 1945 and 1950 the data were estimated from the *Historical Compendium* and *Historical Statistics of Canada*. The 1980 data come from *Advanced Statistics of Education*, Catalogue 81-220 (Ottawa: Statistics Canada, 1979).

58   The projection that between a third and a half of the Big Generation will have at least some post-secondary education is in Z. Zsigmond, G. Picot, W. Clark, and M.S. Devereaux, *Out of School – Into the Labour Force*, Catalogue 81-570 (Ottawa: Statistics Canada, 1978), p. 214. Four projections range from 39.1% to 45.7%.

58   For surveys showing that education polarizes society more strongly than other distinctions, see Donald E. Blake & Richard Simeon, "Regional Preferences: Citizens' Views of Public Policy," Institute of Intergovernmental Relations, Queen's University, in press, or for details of particular studies see the next reference.

58   For analysis of studies of distinctions of opinion on abortion, American influence, and marijuana, see Frederick J. Fletcher and Robert J. Drummond, Institute for Behavioural Research, York University, Toronto, Canadian Attitude Trends Project, various reports (unpublished, 1976-1977).

59   Jeanne Binstock, "The change ... the industrial revolution," in "Issues in Canadian Identity" (unpublished, 1979).

60   At least a third of the population was in school in 1970: there were 6,363,900 full-time students and 312,700 full-time teachers from kindergarten through university, or 31% of the population of 21,297,000; the number of part-time students and teachers was incompletely counted.

60   William Davis, Ontario Minister of Education, "education for years ... government spending," in Kenneth B. Smith, "Education Outlay Expected to be No. 1 Priority for Years," *The Globe and Mail*, January 10, 1968.

60   "Every dollar spent ... the future," in editorial, Toronto *Star*, November 11, 1968. William Davis, "The investment ... to increase," in "No Cut in Education Spending: Davis," Toronto *Telegram*, February 10, 1968. Official of the Ontario Department of Education, "The community colleges ... quick return," in Smith, "Education Outlay ...," *The Globe and Mail*, January 10, 1968, cited.

60   Barry Eakins, "When we went to high school, the message was geared into us: 'Stay in school ... into place," in Harvey Schachter, "Why Kids Drop Out of College," Toronto *Star*, October 10, 1978.

61   Expenditures on education related to gross national product in *Historical Compendium of Education Statistics*, cited.

61   For Dewey's philosophy see, for example, John Dewey, *The School and Society* (Chicago: University of Chicago Press, 1899) and *Elementary School Record* (Chicago: University of Chicago Press, 1900).

61   The attitudes of Dewey's followers in Canadian schools were discussed in a 1960 essay reprinted in D.A. MacIver, ed., *Concern and Competence in Canadian Education: Essays by J.M. Paton* (Toronto: University of Toronto Press, 1973), p. 26.

62   Overcrowding in the schools was described in a report to the Ontario Secondary School Teachers Federation reported in the Toronto *Telegram*, December 29, 1966.

62   Educators did not know in advance how children would react to open

schools. John Wimbs, a school architect, addressing the Ontario Educational Association, said: "We have no idea how this type of teaching and classroom atmosphere will affect a child." He proposed the formation of a development group of educators, architects, and others to build and test prototypes of open schools. Reported in "Expensive 'Flexible' Schools Could Prove Disastrous Architect Says," Toronto *Star*, March 20, 1968.

63   Pamela Jansen, "So if a child ... beginning reader," in John Kelsey, "Teaching with the Walls Down," *The Globe Magazine*, December 14, 1968.

63-4   The 14-grade school was described in Barrie Zwicker, "Cradle-to-Grad Schooling Plan at One Giant Campus-Type Complex Unveiled in Scarboro," *The Globe and Mail*, November 17, 1966.

64   The aging corps of teachers was described in a report in the Toronto *Star*, December 23, 1966.

64-5   The flood of new teachers is documented in *Historical Compendium of Educational Statistics* and in a statistical table showing annual totals of beginning teachers compiled from unpublished data by the Education, Science and Culture Division of Statistics Canada for this book; anecdotal evidence appears in newspaper reports, e.g., Toronto *Telegram*, November 23, 1966, and Toronto *Star*, December 23, 1966.

65-6   Charles E. Phillips, "Because of failure ... in emergencies," in *College of Education, Toronto* (Toronto: Faculty of Education, University of Toronto, 1977), pp. 32-33, 19-20.

66   Barbara Frum, "High school guidance ... and geography," in "From High School to Teacher's Desk in Only 24 Weeks," Toronto *Star*, March 4, 1968.

66   The out-of-province and overseas search for teachers is described in innumerable contemporary reports, e.g. Toronto *Telegram*, February 23, 1967, *The Globe and Mail*, February 25, 1967, January 27, 1968, February 2, 1968, February 6, 1968, April 8, 1968, May 9, 1968, and Toronto *Star*, January 3, 1968.

66   Robert Brooks, "The average tradesman ... technical schools," in "Many High School Teachers 'Unqualified,'" Toronto *Star*, November 24, 1966.

68   Hilda Neatby, *So Little for the Mind* (Toronto: Clarke, Irwin, 1953).

68   On the introduction of novel teaching methods, see Sybil Shack, *Monday Morning*, March 1970: "We have stumbled blindly from one quick cure to another, each time assured by our betters that this time we had it made. 'Use linguistics and you'll have no more reading problems.' 'Teach the new math and everyone will love and understand it.' 'Let children express themselves freely, and they'll learn to use their language beautifully and concisely.' 'Give children independence and they'll love school and learning.' 'Build open area schools and your worries will be over.' 'Use tomorrow's technology and remove all the drudgery from teaching and learning.' 'Pass a law ungrading the schools and all difficulties will vanish.' "

68   The New School in Vancouver: "'What's this? ... the host,'" in Andrew Szende, "Vancouver's New School is Run by Nine-Year-Olds," Toronto *Star*, January 16, 1968.

69   J.M. Paton, "a popular exposition ... and learning," in MacIver, *Concern and Competence in Canadian Education*, cited, p. 70. Hall-Dennis, "The needs of the child ... for their sunrise," in *Living and Learning: The Report of the Provincial Committee on Aims and Objectives of Education in the Schools of Ontario* (Toronto: Ontario Department of Education, 1968), pp. 47, 62.

page
69   William Davis, "There is a growing . . . other endeavor," in "No Cut in Education Spending," Toronto *Telegram*, February 10, 1968.

70   Harry Bruce, "The creed . . . increaseth strength," in "A Tidal Wave of Higher Learning and its Zealous, Stylish Prophet," *The Canadian*, February 18, 1967.

70   The value of a degree was discussed in many reports, e.g., "A Degree is Worth $3,200," Toronto *Star*, December 6, 1966.

71   The warning to the presidents of Ontario universities was described in "Fear and Trembling in the Academy," *Saturday Night*, October 1978.

71   Undergraduate enrolment rates calculated from *Historical Statistics of Canada*. The 1967 forecast of full-time undergraduate university enrolment is in Wolfgang M. Illing and Zoltan E. Zsigmond, *Enrolment in Schools and Universities 1951-52 to 1975-76*, Staff Study No. 20 (Ottawa: Economic Council of Canada, 1967); the actual course of enrolment is recorded in *Fall Enrolment in Universities*, Catalogue 81-204 (Ottawa: Statistics Canada, 1977). Here are two years for comparison:

	Illing-Zsigmond	Actual
1965		188,692
1970	342,600	270,338
1975	475,700	327,220

71   An up-to-date list of universities appears in *Fall Enrolment in Universities*, cited.

72   The report that half the new faculty members were recruited overseas and Dr. John T. Saywell's remark, "In a sellers' . . . responsibilities," both in Warren Gerard, "Room at the Top in Universities," *The Globe and Mail*, December 28, 1966.

72   York's faculty shopping list in Gerard, "Room at the Top . . .," cited. Six out of every ten professors aged under forty, in "Erosion of the Research Manpower Base in Canada," *Science Forum*, February 1977.

72   References to community colleges and provincial variations and their enrolments are in *Canada Year Book 1978-79* (Ottawa: Statistics Canada, 1978).

73   The arrogance of the first post-war undergraduates is documented in Alan Walker, "The Revolt on the Campus," *The Star Weekly*, January 13, 1968.

73   Data on post-war degrees from *Historical Statistics of Canada, Canada Year Book*, and *Education in Canada* (Ottawa: Statistics Canada, various editions).

73   A Toronto school board planner, "The whole system . . . for decline," in "For School and Country," *The Globe and Mail*, May 11, 1978.

73-4   Everette Reimer, "No country . . . at the trough," in *School is Dead: Alternatives in Education* (New York: Doubleday, 1971), p. 23.

74   Sybil Shack, "a growing malaise . . . for the failure," in *Monday Morning*, March 1970.

75   Prof. Lee, "What the [Ontario] . . . I graduate!", in John Alan Lee, "A Ticking Bomb: The Failsafe School Setup," *The Globe and Mail*, December 20, 1978.

75   Dean Kruger, "We have students . . . remedial programs," in Trish Crawford, "Test Controversy Rages 12 Years Later," Toronto *Star*, April 4, 1979.

page
75-6   Quebec's reform proposals were described in William Johnson, "Revive Basics in Education, PQ Proposes," *The Globe and Mail*, October 7, 1977.

76   B.C.'s back-to-basics campaign was reported in John Clarke, "Teachers Bare Teeth for Bigger Apple Bite," *The Globe and Mail*, April 7, 1979.

76   Carla Wolfe, "looking for something . . . new standards," in letter to the editor, *Books in Canada*, May 1977.

77   The total of 469 elementary-school teachers fired by Metropolitan Toronto's six boards of education in the spring of 1978 was a net figure, the excess of firings over intended hirings; it was reported in Robert Sutton, "Teachers Face a Bleak Fall Survey Shows," Toronto *Star*, June 10, 1978. The figure of 499 elementary-school graduate teachers from Ontario Teacher Education College was confirmed by the college registrar's office.

77   Only 2,750 of the 6,300 graduates from Ontario faculties of education in 1977 had found employment in Ontario elementary and secondary schools a year later; reported in Dorothy Lipovenko, "Too Many Teachers Without Work, Education Schools Reduce Enrolment," *The Globe and Mail*, April 28, 1978.

77   There were 73 applicants for each teaching job at one Toronto Manpower office; reported in John Kettle, "It's No Longer Work, Work, Work," *Executive*, April 1977. Dr. Jackson, "Some directors . . . the 1970s," in "Ontario Teaching Jobs Not as Scarce as Feared," *The Globe and Mail*, June 6, 1978.

78   Interprovincial and international migrants: *1971 Census, Population: Internal Migration*, Catalogue 92-719 (Ottawa: Statistics Canada, 1974).

78   Dean Shapiro, "The government . . . open access," in Lipovenko, "Too Many Teachers . . .," *The Globe and Mail*, April 28, 1978, cited.

78   Five to ten applicants for each place at the Ontario Teacher Education College, Hamilton, in Sylvia Stead, "Teacher College Enrolment to be Cut by 50 Per Cent," *The Globe and Mail*, February 17, 1978.

79   The drop in the attrition rate from 15% to 1-2% was reported in "Ontario Teaching Jobs . . .," *The Globe and Mail*, June 6, 1978, cited.

79   The Ontario Secondary School Teachers Federation's pursuit of absolute tenure was described in Dorothy Lipovenko, "School Board Wants to End Tenure for All Teachers and Fire Another 240," *The Globe and Mail*, June 8, 1978. Taxpayers' resistance was reported in Howard Fluxgold, "Toronto Board Rejects Contract with Teachers," *The Globe and Mail*, February 9, 1979.

79   Sherle Perkins-Vasey, "There's a lot . . . their lives," in Peggy McCallum, "Workshops Help 60 Laid-Off Teachers to Rebuild Shattered Self-Confidence," *The Globe and Mail*, June 10, 1978.

79   The Big Generation suffers from firings: "Teachers and board officials are worried that as junior staff gets fired, schools will be left with an aged school staff – the young teachers with fresh ideas tossed out," in Harvey Schachter, "Nearly 90 Schools Face Closings, Mergers," Toronto *Star*, March 18, 1978.

79-80   The shift in Ottawa and district enrolment was in Alison Cunliffe, "Enrolment Drop Means 71 Miles on School Bus," Toronto *Star*, August 5, 1978. The Calgary situation was described in Barry Nelson, "Closed Schools Threat to Residents, Students," *The Globe and Mail*, April 7, 1979. Toronto's dilemma was reported in Marty York, "Ontario Will Pay for a New School While 2 Others in Area Lose Students," *The Globe and Mail*, June 15, 1978, and Marty York, "Construction of Catholic School could Force Razing of 16 Houses," *The Globe and Mail*, June 17, 1978.

80   For fears about the collapse of downtown neighbourhoods, see Nelson, "Closed Schools Threat . . .," *The Globe and Mail*, April 7, 1979, cited.

80   The Kiosk, Ont., children facing 100,000 miles of school-bus riding were reported in Cunliffe, "Enrolment Drop . . .," Toronto *Star*, August 5, 1978, cited.

80   "Many of the schools that are closing have not been paid for. This will lead to problems about who carries the debt and who gets the spoils if a sale is made," in Jack Willoughby, "Alternative Uses are Studied for Empty Schools," *The Globe and Mail*, February 11, 1978.

81-2 Claude Bissell, "University campuses . . . of moronity," in Bruce, "A Tidal Wave . . .," *The Canadian*, February 18, 1967, cited. Douglas Ward, "[Large universities are] . . . economic slot," in Mack Laing, "Why Students Lock Horns with the Establishment," Toronto *Telegram*, January 20, 1967. Lyn Owen, "It's *our* university . . . Kraft cheese," in Walker, "The Revolt on Campus," *The Star Weekly*, January 13, 1968, cited. Edward Harvey, "When a graduate . . . has failed," in "Dimensions of a Decade: Canadian Higher Education in the Sixties," Garnet McDiarmid, ed., *From Quantitative to Qualitative Change in Ontario Education* (Toronto: Ontario Institute for Studies in Education, 1976), p. 19. A biology lecturer, "My students . . . getting a job," in Frank Appleton, "Lowering the Boom," *Weekend Magazine*, May 15, 1976. Mary Hutson, "Right now . . . some brains," in Sylvia Stead, "Degree is Losing its Mystique, Students Not Finishing University," *The Globe and Mail*, December 5, 1977. Barbara Borenstein, "High-school students . . . FORGET IT!", in letter to the editor, Toronto *Star*, November 11, 1978. Howard Pinnock, "I don't think . . . not happy," in Leslie Scrivener, "60,000 Graduates Soon to Spill into Glutted Job Market," Toronto *Star*, April 9, 1979. James Ham, "What does . . . entry into life," in Andrew Weiner, "A Matter of Degree," *Financial Post Magazine*, September 1979.

82   On the idea that a degree led to a job, see e.g., Edward Harvey, "Dimensions of a Decade . . .," cited: "Higher education represented a route to a good job for the returned veteran of World War 2," p. 12.

82   Edward Harvey, "It was around . . . occupational structure," in Harvey, "Dimensions of a Decade . . .," cited, p. 17.

83   The expectations and success of law-school graduates are discussed in David Lancashire, "What are the Prospects?", *The Globe and Mail*, April 6, 1979. The prospects for engineering graduates are discussed in "Surplus of Engineering Graduates Predicted," *Campus Career Directory*, 1977/78, and "Outlook for New Bachelor Grads in Three Job Areas," *The Pathfinder*, 50th Anniversary issue, undated but about March 1978.

83   When the supply of graduates would match the demand was discussed in Zsigmond *et al*, *Out of School – Into the Labour Force*, cited.

84   Richard J. Needham, "When I was . . . on his UIC," in Needham, "A Writer's Notebook," *The Globe and Mail*, March 3, 1978.

84   Dr. Evans, "It's almost . . . to get marks," in Sylvia Stead, "Desire for Security Drives Students to the Professions," *The Globe and Mail*, April 18, 1978. Prof. James Daly, "Cheating has now . . . others behind," in "Cheating Now a Part of University Scene, Educator Says," Toronto *Star*, August 27, 1977.

85   Prof. Webster on an epidemic of cheating, in "U of T Arts Faculty Seeks Expulsions Over Cheating," Toronto *Star*, October 10, 1979. Prof. Daly,

page

    "There's no excuse . . . a decade," in "Cheating Now a Part . . .," Toronto *Star*, August 27, 1977, cited.

85   For details of Humber College's flood of applicants, see Nicolaas Van Rijn, "12,057 Apply but College Limit is only 3,800," Toronto *Star*, August 9, 1977. The experience of Cambrian and other colleges is in Howard Flux-gold, "The Community College Boom," Toronto *Star*, September 2, 1978. Another college eyed half-empty public schools: see "Seneca College to Turn Away 2,000," Toronto *Star*, April 30, 1979.

85   University graduates applying for places at community colleges: personal communication from Dr. Laurent Isabelle, Algonquin College, Ottawa.

85-6   "After more than two decades of steady growth, full-time enrolment in non-university institutions declines slightly from 248,800 to 248,200; enrolment projected for 1981-82 is 243,800, or a loss of 4,400," in "The Classroom in 1980," *Infomat*, October 12, 1979. Prof. Lee, "The temporary shift . . . designers," in Lee, "A Ticking Bomb . . .," *The Globe and Mail*, December 20, 1978, cited.

86   Ontario universities' estimate turned out to be 60% low: see "Fear and Trembling in the Academy," *Saturday Night*, October 1978. The Economic Council's projection of 540,000 full-time undergraduate and graduate students in 1975 was in Illing and Zsigmond, *Enrolment in Schools and Universities*, cited. The actual 1975 total, 363,188, appears in *Canadian Universities: A Statistical Bulletin* (Ottawa: Statistics Canada, 1977).

86   Age distribution of university staff "now" (actually 1982-3), 58.9% in the 36-50 age group, is in "Erosion of the Research Manpower Base in Canada," *Science Forum*, February 1977.

86-7   Prof. Paterson, "We're in imminent . . . demographically," in Helen Worthington, "College Cuts May End Jobs of 2,550 Profs," Toronto *Star*, July 28, 1979.

87   A dean, "I have a faculty . . . place," personal communication. Prof. Desmond Morton, "An age-group bulge of professors in their late 30s and early 40s could mean that people of their generation will dominate the universities until the beginning of the 21st century," in "Aging Professors Create a New Problem for the Universities," Toronto *Star*, August 29, 1977. Prof. S.P. Rosenbaum, "The single most . . . is occurring," in review of Robin Harris, *A History of Higher Education in Canada: 1663-1960, The Globe and Mail*, May 21, 1977.

87-8   Not many professors are moving out; instead they are creating stronger unions: see Morton, "Aging Professors . . .," *The Globe and Mail*, August 29, 1977, cited. The Science Council forecast of professors' age distribution in 1990–61.4% aged 45-59–is in "Erosion of the Research Manpower Base . . ." *Science Forum*, cited. David Inman, "The only thing . . . is fear," is in Worthington, "College Cuts . . .," Toronto *Star*, July 28, 1979, cited.

88   Reports of universities reducing their admission standards appeared in, e.g., Dorothy Lipovenko, "U of T Report Calls for Cut in Arts Admission Standard," *The Globe and Mail*, March 2, 1978, and Dorothy Lipovenko, "First-year Enrolment at 8 Universities Down 5 to 18 Per Cent; Slight Increase at 3 Others," *The Globe and Mail*, July 28, 1978. The use of radio commercials was reported in Trish Crawford, "Universities Face Probe over Wooing of Students," Toronto *Star*, December 7, 1978. Intensification of recruiting generally is in Crawford, "Universities Face Probe . . .," cited, and Dorothy Lipovenko, "Universities Council Plans

page

Watchdog Agency After Recruiting Methods Bring Complaints," *The Globe and Mail*, June 9, 1978.

88-9 News of the universities' growing deficits appeared in Howard Fluxgold, "Declining Enrolment, Small Grants Could Send Universities to the Bank," *The Globe and Mail*, September 11, 1979, and Trish Crawford, "Universities in Financial Peril, Study Says," Toronto *Star*, October 4, 1979. Claude Fortier, "To be effective . . . fifteen years," in "Honeymoon is Over, Universities Warned," *The Globe and Mail* (Canadian Press), November 15, 1979.

Chapter 5

91 Jean-Jacques Rousseau (1712-78), "The first man who, having fenced in a piece of land, said, 'This is mine,' and found people naive enough to believe him, that man was the true founder of civil society," in *Discours sur l'Origine et le Fondement de l'Inégalité parmi les Hommes*; "Man was born free, and everywhere he is in chains," in *Du Contrat Social*.

91 Herman Kahn, "Who has ever . . . anything else?", personal communication.

91-2 Undergraduates, "the life . . . and contemptible," and other characteristics of the between-the-wars elite in Annan, " 'Our Age' . . .," *Daedalus*, cited, pp. 87, 100.

92 Paul Goodman, "unscheduled, sloppy . . . sketchbook," in Goodman, *Growing Up Absurd* (New York: Random House, 1960), reprinted in Ned E. Hoopes, ed., *Who am I?* (New York: Dell, 1969), pp. 139-147.

92-3 Jack Kerouac, "who never yawn . . . the stars," in Kerouac, *On the Road* (New York: Viking, 1957). Walter Pater, "To burn always . . . in life," in *The Renaissance* (London: Macmillan, 1877). Paul Goodman, " 'like' . . . 'cool'," in Goodman, *Growing Up Absurd*, cited, p. 142 in Hoopes.

93 Judith Finlayson, "We read Shelley . . . of love," in Finlayson, "Laying the Love Generation to Rest," *The Globe and Mail*, July 16, 1977.

93 Charles Reich, "The foundation . . . relations between people," in Reich, *The Greening of America* (New York: Random House, 1970, and Bantam, 1971), pp. 241-45 in Bantam.

93 Retrospective articles on the Woodstock festival were useful in recalling details; e.g., Peter Goddard and Bruce Blackadar, "Woodstock: Ten Years After," Toronto *Star*, August 11, 1979.

94 Marshall McLuhan, "Inside the Five-Sense Sensorium," *The Canadian Architect*, June 1961. Jan Cook, "Most rock shows . . . monster sound," in Bruce Ward, "70,000 Turned On by Electric Light 'So Far Out . . . Unreal'," Toronto *Star*, July 20, 1978.

94 Topaz Amber Dawn, "macrame and folk-singing," in Philip Marchand, "Down Looks Up to Me," *Weekend Magazine*, March 4, 1978. "Throwing pots . . . charts with flair," in Paul McGrath, "The Frisbee and the Soul," *The Globe and Mail*, August 3, 1977.

95 The boredom of bright students is documented in L. Beckman, "A Study of the Hip Adolescent, His Family, and the Generation Gap," report submitted to the Committee on Youth, May 1970; cited in Jack Quarter, "Shifting Ideologies among Youth in Canada," Garnet McDiarmid, ed., *From Quantitative to Qualitative Change in Ontario Education* (Toronto: Ontario Institute for Studies in Education, 1976), p. 126. Marijuana users: "Last year 28,767 cases were recorded. Almost 23,000 of these users were under 24," in Judy Dobbie, "The New Lost Generation: Telling Us Truths

We Don't Want to Know?", *Weekend Magazine*, June 25, 1977. "Alcohol actively facilitates aggression: marijuana actively inhibits it," in Jeanne Binstock, *Issues in Canadian Identity*, cited.

96 For trends in adolescence and age at menarche, see J. M. Tanner, *Education and Physical Growth* (London: University of London Press, 1961), p. 117; Ellie Tesher, "The Teen Pregnancy Explosion," Toronto *Star*, October 20, 1978; "Girl Puberty Age Drops," Toronto *Star* (Associated Press), October 24, 1978.

96 Dr. Eleanor Hamilton, "Until just ... without functioning," in *Book-of-the-Month Club News*; Dr. Hamilton is author of *Sex, With Love*. "1 in 5 U.K. Teens Have Had Sex Before 16: Study," Toronto *Star*, July 20, 1978.

96 Dr. Devlin, "An intercourse ... traumatized by it," in Leslie Scrivener, "Teen Sex: Too Far, Too Soon," Toronto *Star*, August 13, 1979, and Ellie Tesher, "The Teen Pregnancy Explosion," Toronto *Star*, October 20, 1978.

96 Young prostitutes in Vancouver were reported in "Workers Fight Juvenile Prostitution," *The Globe and Mail* (Canadian Press), December 7, 1979.

96-7 Robertson Davies, "[homosexuals] want ... bourgeois," in Davies, "Past Imperfect, Future Tense," *The Globe and Mail*, December 18, 1979.

97 The poll on individualism and family life is reported in *DataTrack 4*, Summer 1978 (American Council of Life Insurance), p. 12.

97-8 Abraham H. Maslow, *Motivation and Personality* (New York: Harper, 1954).

98 On the proliferation of professors of psychology, see Dr. Max von Zur-Muehlen, "Some Characteristics of Full-Time University Teachers, 1956-57 to 1977-78," *Canadian Statistical Review*, July 1978.

98 Jane Newitt, "A heightened sense ... through life," in Newitt, *A Social Trends Handbook for Health Services*, cited, p. 42.

99 Kenneth Clark, *Civilisation* (London: British Broadcasting Corporation and John Murray, 1969).

99 Paul Goodman, "[1] attachment ... all their ways," in Goodman, *Growing Up Absurd*, cited, p. 142 in Hoopes. Reich, "without the guideposts ... a life," in Reich, *The Greening of America*, cited, p. 235.

100 The poll of students was carried out by J. Richard Finlay and described in Finlay, "The Strange, Skeptical Mood of the Campus," *Saturday Night*, October 1979.

100 Harvard sophomore, "They never did ... believe in," in Steven Kelman, "These are Three of the Alienated," The New York *Times*, 1967; reprinted in Ned E. Hoopes, ed., *Who Am I?* (New York: Dell, 1969), p. 164. Ernest Van den Haag, "it is no fun to fight pudding," in *The Public Interest*, Fall 1976, p. 121.

100 Geoffrey Vickers, "Literally ... responsible person," in "The Weakness of Western Culture," *Futures*, December 1977, p. 469.

101 Jack Quarter, "expressed a higher ... authoritarian thinking," in "Shifting Ideologies among Youth in Canada," cited in note to page 95, pp. 124-30.

102 Dean Davidson, "temporarily camouflaged ... the early 1970s," in H. Justin Davidson, "The Top of the World is Flat," *Harvard Business Review*, March-April 1977.

103 For details of the Big Generation's locating in rural non-farm areas, see *1976 Census of Canada: Population: Demographic Characteristics: Five-Year*

Age Groups, Catalogue 92-823 (Bulletin 2.4) (Ottawa, Statistics Canada, 1978).

103   Evidence of student activists' moods and expectations can be found in their own writings collected in Alexander Cockburn and Robin Blackburn, eds., *Student Power: Problems, Diagnosis, Action* (Harmondsworth: Penguin, 1969).

104   News of the girl in the hippie commune appeared in *The Observer*, September 2, 1979.

105   Dr. Levine, "On the average ... the overcrowding," in Judy Dobbie, "The New Lost Generation ... ," *Weekend*, cited.

106   Dave Reason, "The violence ... the overcrowding," in Trish Crawford, Toronto *Star*, March 23, 1979.

106   Ellen Dudley, "A growing number of homeless children have not left of their own volition, but are 'trashed kids,' 'pushouts,' 'throwaways.' ... Some shelters report that the majority of their children are now throwaways," in "Rainbows and Realities: Current Trends in Marriage and Its Alternatives," *The Futurist*, February 1979.

106   The cost of vandalism in 1978 was $100 million; see Rosemary Speirs, "Judge Appointed to Vandalism Probe," *The Globe and Mail*, December 18, 1979. "While a noisy party complaint once meant 30 people and a blaring stereo, Canada's westernmost provinces have more recently given birth to their own perplexing version of Saturday night fever. Most weekends, hundreds of falling-down drunks, plugged into a grapevine that always knows where the party is, cram suburban houses or throng outdoor recreational areas in scenes that would make the movie *Animal House* seem tame as a tabby. ... The vast majority of partygoers are 18 to 24. ... In the view of Charles Costello, a psychologist at the University of Calgary, 'good, healthy anarchy' would be easier to deal with than the 'reflex thing' that turns partygoers into savages. ... 'It's similar to the situation of blacks in the U.S., except we're dealing with the other end of the socioeconomic spectrum. These kids are frustrated because they can't get a hold on life so they act out, they destroy,'" in Suzanne Zwarun, "Getting Together for Beer and Destruction," *Maclean's*, August 11, 1980. In schools: "Ontario's task force on vandalism reported yesterday that more than 88 per cent of high school students surveyed this spring committed acts of vandalism over the past year. The acts of vandalism identified in the survey included scratching a school desk, breaking a bottle, writing graffiti, and more serious acts such as slashing tires or breaking windows. The average student admitted to an average 12 acts of vandalism and that number is likely low, the task force director of research said," in Sylvia Stead, "Committed Vandalism, 88% of Students Say," *The Globe and Mail*, August 9, 1980.

107   The City of Mississauga study found that vandalism is not senseless and that its target is more often public than private property, in Alden Baker, "Vandalism: Cost to Metro is $2 Million a Year," *The Globe and Mail*, July 26, 1977. Gillian Campbell, "Vandalism ... for their frustrations," in Julia Turner, "Riverdale Project Sets Out to Stop Vandals," *The Globe and Mail*, September 21, 1978. Grant Lowery, "If we learned ... left out," in Leslie Scrivener and Jackie Smith, " 'We Throw Rocks, Kick in Cars for Something to Do,' Youth Says," Toronto *Star*, April 10, 1979.

107   The three cases of assaults on teachers were reported in Helen Bullock,

"Kicked, Punched But Teacher Feels for Hostile Teen," Toronto *Star*, June 16, 1979; Mary Kate Rowan, "Teacher Hurt in Struggle with Intruder, Meeting Told," *The Globe and Mail*, March 20, 1979; and Mary Kate Rowan, "Violence Under Wraps," *The Globe and Mail*, June 7, 1979.

107   William Butt, "They were too ... the floors," in Dorothy Lipovenko and Denys Horigan, "Student Suspensions Soar in Ontario, Many for Drinking and Fighting," *The Globe and Mail*, December 8, 1978. Alan Murray, "It's people ... their being expelled," in Mary Kate Rowan, "Teacher Hurt ... ," *The Globe and Mail*, cited.

107-8 Dr. Wilkes, "Kids are unable ... anything's wrong," in Liane Heller, "Teen Timebomb Set to Explode," Toronto *Star*, March 8, 1979.

108   "We must start ... riot squads," in Dorothy Lipovenko, "32 Teachers Assaulted by Students in 3 Months," *The Globe and Mail*, March 1, 1979. The survey of 652 teachers was reported in David Vienneau, "Put Thugs in Own Schools–Teachers," Toronto *Star*, May 16, 1979.

108   Detective Earl Gibson, Ontario Provincial Police, "When I started in the force 19 years ago, armed robbery was unusual; it created a major investigation. Now armed robberies are much more common. People are much more prone to using violence, too, and I don't know why that is," in "Rash of Armed Robberies Hits Brockville," *The Globe and Mail* (Canadian Press), August 7, 1980. Half the prisoners in 1974 were aged 15 to 24; Dr. Hagan, "There is no ... of society"; and almost all racial assaults are perpetrated by people aged 18-21, are all in Judy Dobbie, "The New Lost Generation ... ," *Weekend*, cited. Twenty-two per cent of female prisoners were in their teens, in Helen Bullock, "New Crime Menace is Violence in Skirts," Toronto *Star*, September 15, 1978.

109   Teenagers' involvement in alcohol-related collisions was discussed in Jonathan Manthorpe, "Drying Out the Teens," Toronto *Star*, May 25, 1978.

109   Cpl. Wes Prosser, "We expected ... wild as it was," in " 'Wild' Beach Party," Toronto *Star*, May 21, 1979. Police spokesman, "Things have gone ... control in there," in "Dare Not Enter Mosport Grounds to Control Crowd, OPP Say," *The Globe and Mail*, July 4, 1977.

109-10 Age-specific death rates are given in annual editions of *Vital Statistics, Volume III, Mortality*, Catalogue 84-206 (Ottawa: Statistics Canada, 1980) or earlier equivalents. Suicide as top cause of death in cities is in Trish Crawford, "From 15 to 44 Suicide City's Biggest Killer," Toronto *Star*, September 13, 1978.

110   Nadine Mayers, "The individual ... accomplish in life," in letter to the editor, *The Globe and Mail*, March 13, 1979. Dr. Diane Syer, "With young people ... is negative," in Peggy McCallum, "Impact of Divorce, Uncertainty about Future Linked to More Suicides," *The Globe and Mail*, September 29, 1977. Dr. Quentin Rae-Grant, "Adolescents ... to alleviate it," in Margaret Mironowicz, "Teenage Suicide: When Cries, Whispers Go Unheard," *The Globe and Mail*, March 29, 1979.

110-1 The relation of suicide rates for people aged 15-24 to the relative size of the 15-24 age group can be seen in some figures from the past 30 years. The coefficient of correlation is 0.929. The source for suicide rates is *Vital Statistics*, cited; the relative size of the 15-24 age group was calculated from *Population: 1921-1971*, Catalogue 91-512 (Ottawa: Statistics Canada,

	Suicides per thousand people aged 15-24	*People Aged 15-24 as % of total population*
1950	4.6	15.9
1955	2.9	14.4
1960	5.2	14.3
1965	5.7	16.0
1970	10.3	18.3
1975	14.4	19.3

1973) and "Intercensal Estimate of the Population by Sex and Age, June 1, 1975" in *Statistics Canada Daily*, July 21, 1978.

111   "Ontario coroners will not call the deaths of children 14 and under suicide, [Dr. Diane Syer] said, because they feel the children are too young to understand the nature of the act or the meaning of death," in Peggy McCallum, "Impact of divorce . . . ," *The Globe and Mail*, September 29, 1977, cited. Guidance teacher, "They feel . . . language they use," in Margaret Mironowicz, "Teen-Age Suicide . . . ," *The Globe and Mail*, March 29, 1979, cited.

111   The Salvation Army's suicide prevention centre was described in Don Dutton, "Teens of 1960s Today's Suicides," Toronto *Star*, September 14, 1978. The study of more than 500 would-be suicides under 15 was reported in Joan Hollobon, "Youthful Suicides Growing in Ontario," *The Globe and Mail*, January 26, 1979. The study of 153 would-be suicides was reported in "Common Factors Pinpointed in 153 Attempted Suicides," Toronto *Star*, September 9, 1978.

Chapter 6

115   "The young people . . . life-style," in advertisement for *Oui* magazine, New York *Times*, June 3, 1976.

116   Angela Gibson, "I bought four . . . much money," in letter to editor, Toronto *Star*, August 2, 1979.

116   "During the last fifteen years the average pocket money of teen-agers in the United States has increased from $2.50 to $10.00 a week," in "Youth–the Young Go Boom," *The Great Ideas Today 1961* (Chicago: Encyclopaedia Britannica, 1961), p. 134. Teenagers' purchases in Paul C. Harper, Jr., "What's Happening, Baby?", Ned E. Hoopes, ed., *Who Am I?* (New York: Dell, 1969), pp. 157-160.

116-7 Ed and Annette Buckley, "We couldn't . . . two salaries," and Bob and Jeannette Baxter, "We want . . . tied down," in Sylvia Stead, "The New Lifestyle: Spend While Young," *The Globe and Mail*, January 31, 1979.

117   The changing proportion of teenagers in the population was estimated from *Population: 1921-71*, cited, and annual estimates in *Statistics Canada Daily*.

117   CHUM's claim to "the youth audience" in Lee Belland, "CHUM Sees Eight More Years of Rock," Toronto *Star*, June 2, 1977.

117-8 *Oui* magazine's claim to "the faster crowd" in their advertisement in New York *Times*, June 3, 1976.

118 McDonald's best customers are aged 20-34 in "Big Macs are Big Business," *Intercom*, February 1977.

118-9 Richard Flohil, "Their audience ... in their thirties," personal communication.

119 Paul McGrath, "what they assume ... co-opted," in "Diapers and the Decline of Rock," *The Globe and Mail*, July 16, 1977.

119 Levi Strauss's past achievements and present plans were reported in Vianney Carriere, "Maker of Levis is Fined $150,000," *The Globe and Mail*, January 30, 1979, and Gillian MacKay, "Levi Strauss has No Intention of Losing Baby Boom Market to Ravages of Age," *The Globe and Mail*, March 10, 1979.

119 The pattern of spending by households headed by people of various ages was detailed in *Urban Family Expenditure 1976*, Catalogue 62-547 (Ottawa: Statistics Canada, 1979). Similar surveys were reported in publications of the same title for 1964, 1967, 1972, and 1974.

120 Forecasts of the Big Generation's future spending as a proportion of total household spending were based on *Urban Family Expenditure 1976* combined with a projection of the number of households by age of the head of the household in *Household and Family Projections for Canada and the Provinces to 2001*, Catalogue 91-517 (Ottawa: Statistics Canada, 1975), Projection 2.

122 Charles Reich, "a deliberate rejection ... no elitism," in Reich, *The Greening of America*, cited, pp. 252-56.

123 Mary McCarthy, "Look at the face ... abstraction," in Miriam Gross, "A World Out of Joint," *The Observer*, October 14, 1979. Some interesting comments on self-absorption are to be found in Christopher Lasch, *The Culture of Narcissism* (New York: W.W. Norton, 1979, and Warner, 1979).

124 Involvement in various recreational activities by age group from *Culture Statistics: Service Bulletin*, Catalogue 87-001, January 1979 (Statistics Canada), interpreted by reference to "Intercensal Estimates of the Population by Sex and Age" for various years in *Statistics Canada Daily*.

124-5 Drinking pattern by age in "Back to Basics?", *Wall Street Journal*, August 24, 1978, and Edward Clifford, "Rising Age of U.S. Drinkers May Aid Canada's Distillers," *The Globe and Mail*, September 23, 1978.

125 Comments on the "bosoms and bullets" formula in Edward Clifford, "Buyers Hope to Find Effective Medium in New Paper," *The Globe and Mail*, November 21, 1979.

125 Comparisons of the cost of advertising to adults and adolescents on radio and television were made in "Radio Advertisers have Edge on U.S. Counterparts," *The Globe and Mail*, November 28, 1979.

126 "Average Annual Growth Rates of Some Leisure Activities if Participation Rates, by Age and Education, Remain at the 1978 Level" was the title of a table in *Culture Statistics*, Catalogue 87-610 (Ottawa: Statistics Canada, 1980).

Chapter 7
There are two main sources for the data and projections in this chapter. Both are publications of the 1976 Census of Canada series, *Population: Demographic Characteristics* (Ottawa: Statistics Canada, 1978). One is *Five-year Age Groups*, Catalogue 92-823 (Bulletin 2.4), the other is *Mobility Status*, Catalogue 92-828 (Bulletin 2.9); these titles are used as sources without further identification in the notes to this chapter.

127   The forecast of the number of Big Generation members who will move between 1981 and 1986 is based on *Mobility Status*, from which was calculated the rate at which people in the age group 20-34 move – that is, the
number of moves per thousand people of that age – including estimates for
immigrants, emigrants, and deaths. It was assumed that the Big Generation will move at the same rate as its predecessors. The source for the
number of people in the age group 20-34 in the year 1986 was *Population
Projections for Canada and the Provinces 1976-2001*, Projection 4, cited. The
forecast is the sum of the products of the historic rate and projected number in each five-year age group.

127   Robert Louis Stevenson, "Youth is ... town and country," in "Crabbed
Age and Youth," *Virginibus Puerisque* (London: C.K. Paul, 1881).

127-8 The calculation of the size of the median location for each age group was
made from Census counts of the population by age, sex, and urban size
group in different years, e.g., *Five-Year Age Groups* for 1976. The pattern
takes people from smaller places to larger places: follow any cohort – e.g.,
aged 10-14 in 1956, 20-24 in 1966, 30-34 in 1976. The jump between 15-19
and 20-24 is the largest. Here are some years and age groups to show this
pattern:

Size of Median Location for Each Age Group at Three Censuses

Age	1956	1966	1976
0-4	12,100	58,300	68,600
5-9	9,000	49,700	70,900
10-14	7,100	38,100	66,600
15-19	8,300	51,700	83,700
20-24	32,700	123,800	210,500
25-29	53,700	148,200	224,200
30-34	56,800	151,100	197,500
35-39	46,300	143,300	202,200
40-44	44,500	133,800	217,100
45-49	40,200	96,000	220,400
50-54	40,000	92,600	206,800
55-59	34,800	83,800	139,400
60-64	30,900	76,700	109,000
65-69	27,700	70,000	96,100

128   A table in *Mobility Status* shows the number of people in the country and in
each metropolitan area who had arrived from overseas in the previous five
years, by age.

128   The possible start of a movement of younger adults away from the
metropolitan areas; the fact that farm populations are not increasing; and
the observation that the increase in rural non-farm residents was largest
among those born between 1941 and 1956, were all calculated from data in
Five-Year Age Groups and *Mobility Status*. Peter A. Morrison with Judith P.
Wheeler, "Rural Renaissance in America?", *Population Bulletin*, October
1976, was a useful starting point. Robert Parenteau, "Is Canada Going
Back to the Land?", Working Paper No. 11-GEO 79 (Ottawa: Statistics
Canada, 1980), published after this book was completed, considers the Canadian evidence: "The increase in the rural proportion of the total popula-
tion between 1971 and 1976 ... may signify the end of the increasing trend

toward urbanization. ... This new movement of ruralization ... could significantly alter the foundations of Canadian society," p. 29.

128-9   The movement of people aged 20-34 in and out of metropolitan areas was calculated from *Mobility Status*.

129   David Lewis Stein, "Now the subdivisions ... children alone," in "Turmoil in the Suburbs," Toronto *Star*, April 8, 1979.

129-30 The cities most affected by the influx of young adults were identified by calculations from *Mobility Status*, which also revealed which were most affected by internal migration and which by immigration from abroad.

130   The concentration of young adults in central cities was derived from *Five-Year Age Groups*.

130   Some communities experienced near-riot conditions: e.g. Fort McMurray. "The adult crime rate is considerably higher than in the rest of the province, particularly for alcohol-related offences, as are rates of juvenile offences and sexual deviation. ... The annual turnover in school enrolments is around 50 per cent. In one survey ... more than 40 per cent of residents had been in Fort McMurray less than two years. ... 'The town has changed from an open, friendly place to one characterized by cliques,' [according to a socio-economic study of the impact of the two oil-sands plants]," in Anne Penketh, "The Bleak Side of Boom Town," *The Globe and Mail*, August 8, 1980.

131   K.S. Gnanasekaran, *Migration Projections for Canada 1969-84*, cited, gives the average age distribution of immigrants and emigrants in the period 1956-66. In summary they are:

Age	Immigrants		Emigrants	
0-14	23.3%		29.5%	
15-19	7.9%		6.3%	
20-24	19.4%)		12.5%)	
	)		)	
25-29	17.2%)	47.2%	13.7%)	37.4%
	)		)	
30-34	10.6%)		11.2%)	
35+	21.6%		26.8%	
TOTAL	100.0%		100.0%	

The distribution of Canadian emigrants could be expected to vary more from year to year than the immigrant distribution because the age distribution of the whole Canadian population varies more rapidly than that of the population that is the source of immigrants. For this reason, some demographers think it advisable in long-term population projections to total up the number of expected emigrants from the projected population distribution and age-related emigration rates rather than to start at the other end and distribute the estimated total according to a fixed pattern. In the short term the difference is small. A 1977 Gallup Poll survey asked, "Can you think of any other country that you would prefer to be a citizen of?" The published response was:

Age	Yes	No, prefer Canada	Don't Know
18-29	13%	84%	3%
30-49	10%	89%	2%
50+	4%	94%	3%

131 The rise in emigrants was calculated from figures in *Mobility Status*. The drop in emigrants during the Vietnam war was explained in John Kettle, "The U.S. in Our Future," *Executive*, August 1978, p. 39: "The actual number of Canadian emigrants to the U.S. from 1965 through 1976 was 314,000. If the trend of the post-war years had continued, there would have been 713,000 emigrants, or some 400,000 more."

132 The two sources of estimates of the number of people who moved in the years 1971-76 are *Mobility Status* and *International and Interprovincial Migration in Canada 1961-62 to 1975-76*, Catalogue 91-208 (Ottawa: Statistics Canada, 1977). The first records the position after five years, the second records each move.

132 A useful compilation of migration statistics from 1852 is in Constantine Passaris, *Understanding Canadian Immigration* (Toronto: Canadian Foundation for Economic Education, 1978). Immigrants of the same age as the Big Generation were calculated from annual immigrant totals distributed by age according to figures in Gnanasekaran, *Migration Projections for Canada 1968-84*, cited.

133 The inverse relation between unemployment and immigration is not official government policy, but the post-war data make it evident (see for example Zsigmond *et al., Out of School – Into the Labour Force*, cited, p. 79), and officials have confirmed privately that the relation exists.

Chapter 8

134 The headings appeared in Toronto *Star*, May 17, 1977, May 7, 1977 and April 8, 1979, and *The Globe and Mail*, December 1, 1979; the first was in fact not a front-page story. The theory of human capital "holds that an individual's level of earning depends on the amount that [he] has *invested* in acquiring skills of value in the labour market," in G. Picot, *The Changing Education Profile of Canadians, 1961 to 2000* (Ottawa: Statistics Canada, 1980), p. 19. See, e.g., G.S. Becker, *Human Capital* (New York: Columbia University Press, 1964). Federal government briefing paper: *"A Background Paper Reviewing Unemployment and Underemployment among Canada's Educated Youth"*, Canada Employment and Immigration Commission, unpublished, undated, but about 1977, p. 5. The degree-salary relation: see Zsigmond *et al, Out of School – Into the Labour Force*, cited, pp. 183-89.

134-5 Ronald Anderson, "The argument . . . to their training," in "The Missing Jobs," *The Globe and Mail*, June 1, 1977.

135 "If, indeed . . . graduates," in *A Background Paper Reviewing Unemployment . . .*," cited, p. 5.

135 "at least ten . . . education," in John A. Buttrick, *Educational Problems in Ontario and Some Policy Options*, Occasional Paper 4 (Toronto: Ontario Economic Council, 1977), pp. 17-18.

135 Three examples: Robert Cook in "The Fading Dream: Children of Baby Boom Try to Keep Job Hopes Alive," *The Globe and Mail*, December 1, 1979. Vera Mikolajiw in Frank Jones, "The Unwanted Graduate: Who's to Blame?", Toronto *Star*, May 7, 1977. Wolf Ballman in Trish Crawford, "University Grads Seek Job Skills at Trade Schools," Toronto *Star*, April 16, 1979.

136 "The teaching profession . . . has been a major employment sector for university graduates: in 1973 36% of all employed degree-holders in Canada, 28 or younger, were in education," in Zsigmond *et al, Out of*

School – *Into the Labour Force*, cited, p. 59.

136   Ruben Bellan, "The Canadian economy ... system," in "Ottawa's Policies are Frustrating Young Grads, Economist Says," Toronto *Star*, July 11, 1978. Stephen Threlkeld, "We're going ... bright young people," in Trish Crawford, "A New Brain Drain," Toronto *Star*, August 2, 1979. Pierre Elliott Trudeau, "If they don't ... that's all," in "Long-run Prospects: Good," *The Globe and Mail*, March 29, 1977.

136   Surplus of Ph.D.s from Zur-Muehlen (Statistics Canada), "The Age Structure of University Teachers by Provinces," March 1977, cited in Lewis Auerbach, "Implications of the Changing Age Structure of the Canadian Population" (Ottawa: Science Council of Canada, 1977).

137   Journalism graduate in Peggy McCallum, "They Graduate into Unemployment," *The Globe and Mail*, March 17, 1977.

137   Janet King, "because I can't ... political science," in McCallum, "They Graduate ... ," cited.

137   Jack Quarter, "A youth who ... his outlook," in "Shifting Ideologies among Youth in Canada," cited, p. 129. U.S. Supreme Court, "There is no more ... employer," quoted in *Wall Street Journal*, May 1, 1978.

137-8 Daniel Yankelovich, "The New Breed ... value system," in "Work Values and the New Breed," Clark Kerr and Jerome Rostow, eds., *Work in America: The Decade Ahead* (New York: Van Nostrand, 1979), quoted in Richard Sennett, "The Boss's New Clothes," *The New York Review of Books*, February 22, 1979.

138   Richard Sennett, "The demand of employees ... Evidently not," in "The Boss's New Clothes," *The New York Review of Books*, February 22, 1979.

138   Torsten Husén, "Young people ... articulate groups," in "Changing Attitudes to Education and Work among Youth," *OECD Observer*, January 1978.

139   Dr. Clarkson, "There are some ... dead-end," (edited down from original), in Bill Dampier, "What Do the '80s Hold in Store?", Toronto *Star*, December 30, 1979.

139   Prof. Husén on common working ideals of young people, in "Changing Attitudes to Education ... ," *OECD Observer*, cited.

139   Max Weber, "in building ... glory of God," in *The Protestant Ethic and the Spirit of Capitalism*, translated by Talcott Parsons (New York: Scribners, 1958), pp. 181, 158. Stanley R. Parker, "for most of history ... himself," in *The Future of Work and Leisure*, 1971, cited in "The Changing Nature of Work," *Trend Analysis Report 17*, undated, American Council of Life Insurance.

139-40 Arthur B. Shostak, "It's a generation ... at work"; Yankelovich poll; Jerome Rosow, "They want ... the individual"; all in "Americans Change," *Business Week*, February 20, 1978. Controller Orlando Zamprogna, "They might look ... process," in "City Warned about Overqualified Workers," *The Globe and Mail*, September 7, 1978. The source of the survey on career and job aspirations was Strategic Planning & Research, *Canadian Work Values* (Ottawa: Department of Manpower and Immigration, 1975), pp. 39, 44, cited in Kevin Collins, *Youth and Employment: A Source Book* (Ottawa: Canadian Council on Social Development, 1976), p. 54.

140   Ian Wilson, "From consideration ... towards participation," (edited down from original), in "Issues of the 1980s: The Blooming Baby Boom," *Planning Review*, September 1979.

140-1 Eugene Cass and Frederick Zimmer, "The oncoming generation ... in history," in *Man and Work in Society* (1976), cited in "The Changing Nature of Work," *Trend Analysis Report 17*, cited.
141 For discussion of the New Class, see, e.g., B. Bruce-Briggs, ed., *The New Class?* (New York: Transaction Books, 1979). Richard Finlay, "A message ... shape society," in "The Strange, Skeptical Mood ...," *Saturday Night*, cited.
141-2 Evidence of the effects of changes in unemployment insurance regulations on the Big Generation can be found in John Kettle, "It's No Longer Work, Work, Work," *Executive*, April 1977; "Anomalies in Jobless Rates are Blamed on UIC Changes," *The Globe and Mail* (Canadian Press), May 21, 1977; John Kettle, "The Trouble with the Economy," *Executive*, December 1977; "Loosening of UIC Benefit Rules Called Big Break for Job Seekers," *The Globe and Mail* (Canadian Press), July 21, 1978; and Denys Horigan, "225,000 Quit to Take Jobless Pay," *The Globe and Mail*, October 20, 1979.
142 Arthur Donner and Fred Lazar, "It is natural ... employment opportunity," in "Finding Work for the Young," *The Globe and Mail*, December 13, 1977.
142 Amy Bearg, "I can't find ... constantly late," in Elaine Carey, "Youth Squeezed Out in Search for Jobs," Toronto *Star*, April 8, 1979.
142 Young people shed unsatisfactory jobs quickly, Statistics Canada survey, in Toronto *Star*, November 13, 1976. Economic Council of Canada, "More people can ... several options," in Ronald Anderson, "Estimates on Jobless Show Range of Values," *The Globe and Mail*, December 19, 1979. Gwen Bedville, "There are jobs ... on the job," in Peggy McCallum, "They Graduate into Unemployment," *The Globe and Mail*, March 17, 1977.
143 The unemployed: Barry Switzer in letter to the editor, *The Canadian*, August 20, 1977. Topaz Amber Dawn in Philip Marchand, "Down Looks Like Up to Me," *Weekend Magazine*, March 4, 1978: the lyric of Mick Jagger's "Ruby Tuesday" actually says that what you lose is your mind, not your life. Anthony Iamundo in Paul Palango, "The Future: For Many of Canada's Young, it's a Big Question Mark," *The Globe and Mail*, June 12, 1978. Doug Skelton in Marchand, "Down Looks Like Up to Me," cited.
143 Canadian suicide study in "Common Factors Pinpointed in 153 Attempted Suicides," Toronto *Star*, September 9, 1978. Johns Hopkins University study in "A Job Means More than Money," Toronto *Star*, December 4, 1978.

Chapter 9
The economic growth rate data and projections in this chapter are calculated from or based on CANSIM Matrices 526 and 598 and *Canadian Statistical Review: Historical Summary*, Catalogue 11-505 (Ottawa: Statistics Canada, 1972) from 1926 on, and from data in *Historical Statistics of Canada* up to 1925, unless otherwise stated.
146 Herman Kahn's forecast is contained in *World Economic Development* (Boulder, Colorado: Westview, 1979); the numbers given here were calculated from data on pp. 86-87 and equations on pp. 506-07.
146-7 French auto industry figures were calculated from data in Barbara Ward, "Small Steps Towards a More Civilized World," *The Observer*, November 18, 1979.

147-8   Max Weber, "But a peculiar . . . for that purpose," in *The Protestant Ethic and the Spirit of Capitalism*, cited, pp. 59-60.
148   Future population growth at only 0.5-1.25% a year on average, calculated from *Population Projections for Canada and the Provinces, 1976-2001*, cited.
149   The observation that 100,000 immigrants will typically include 50,000 workers is based on the experience of the period 1955-79, when there were 1,788,000 immigrants who intended to join the labour force among the total of 3,599,000 immigrants; or 49.7%. In the last five years, however, the proportion of workers has been only 42.1%. The source of this information is CANSIM Matrix 3.
150   One-person households rose from 11.4% of the total in 1966 to 16.8% in 1976: *Canada Year Book 1978-79*, cited, p. 163. The age distribution of one-person households can be found in *Private Households by Marital Status, Sex, and Age of Head*, Catalogue 93-809 (Bulletin 3.10) (Ottawa: Statistics Canada, 1978).
150   Household spending patterns were derived from *Urban Family Expenditures 1976*, cited. For the forecast these age-related rates were applied to the projected numbers of households characterized by age of the head of the household in *Household and Family Projections for Canada and the Provinces to 2001*, cited, Projection 4; since those projections were made on the basis of earlier population projections, they were recalculated according to later projections.
151   Robots in automobile plants in New York *Times*, November 5, 1979.
151-2   Kimon Valaskakis, "What with robotics . . . by 1990," in *Executive*, February 1980, p. 9.
153   "Many of the women . . . labor force," in *People and Jobs* (Ottawa: Economic Council of Canada, 1976), cited in Wayne Cheveldayoff, "Working Women – Force of the Future," *The Globe and Mail*, February 28, 1979. The rising participation rate of women is documented in CANSIM Matrix 2074; a forecast through 1990 appeared in *Executive*, February 1980, p. 18.
153-4   The relation between labour force participation rate and level of education for women in 1976 is apparent in these figures. The 1961 rates are included here for easier comparison:

Years of Schooling	Participation rates, 1976	Participation rates, 1961
less than 5	16.9%	14.3%
5-8	27.5%	23.1%
9-10	37.7%	31.0%
11	45.6%	31.0%
12	55.1% ⎫	
13	59.0% ⎬	40.6%
14	64.0%	47.3%
16	70.5% ⎫	
18	74.0% ⎬	47.9%
20	76.6% ⎭	

A curve fitted to the pairs of 1976 data gives a participation rate of 38% for women with Grade VIII, 53% for Grade XII, and 68% for women with 16 years of education. The co-efficient of correlation is 0.983. The source for the 1976 data was *Population by Age and Level of Schooling*, Catalogue 94-806 (Ottawa: Statistics Canada, 1976). For 1961 data the source was Sylvia page

Ostry, *The Female Worker in Canada* (Ottawa: Statistics Canada, 1968).

154   "The participation rate of divorced or separated women is higher than the participation rate of married women," in "Divorced Persons Grow in Workforce," *The Globe and Mail* (Canadian Press), December 9, 1978. "Reflects, at least ... in marriage," in Douglas R. Sease, "Women at Work: Marital Relationships Often Undergo Strain When Wives Get Jobs," *Wall Street Journal*, September 19, 1978.

155   Jeanne Binstock, "In industrial societies ... and growth," in *Dr. Spock's Babies Take Charge*, book in process.

155   An interview with the Buckleys appeared in Sylvia Stead, "The New Lifestyle: Spend While Young," *The Globe and Mail*, January 31, 1979. "... 70% of married women ... work to bring their husband's income above the poverty line," in Michele Landsberg, "Tell Ottawa You're Not Secondary," Toronto *Star*, January 16, 1979.

155   The survey asked, "Given the choice, do you think you would prefer to work full-time as a homemaker, work as a homemaker with a part-time job outside the home, or be employed full-time outside the home?" The answers by level of education were:

	Grade-school education	High-school education	College or University
Homemaker	50%	33%	25%
Homemaker & part-time	28%	45%	43%
Full-time	17%	19%	28%
Don't know, no answer	4%	3%	5%

Not all columns add up, because of rounding. The survey was carried out by CROP Inc.

155-6   The estimate of women's participation rate at the end of the century was worked out in this way:

50% of women will have participation rate like men today	=75.5 %
25% of women will have participation rate like all women today	=45.0 %
25% of women will have participation rate in between these rates	=60.25%
Weighted average for all women	=64.1 %

The 1976 figures were used because they were obtained at the census and are thus more reliable than the estimates produced monthly in the Labour Force Survey. If April 1980 figures are used, the weighted average would be 67.9%. The source for the Census figures is *Population by Age and Level of Schooling*, cited; for the 1980 figures, *Canadian Statistical Review*, May 1980.

156   The projected labour force participation rates referred to are unofficial figures produced by a unit of Statistics Canada and not published or given agency sanction for outside use; received by personal communication.

Average spring unemployment rates for people aged 15-24 in the period 1974-77, by level of education:

Elementary	23.2%
Secondary	13.5%
Some post-secondary	9.5%
Post-sec. diploma or certificate	6.3%
Degree	5.4%

The source for these data is Zsigmond *et al, Out of School – Into the Labour Force*, cited, p. 54.

157 A quarter of the Ontario workforce in 1971 was immigrant: see *Canada Year Book 1978-79*, p. 363. A seventh of the Canadian population in 1971 was immigrant: see *Canada Year Book 1978-79*, p. 162.

157 The equation can be stated as

$$P + C = W + O$$

where P is the growth rate of the population, C the growth rate of consumption per person, W the growth rate of the employed, and O the growth rate of output per worker. This assumes that growth rates are being expressed as a percentage. A slightly more exact and complicated form of the equation substitutes the growth multiplier for the growth rate – i.e. 1.02 rather than 2% – and then reads

$$P \times C = W \times O$$

Where growth is less than 10% the difference is negligible. The equation is a truism, stating only that growth of consumption equals growth of production, but it is nonetheless a useful device.

158 Behind the workforce projections for 1996 are these assumptions about participation rates:

Age	Men	Women
15-19	40.0%	40.0%
20-24	75.0%	72.5%
25-34	95.0%	75.0%
35-44	97.0%	75.0%
45-54	93.0%	75.0%
55-64	77.5%	50.0%
65+	9.5%	2.5%

They are conservative extrapolations of recent trends.

158-9 Participation rates and unemployment rates for the ten provinces in 1979 are in *Canadian Statistical Review*, May 1980. Regression of these pairs of data yields a coefficient of correlation of −0.893, and suggests that every increase of 1% in the unemployment rate will produce a reduction of 1.2% in the participation rate.

159 Here are the three "solutions" to the growth rate equation:

	Population		Consump- tion per person		Output per worker		Employ- ment
Pessimistic	0.7%	+	2.0%	=	2.2%	+	0.5%
Standard	1.0%	+	2.0%	=	2.0%	+	1.0%
Optimistic	1.0%	+	2.2%	=	1.7%	+	1.5%

159   Margaret Garritsen de Vries, "stimulating the economy . . . less inflation," in *IMF Survey*, January 7, 1980, quoted in Ronald Anderson, "World Economy in '70s Appeared out of Control," *The Globe and Mail*, January 22, 1980.

160   There were 21,290 physicians in Canada in 1961, 40,130 in 1976. The sources for these data are *Canada Year Book 1973*, p. 275, and *Canada Year Book 1978-79*, p. 234.

160   The two bulges in civil service hirings are most clearly visible in data contained in the *Annual Report of the Public Service Commission of Canada 1974*, p. 44, and the *Annual Report of the Public Service Commission of Canada 1978*, Volume 2, Statistics, p. 9. A fact sheet issued at the time of publication of the 1978 annual report showed the following applications and hirings:

Graduates of Community Colleges, etc.

	Applicants	Hired	Percent Hired
1977	4,047	354	8.7%
1978	2,829	273	9.7%

Universities Graduates

1977	25,027	1,008	4.0%
1978	26,093	1,051	4.0%

Chapter 10

161   A quarter of the people employed in 1976 were under 25 years old, as were a third of those employed in wholesale and retail trade: the source for these statements is an unpublished Statistics Canada tabulation, "Employed in Industry by Age and Sex, Canada, Annual Average 1976." Only 15% of the employed in the year 2001 will be under 25: based on an estimate derived from participation rate trends and population forecast described in a note to p. 158.

161-2   Sources for observations on labour shortages: sewing-machine operators, motor vehicle mechanics, etc., in 1977, in "Help Needed Despite Rise in Unemployed," *The Globe and Mail* (Canadian Press), August 19, 1977; mechanics and tool-makers in Ontario in 1978, in Pat McNenly, "Pay is $500 but He Still Can't Hire Skilled Men," Toronto *Star*, February 25, 1978; skilled tradesmen in Ontario in 1979, in "Skilled Labor Shortage," *The Globe and Mail*, November 22, 1979; journeymen for General Motors, in Rosemary Speirs, "Failure by Firms to Train Apprentices Blamed for Need to Recruit Overseas," *The Globe and Mail*, May 2, 1979; welders in Alberta, in David Hatter, "Shortage of Workers?", Calgary *Albertan*, August 23, 1979; skilled aerospace technicians, in Ken Romain,

"Manpower Shortage Held Threat to Aerospace Industry," *The Globe and Mail*, September 26, 1978; millwrights, machinists, etc., in Wayne Cheveldayoff, "Job Training," *The Globe and Mail*, January 10, 1979.

162 The unions are not enthusiastic about apprenticeship, in Douglas Fullerton, "The Unemployed Young People are the Economy's New Chronic Disease," Toronto *Star*, March 28, 1977. Employers are not enthusiastic about apprenticeship, in "Parents' Attitudes about Job Status Blamed for the Critical Shortage of Skilled Workers," *The Globe and Mail*, January 29, 1980.

162 John Cyr, "a lot of applications ... part-time jobs," in Dorothy Lipovenko, "Job-sharing Favored by Working Mothers," *The Globe and Mail*, January 17, 1980.

163 The trend of part-time employment is documented in CANSIM Matrix 2074. An extrapolation of the trend appeared in *Executive*, August 1979, p. 16.

163 Dr. Eva Rudnicki and Dr. Linda Lee share a dentist's office, and 16 educators share eight jobs, in Dorothy Lipovenko, "Job-sharing Favored . . . ," cited.

164 This table shows three ways of spreading work and their effects on the people in the labor force. The solutions all reduce unemployment to four per cent.

	Unemployed	*Part-time* (15 hrs/wk)	*Job Sharing* (20 hrs/wk)	*Full Time* (40 hrs/wk)
The Problem	2,000,000	1,600,000	—	6,400,000
Solution 1: Part time	400,000	4,160,000	—	5,440,000
Solution 2: Job-sharing	400,000	1,600,000	3,200,000	4,800,000
Solution 3: Reduced Hours	400,000	1,920,000 (12.5 hrs/wk)	—	7,680,000 (33.3 hrs/wk)

165 Forecasts of youth unemployment rates in various countries in 1981, from *OECD Economic Outlook*, July 1980:

United States	16.0%
Japan	4.0%
West Germany	5.5%
France	16.5%
Britain	14.0%
Canada	14.5%
Average of these	13.0%

Source: Wayne Chevaldayoff, "Sharp Rise in Youth Unemployment

Forecast Except in Canada, Japan," *The Globe and Mail*, July 12, 1980.

165   Less than one third of the workers in industry, two thirds in services: data in CANSIM Matrix 2074. Figures for 1979 were: agriculture, 5.7%; industry, 27.7%; services, 66.6%.

166   Shifts in industry's share of output are documented in CANSIM Matrix 563, covering gross domestic product from 1926 on; before that the source is *Historical Statistics of Canada*. Industry's share of employment from 1911 on is documented by R. Marvin McInnis in "Long-run Changes in the Industrial Structure of the Canadian Work Force," *Canadian Journal of Economics*, August 1971, subsequently updated by McInnis to include data for 1971; before that the source for estimates is *Historical Statistics of Canada*.

166   In the 1970s, 72% of the net new jobs were in businesses employing fewer than twenty people: the source was the Canadian Federation of Independent Business, in "Where the Jobs Are," *Executive*, June 1979, p. 16: "In manufacturing, small firms created 317,800 new jobs [in the past eight years] while large firms actually got rid of 124,800 employees."

167   "There are at least 80 [theatre] schools in Canada," in Boyd Neil, "Theatre Schools Over-producing, Under-preparing," *The Globe and Mail*, January 26, 1980. "77.6% of our 6,600 members earn less than $4,000 a year in our jurisdiction," according to a spokesman for the Association of Canadian Television and Radio Artists.

168   The proportion of information work in the nation's work is hard to calculate. Pioneering work on this question in North America was done by Fritz Machlup, *The Production and Distribution of Knowledge in the United States* (Princeton: Princeton University Press, 1962), and more recently by Marc Uri Porat, *The Information Economy*, nine volumes (Washington: U.S. Department of Commerce, Office of Telecommunications, 1977). Porat calculated that 25.1% of Gross National Product was created in the primary information sector (e.g., the media) and 21.1% in the secondary information sector (e.g., industrial research); volume 1, p. 7. He calculated that 53.5% of total employee compensation was paid to information workers; Vol. 1, p. 107. Canadian work by, e.g., Canada Department of Communication and GAMMA (Universite de Montreal/McGill University) Information Society Project suggests that Canadian output and employment is about five percentage points lower. On tourism: "Tourism will become Canada's leading industry by the year 2000 in terms of income, export earnings, and employment," in L.J. D'Amore, "The Significance of Tourism to Canada," *The Business Quarterly*, Autumn 1976; Guy Chiasson, "The Canadian tourism industry . . . is the largest employer in Canada, with one million workers. . . . It is often the only industry in a particular region," in Ken Romain, "Tourism Industry Seen as 'Neglected Orphan'," *The Globe and Mail*, March 25, 1980; tourism is Quebec's leading revenue producer, ahead of pulp and paper and mining, in Wendie Kerr, "Quebec's Top Revenue Producer, Tourism Wants Clout in Cabinet," *The Globe and Mail*, September 8, 1977.

Chapter 11

169-70 Statistics Canada's first published shot at population forecasting was *The Population Projections for Canada, 1969-84*, Analytical and Technical Memorandum No. 4 (Ottawa: Statistics Canada, 1970). The high and low Total Fertility Rates (TFR) used in the projections were 2.8 and 2.2; a year

page

    later the actual TFR was below 2.2. Their first population forecasts to the end of the century were published in *Population Projections for Canada and the Provinces, 1972-2001*, Catalogue 91-514 (Ottawa: Statistics Canada, 1974). The high and low TFRs were 2.6 and 1.8; four years later the actual TFR was below 1.8. The latest forecasts are in *Population Projections for Canada and the Provinces, 1976-2001*, Catalogue 91-520 (Ottawa: Statistics Canada, 1979). The high and low TFRs are 2.1 and 1.7. The Total Fertility Rate is the number of children that would be born to a woman who had children throughout her fertile years at the present rate for each five-year age group. It is an approximation for the Completed Fertility Rate, which is the actual number of children the women of a particular cohort had on average during their fertile years, but the TFR swings higher and lower than the CFR.

170   For references to the Easterlin hypothesis, see notes to p. 33.

170-1 The new pattern of women's lives described in the last chapter gives rise to this suggestion of a new pattern of fertility, toward which women are now moving:

50% of women will have the same Total Fertility Rate as men   = 0.00
25% of women will have the average TFR of the past 20 years   = 2.68
25% of women will have a rate between these two   = 1.34
Weighted average TFR for all women   = 1.005

The average TFR of the period 1921-78 is 3.05. This seems too high to be the "historic" figure in this calculation, but if it was used the weighted average for the new pattern would be 1.15, a figure still strikingly lower than anything now considered in the Canadian literature.

171   Joanne Kates, "We are all talking . . . on parenting," in "Infant Dreams," *The Globe and Mail*, May 4, 1977. Phyllis Chesler, "To some extent . . . feminine pride," in Judith Finlayson, "Babies: A New Vogue?", *The Globe and Mail*, January 12, 1980.

171-2 "The institutionalization of motherhood as the dominant role for women and discrimination against women who would seek a life course independent of raising a family headed the list of pronatalist forces," in Masnick and McFalls, "Those Perplexing U.S. Fertility Swings," *PRB Report*, November 1978, cited. Judith Blake, "A willingness to regard . . . is still rare," in "Can We Believe Recent Data on Birth Expectations in the United States?", *Demography*, February 1974. "Psychological propensity . . . North American women," in *Population Projections for Canada and the Provinces, 1972-2001*, Catalogue 91-514, cited, p. 30.

172   Prof. Easterlin, "Demographers should . . . relative affluence," in Glenn Collins, "The Good News About 1984", *Psychology Today*, January 1979.

173   Unwanted pregnancies among teenagers are continuing to increase, in Rudy Platiel, "Teen Pregnancies Increase is Slowing, Professor Says," *The Globe and Mail*, June 16, 1979.

"Do not and will not have children," in "To Most Canadians 'Upper Class' Means 'Rich'," *Weekend Magazine*, February 25, 1978; telephone survey of 1,006 people conducted in 30 large urban centres by Data Laboratories Research Consultants, Montreal. "It is perfectly all right to be married and to choose not to have children. Agree – 83%," in "Households and Families," *DataTrack 4*, Summer 1978 (American Council of Life Insurance).

242

174   "What do you think is the ideal number of children for a family to have?" the Gallup Poll asked Canadians over the years. The answers given in various years are shown below (the estimated median answer is my addition):

	Two or fewer	Three	Four or more	Estimated median
1945	17%	23%	60%	4.5
1957	22%	23%	55%	4.2
1970	34%	33%	33%	2.5
1977	55%	29%	15%	1.8
1977 all respondents aged 18-29	59%	31%	10%	1.7

174   Ellen Dudley, "a new phenomenon has emerged in recent years: divorces in which neither mother nor father wants to take the children," in "Rainbows and Realities," *The Futurist*, February 1979. Michele Landsberg, "Do we fear . . . forty any more," in "Do We Fear and Loathe Unknown in Kids?", Toronto *Star*, May 18, 1978.

175   Marvin Novick, "In the Fifties and Sixties, Ontario invested heavily in schooling . . . , but it was easy then. We had enough for our private needs. When we come to the Seventies, we have some hard choices. There is a feeling among many adults that 'I paid for my children, why should I go on paying for somebody else's children?'," in Kathleen Rex, "Unfairness to Young Widespread, Meeting Told," *The Globe and Mail*, June 1, 1979. "A sharp increase in the number of child abuse cases," in Liane Heller, "Increasing Child Abuse Called Symptom of a Sick Society," Toronto *Star*, April 27, 1979. Barbara Chisholm, "visible anger against children," and "One group uses the slogan 'None is Fun'," both in "Anger Building Up against Children Consultant Says," Toronto *Star* (Canadian Press), May 15, 1979.

175   Michele Landsberg, "The parent's only . . . automotive subculture," in "Do We Fear and Loathe the Unknown in Kids?", Toronto *Star*, May 18, 1978.

175   Brian Emmons, "We analyzed it . . . responsibility," in Dorothy Lipovenko, "The Child-free are Care-free," *The Globe and Mail*, November 1, 1979. "Be fruitful . . . replenish the earth," in *Genesis*, i, 28.

175   "A community of detached homes for adults only," in "Adults-only Housing Development near Ottawa a Success," *The Globe and Mail*, November 5, 1979. The article quoted a resident: "I know people will say we don't like children. That just isn't true. We had four of our own, but now we want a different kind of life where the living is relaxed and quiet."

176   "In contrast . . . as they like," in "New Breed of Parents have New Values," Toronto *Star* (Reuter), April 25, 1977.

176   The 34 women graduated with 742 men in the Harvard MBA class of '73; in Wyndham Robertson, "Women M.B.A.'s, Harvard '73 – How They're Doing," *Fortune*, August 28, 1978. The education-fertility relation for 1971 is shown by a chart, "Children Born per 1000 Women Ever Married

by Present Age and Level of Schooling for Canada, 1971," in *1971 Census of Canada, Profile Studies: Fertility in Canada*, Catalogue 99-706 (Ottawa: Statistics Canada, 1976). Data for the chart have not been published. A less detailed breakdown of fertility by level of education for all women aged 15 and over was published after the 1961 census:

Elementary	3.70
Secondary	2.44
University without degree	2.10
University with degree	2.02

The source is *1961 Census of Canada, General Review: Fertility Trends in Canada*, Catalogue 99-527 (Bulletin 7.2-2) (Ottawa: Statistics Canada, 1968).

177 Here are the participation and fertility rates for women aged 20-24 in some years in the past quarter century:

	Participation rate	Fertility rate
1953	47.2%	208.2
1958	47.4%	226.5
1963	50.3%	226.0
1968	58.4%	152.6
1973	64.7%	117.7
1978	70.3%	103.1

The coefficient of correlation for the full set of data is −0.971. The source of the participation rates is CANSIM Matrix 2074; of the fertility rates, *Vital Statistics Volume I, Births*, Catalogue 84-204, cited.

177 Dr. Westoff, "which in turn ... have any children," in "Some Speculations on the Future of Marriage and Fertility," *Family Planning Perspectives*, March/April 1978, pp. 79-83.

177-8 Judith Finlayson, "I'll never have ... suitable man," in "Babies: A New Vogue?", cited. Joanne Kates, "We watched ... any of it," in "Infant Dreams," cited.

178 "A University of Toronto survey showed that female undergraduates now have about the same number of sex partners before marriage as males," in Edward Shorter, "25 Years on the Pill," *Weekend Magazine*, August 18, 1979. "There is no such thing as an instinctive urge to bear and raise children," quoting Dr. G. N. Ramu, in "Professor Says Ottawa Should Aid Birth Rate," *The Globe and Mail* (Canadian Press), December 11, 1979. *New Society*, "a society ... equal rights," in "Magazine Cites Women's Rights for Drop in Birthrate in U.K.," *The Globe and Mail* (Reuter), January 1, 1976.

179 Jeanne Binstock, "Many of the young ... traps for men," in "Motherhood: An Occupation Facing Decline," *The Futurist*, June 1972.

179 Warner Troyer, "Many girls ... in later years," in *Divorced Kids*, cited, p. 145.

179-80 More teenagers decide to keep their babies, in Dorothy Lipovenko, "Too

Young to Vote, Old Enough to Have a Baby," *The Globe and Mail*, January 10, 1980. Age-specific fertility rates for the Big Generation are in *Vital Statistics, Births*, cited.

180 At current age-specific divorce rates, the proportion of marriages remaining intact at age 50 was 77.6% in 1971, 70.0% in 1976; estimated from *Vital Statistics, Volume II, Marriages and Divorces*, Catalogue 84-205, various years. This was also the source for the statement that the highest age-specific divorce rates are for people aged 25-29. Jay Scott, "Her story is a seventies archetype," in "Kramer vs. Kramer an Emotional KO," *The Globe and Mail*, December 15, 1979. Joanne Kates, "We've seen marriage ... five years," in "Infant Dreams," cited.

180-1 The source for data on marriages and divorces is *Vital Statistics, Marriages and Divorces*, various years, cited. This table gives some idea of the trends of recent years:

	Number of Marriages	Number of Divorces	Ratio of Marriages to Divorces
1950	125,083	5,386	23.2 : 1
1965	145,519	8,974	16.2 : 1
1970	188,428	29,775	6.3 : 1
1978	185,523	57,155	3.2 : 1

The same source gives the median ages of brides at marriage in recent years:

181-2 Observations about marriage rates, marriageable age, age of marriage, and so on, based on tables in *Vital Statistics, Marriages and Divorces*, cited, and *Population 1921-1971*, cited. The Total Marriage Rate, a figure I have calculated on the same basis as the Total Fertility Rate, was 73.2 in 1977. It was calculated from the age-specific marriage rates for single women. It means that at the current rates 27% of women would never get married. By comparison, the TMR as recently as 1971 was 91.0, meaning that only 9% of women would never get married. It is not a reliable measure, but it serves to indicate that marriage rates have dropped dramatically in the 1970s.

182 The marriage squeeze is calculated from the latest available count of the population by single years of age, matching women of each age with men two years older. The last actual count was the 1976 Census; the latest estimate is in *Estimates of Population by Sex and Age for Canada and the Provinces, June 1, 1978*, Catalogue 91-202 (Ottawa: Statistics Canada, 1980). A graphic representation of the squeeze appeared in "Women Will Have Larger Choice of Mates," *Executive*, May 1979.

182 Donald Symons, "Competition over women ... cause of violence," in *The Evolution of Human Sexuality* (Oxford: Oxford University Press, 1979), reviewed in Clifford Geerts, "Sociosexology," *The New York Review*, January 24, 1980.

182-3 The rise of the live-alones was calculated from *1976 Census of Canada: Dwellings and Households*, Catalogue 93-804, and *Households and Family Projections ...* , cited.

183 Dr. Leonora Butler, "Young loners are likely first-borns. They are more independent. Later-borns need fraternity," in Eileen Morris, "The Lone

Generation," *Weekend Magazine*, April 30, 1977. Meg Pettie, "How to deal with . . . depression," and Bob Bechthold, "They say they . . . need friends," both in Peggy McCallum, "Singles in a World of Couples," *The Globe and Mail*, October 19, 1978.

183 Herbert Passin, "For the first . . . and whole," in Morris, "The Lone Generation," cited. Frank Furstenberg, "separate economic . . . transitory arrangements," in June Kronholz, "On Their Own: A Living-Alone Trend Affects Housing, Cars and Other Industries," *Wall Street Journal*, November 16, 1977.

183 In 1976, 54,095 out of 160,200, or 34%, of Vancouver households contained only one person, in City of Vancouver Planning Department *Quarterly Review*, July 1978.

184 Mothers' ages at the birth of their children derived from data in *Vital Statistics, Births*, cited. The risk of giving birth to a mongoloid child has often been said to rise with age. E. Matsunaga, "Parental Age, Live-Birth Order and Pregnancy-Free Intervals in Down's Syndrome in Japan," in G.E.W. Wolstenholme and Ruth Porter, eds., *Mongolism* (Boston: Little, Brown, 1967) is the source for this table:

Age of mother at child's birth	Relative incidence
Under 20	0.40
20-24	0.61
25-29	0.55
30-34	0.82
35-39	2.33
40-44	5.20
45-49	10.11

Matsunaga's work has been regarded as conservative: some studies show a sharper increase with age.

184-5 "A Baby Boom . . . Over 30," heading on article by Carola Vyhnak, Toronto *Star*, October 3, 1977. The observation that fertility rates of women over 30 are close to their all-time low is based on data in *Vital Statistics, Births*, cited. A calculation based on first-child fertility rates shows that if the cohort of women born 1946-50 is to achieve the same cumulative first-born fertility rate by age 30-34 – that is, by 1980 – as the cohort born in 1941-45 had achieved at the same age – that is, by 1975 – the first-child fertility rate for women 30-34 would have to rise from 12.7 children per 1000 women of the older cohort in 1975 to 24.8 children per 1000 women of the younger cohort in 1980. Such a rise seems unlikely. On present trends, it is more likely that 85% of the younger cohort will still be childless at 35, compared with 90% of the older cohort. The relation between age at marriage and number of children can be seen in this table, which deals with women aged 45 and over, who have probably completed their families:

Age at marriage	Number of children
15-19	4.55
20-24	3.61
25-29	2.80
30-34	2.09
35-39	1.41
40-44	0.89

The source is *1971 Census of Canada, Population: Women Ever Married by Number of Children Born*, Catalogue 92-718 (Ottawa: Statistics Canada, 1973). Ruth Wright, "I suspected also ... motherhood," in letter to the editor, *The Globe and Mail*, January 26, 1980. Ivan Timonin, "Fertility delayed is fertility denied," in "Age Structure Changes and Public Policy: Some Aspects," unpublished. The typical pattern of deciding never to have children is in Jean Veevers, *Childless by Choice* (Toronto: Butterworths, 1980).

185 The best-known book on zero population growth in the 1960s was Paul R. Ehrlich, *The Population Bomb* (New York: Ballantine, 1968). Women under 20 had 18,826 abortions in 1978 and bore 34,031 live children; that is, 36% of these 52,857 pregnancies ended in abortion; sources, *Therapeutic Abortions 1978* Catalogue 82-211 (Ottawa: Statistics Canada, 1980) and *Vital Statistics, Births and Deaths, 1978*, cited. U.S. sterilization rates in "Sterilization Leading Birth-Curb for Married Couples, Study Finds," *The Globe and Mail* (Associated Press), July 22, 1977.

185-6 In the population forecasting model, it is assumed that the slow decline in death rates continues; that emigration continues at the same rate for each age group – i.e., when there are more people aged 20-24 there will be more emigrants aged 20-24, and so on; and that the Total Fertility Rate declines to 1 by the end of the century and remains at that level. Some results of three runs of the model are shown below. The difference between them is the level of immigration, whether rising steadily to 100,000 or 200,000 at the end of the century; a zero-immigration run is included so that the effects of immigration can be isolated.

The zero-immigrants model

	No. of immigrants	Total Population	% Aged 0-20	% Aged 60+
1981	0	23,363,000	32	14
1991	0	23,351,000	26	17
2001	0	22,304,000	21	20
2011	0	20,632,000	17	26
2021	0	18,571,000	14	33
2031	0	16,245,000	12	39
2041	0	13,854,000	11	45
2051	0	11,584,000	9	50

page

The 100,000-immigrants-in-2000 model

	No. of immigrants	Total Population	% Aged 0-20	% Aged 60+
1981	92,000	23,837,000	32	14
1991	96,000	24,862,000	27	16
2001	100,000	24,879,000	22	19
2011	103,000	24,266,000	18	24
2021	107,000	23,241,000	16	29
2031	111,000	21,892,000	14	34
2041	115,000	20,408,000	13	38
2051	119,000	18,977,000	13	41

The 200,000-immigrants-in-2000 model

1981	111,000	23,896,000	32	14
1991	153,000	25,350,000	27	16
2001	196,000	26,205,000	22	18
2011	238,000	26,825,000	19	22
2021	280,000	27,422,000	17	26
2031	323,000	28,050,000	16	30
2041	365,000	28,861,000	16	32
2051	407,000	30,009,000	16	32

Projections of the demand for housing from Central Mortgage and Housing Corporation:

	total	annual average
1976-81	1,170,000	234,000
1981-86	1,040,000	208,000
1986-91	989,000	198,000
1991-96	872,000	174,000
1996-2001	849,000	170,000

The immediate source of this report was "Housing Industry in Canada Seen as Heading Into Worst Period in 10 Years," *The Globe and Mail* (Canadian Press), January 17, 1980

186 Peter Carter, "The picnic ... in the industry," address to Toronto Home Builders' Association, December 5, 1979.

186 Michael Walker's comments on immigration and housing, in "Demand for Housing Expected to Decline," *The Globe and Mail* (Canadian Press), January 16, 1980.

187 Peter Carter, "It seems clear ... and downtown," address to Toronto Home Builders' Association, December 5, 1979.

187 George Sternlieb and James W. Hughes, "This desperate feeling ... a house," in "The Post-Shelter Society," *The Public Interest*, Fall 1979, p. 47. Most young people want to buy a house of their own, in "9 out of 10 Young Canadians Hope to Own a Home," *Weekend Magazine*, March 17, 1979; telephone survey of 1,103 people in 32 large urban centres by Data Laboratories Research Consultants, Montreal. Gerald Long, "a pent-up demand for housing," in "B.C. Program ... ," *The Globe and Mail*, January 17, 1980.

Chapter 12

191 The statement that the Big Generation will be close to half the labour force is based on conservatively projected labour force participation rates by age and sex applied to Statistics Canada's latest population projections for 1996, *Population Projections for Canada and the Provinces 1976 to 2001*, cited, Projection 4.

191 "If this process . . . substantially eroded," in "Youth Employment and Unemployment," *OECD Observer*, July 1977.

191-2 R.W. Reid, "Otherwise, five . . . human misery," in Ronald Anderson, "The Job Hunters," *The Globe and Mail*, May 3, 1977. Father Desmond McGrath, "We may be . . . but unemployable," in Ed Finn, "Unemployed Young May Soon Become Unemployable," Toronto *Star*, August 14, 1978. Judith Maxwell, "A certain amount . . . of their talents," in "Canada Can't Afford to Create Jobs for Everyone, Policy Analyst Says," *The Globe and Mail*, August 4, 1977.

192 The assertion that most discoveries are made by young scientists appeared in a Johns Hopkins University Bulletin, reported in *Science Digest*, January 1961, and quoted in "Youth–The Young Go 'Boom'," *The Great Ideas Today 1961* (Chicago: Encyclopaedia Britannica, 1961), p. 131. Average age at winning Nobel prizes in science: see Lincoln H. Day, "What Will a ZPG Society be Like?", *Population Bulletin*, June 1978, p. 33.

192 The peak years for futurists were calculated from a list of 552 futurists who gave their birth dates, in *The Future: A Guide to Information Sources* (Washington: World Future Society, 1979), pp. 123-387. No members of the Big Generation made it into the list; the youngest futurist listed was born in 1949.

192-3 "Large numbers . . . move up quickly," and Roger Revelle, "A lot of people . . . executive positions," both in Caroline Donnelly, "A Free-Spending, Job-Squeezed, House-Proud Future," *Money*, May 1976.

193 Promotability must depend on average on the number of people who could be given a management position and the number of people there are for them to manage. The Big Generation loses out on both scores: it is high in numbers who could be given a management position, and the numbers following are notably lower than has ever been the case before. One promotability measure used here was calculated by looking at the ratio of each five-year age group in the labour force to all those who are younger, the other by calculating the ratio of each group to a 20-year age group of which it is the oldest part. The Big Generation's promotability was then compared with the average promotability of all other groups. The "notoriously lucky cohort" is the group of Canadians whose numbers fall furthest below a standardized age distribution. It includes most people born in the 1930s and a few in the early 1940s; the "luckiest" year to have been born was 1938.

193 "Koppers Co. last January assigned the duties of its retiring president to five new group presidents," in Roger Rickles, "Golden Handcuffs: Many Firms Step Up Inducements to Keep Executives in the Fold," *Wall Street Journal*, August 31, 1978.

Chapter 13

194 The story of 70 policemen injured in an unemployment demonstration appeared in "Riots Rock Paris During Jobs March," Toronto *Star* (Reuter), March 24, 1979. "Red Brigades seem to be gaining favor among

some of [Italy's] dissatisfied youth," in Theodora Lurie, "Wave of Violence Heightens Political Confusion in Italy," *The Globe and Mail*, June 22, 1977.

194 Bill Cumpsty, "In all my years ... to get them," in Rosemary Speirs, "Unemployed Speak Out: Be Ready for Violence," Toronto *Star*, October 23, 1977.

194 Dr. Levine, "One thing common ... and crime," in Ellie Tesher, "Jobless Young Could Turn to Terrorism – MD," Toronto *Star*, January 29, 1979.

195 In 1983 there will be 6,840,000 members of the Big Generation in a total electorate of 17,970,000; or 38% of the total. Source for basic data: *Population Projections ... 1976-2001*, cited, Projection 4.

195 Richard Finlay, "While only 22% ... same period," in "The Strange, Skeptical Mood of the Campus," *Saturday Night*, October 1979.

195 Fewer young people vote: see "Study Blames Youth of Potential Voters for Lower Turnout," *Wall Street Journal*, April 14, 1978. "Only 38 per cent of the people aged 18-19 voted [in the U.S. presidential election of 1976]; about half of those 25-29 voted; but 70 per cent of those 55-64 did so," in Leon F. Bouvier, "America's Baby Boom Generation: The Fateful Bulge," *Population Bulletin*, April 1980, p. 27. Lower estimates by the Committee for the Study of the American Electorate, in "A 'Lost Generation'," *The Globe and Mail* (Associated Press), September 6, 1976. Figures in the text were calculated from figures in this article.

196 Peter Walker, "Never let it ... of inflation," in "March Rights are Defended in U.K. Riot," *The Globe and Mail* (Associated Press), August 15, 1977. Data on support by age for the PQ, in William Johnson, "Strike Ironic Clash of Aims," *The Globe and Mail*, December 5, 1978. Ratio of the unemployment rate of people aged 14-24 to the unemployment rate of people 25 and over in 1975:

Atlantic	2.13:1
Quebec	2.44:1
Ontario	2.56:1
Prairies	2.86:1
Pacific	2.56:1

Source: Kevin Collins, *Youth and Employment: A Source Book*, cited, p. 13. In France, voting by unemployed youths helped the leftist upset, in Eric Morgenthaler, "European Youths, Hard Hit by Unemployment, Are Posing Major Political and Social Problems," *Wall Street Journal*, June 21, 1977.

196-7 Here are some other potential blocs in the electorate in 1983; some are overlapping:

The Big Generation	6,840,000
Men older than the Big Generation	5,350,000
Women older than the Big Generation	5,785,000
All Ontario electors	6,500,000
All Quebec electors	4,730,000
All Western electors	5,120,000
All Atlantic electors	1,630,000

Eric Jackman, "I don't know ... my own man," in Paul Palango, "The Butterfly Campaign," *The Globe and Mail*, February 8, 1980.

197 Aristotle's cyclical theory of governance, based on his study of 158 constitutions of Greek cities, was modified in Herman Kahn and Anthony J. Wiener, *The Year 2000* (New York: Macmillan, 1967), pp. 31-3.

198 Ernest Callenback, *Ecotopia* (Berkeley: Banyan Tree, 1975; New York: Bantam, 1979); in 1976 appeared the first issue of *Seriatim: Journal of Ecotopia*, published in El Cerrito, California. Jonathan Mills, "The matter can ... old age pensions," in letter to the editor, *The Globe and Mail*, August 13, 1979.

198 Dr. Levine, "They form a fertile ... youth population," in Ellie Tesher, "Jobless Young Could Turn to Terrorism – MD," Toronto *Star*, January 29, 1979.

198-9 Dr. Knutson and the case of Zvonko Busic, in Rochelle Semmel Albin, "The Strange Bond that Grows between Terrorist and Hostage," *The Globe and Mail*, November 24, 1979.

199 Robert Spencer, "We thought ... would cause it," Peter Warrian, "I'm surprised now ... we were fighting," and Steven Langdon, "The student movement ... society," all in Sylvia Stead, "Sixties' Radicals Say They Really Haven't Changed," *The Globe and Mail*, November 21, 1977.

199 Here are two calculations of the median age of the electorate:

	Projection 4	Projection 7
1961		44.3
1971		42.7
1981	38.6	38.8
1991	40.5	41.0
2001	43.6	44.2
2011	46.6	47.5
2021	48.4	49.7

Source: *Population Projections ... 1976-2001*, cited.

200 A study of the changing political voting patterns of college generations as they age is in Seymour Martin Lipset and Everett Carll Ladd, Jr., "College Generations – from the 1930's to the 1960's," *The Public Interest*, Fall 1971, pp. 99-113. The median ages of British voters in 1969 (45.6) and Swedish voters in 1967 (46.0) were calculated from data in Lincoln H. Day, "The Social Consequences of a Zero Population Growth Rate in the United States," Commission on Population Growth and the American Future, Charles F. Westoff and Robert Parke, Jr., eds., *Research Reports, Volume 1, Demographic and Social Aspects of Population Growth*, cited, p. 669.

Chapter 14

202 The rarity of old people in the past and their abundance in the future can be seen from this table, which shows what proportion of the whole Canadian population was or will be aged 65 or more over a 200-year period:

1851	2.7%	1921	4.8%	1991	11.3%
1861	3.0%	1931	5.6%	2001	12.7%
1871	3.7%	1941	6.7%	2011	14.4%
1881	4.1%	1951	7.8%	2021	19.1%
1891	4.6%	1961	7.6%	2031	24.2%
1901	5.0%	1971	8.1%	2041	25.2%
1911	4.7%	1981	9.5%	2051	25.2%

The source for the period 1851-1911 is *Historical Statistics of Canada*, cited; for 1921-71, *Population 1921-1971*, cited; for 1981-2051, F. Denton, C. Feaver, and B. Spencer, "The Future Population and Labour Force of Canada: Projections to the Year 2051," background paper prepared for the Economic Council of Canada, 1979, Projection P-05, quoted in *One in Three: Pensions for Canadians to 2030* (Ottawa: Economic Council of Canada, 1979), p. 127.

202 "One fairly conservative estimate":

Age	Number	Proportion
0-19	5,600,000	22%
20-39	6,330,000	24%
40-59	6,780,000	26%
60+	7,240,000	28%
Total	25,960,000	100%

Median age	42.9
Median age of electors	50.1

Based on data in *Population Projections . . . 1976-2001*, cited, Projection 7.

202 The age distribution of a hypothetical stationary population for the United States is given in Lincoln H. Day, "The Social Consequences of a Zero Population Growth Rate in the United States," *Demographic and Social Aspects of Population Growth*, cited, p. 669;

Age	Proportion
0-19	27%
20-39	27%
40-59	25%
60+	21%

202 Ronald Blythe, "The reason why . . . ordinary multitude," in *The View in Winter* (London: Allen Lane, 1979), reviewed and quoted in *The Observer*, October 14, 1979, and *The New York Review of Books*, November 8, 1979. Marion Levy, "We take it . . . into senility," in Martin Mayer, *Today and Tomorrow in America* (New York: Harper & Row, 1976), p. 69.

202-3 Jonathan Swift, "Every man desires . . . be old," in *Thoughts on Various Subjects* (1711).

203 Out of every 100,000 male children born in Canada, the table shows the number surviving at various ages:

page

At age	Survivors
0	100,000
10	98,041
20	97,108
30	95,490
40	93,742
50	89,666
60	79,784
70	60,261
80	31,475
90	6,874
100	189

Source: *Life Tables, Canada and Provinces, 1975-77* (Ottawa: Statistics Canada, 1979). The publication includes tables for women as well as men, for each province as well as for Canada. "Curve-squaring" would keep the number of survivors high for much longer; but the number would still drop to zero soon after age 100.

203 Theodore Gordon, "Since the lifespan-extending ... many years," and discussion of curve-squaring, both in "Lifestyle of the Future: Conspicuous Conservation," address to the Conference Board, May 19, 1977, in *Vital Speeches of the Day*, July 1, 1977, pp. 557-63. See also *Death, Dying, and Life Extension*, Trend Analysis Program 16, Winter 1978.

204 Death rates and causes of death are given in *Vital Statistics, Volume III: Deaths*, Catalogue 84-206 (Statistics Canada), annually.

204-5 "Peter Drucker, a leading U.S. management consultant, said ... that the age 65 cutoff for employment is an anachronism. It was selected as the retirement age almost a century ago in Germany," in Ronald Anderson, "Retirement Age," *The Globe and Mail*, November 28, 1978.

205 "A method by which ... the aged," in Frank Blackaby, "Income Policies and Inflation," *National Institute Economic Review*, November 1971, p. 38; quoted in *One in Three* ... , cited, p. 77.

205 Lou Harris, "It is impossible ... inflation," in "Americans Expect to Delay Retirement, Says Harris Survey, Reversing Trend; Inflation Seen as Prompting Change," *World of Work Report*, April 1979. Prof. Pesando, "Under private pension ... not indexed," in Rosemary Speirs, "Report Defends Retiring at 65," *The Globe and Mail*, October 24, 1979. The retirement poll, by CROP Inc., July 1978, showed that after retirement people would make these choices:

Part-time job	55%
Not work at all	25%
Full-time job	2%
Don't know, etc.	18%

205 Hideo Shiremura, "Our government pensions ... ends meet," in Stephen Handelman, "Japan 'Graying' Crowded Elderly Turn to Suicide," Toronto *Star*, January 31, 1979.

206 Sen. Croll, "poverty, aimlessness, and loneliness," in "Out at 65 Not All

Bad," *Financial Post*, December 29, 1979. American Medical Association study, "often leads to ... premature death," in "Compulsory Retirement at Age 65 is New U.S. Human Rights Issue," *The Globe and Mail*, August 22, 1977. One in four people retiring from employment in Britain's National Health Service at 65 dies within six months, and David Simmonds, "When people feel ... go on living," both in Leslie Holbrook, "Doing Nothing Forever a Hellish Eternal Vision," *The Globe and Mail*, January 17, 1980.

206   "Effective next January 1, the law raises from sixty-five to seventy the age at which the vast majority of employees can be forced to retire," in Irwin Ross, "Retirement at Seventy: A New Trauma for Management," *Fortune*, May 8, 1978.

206   The Sears, Roebuck estimates were in Ross, "Retirement at Seventy ...," *Fortune*, cited. The French government pays workers to retire early, in "Europeans Struggling with Pros, Cons of Early Retirement," *The Globe and Mail* (New York Times Service), December 6, 1977.

207   The ideal age to retire: 61 was the median answer, calculated from data in a survey conducted by CROP Inc., July 1978.

207   The problem of dismissing "deadwood," in Dennis Slocum, "Caution Advocated on Retirement Issue," *The Globe and Mail*, November 21, 1979. "Increasing offers of early retirement to salaried workers over 55 years of age," in "U.S. Firms may Use Small Cars to Lure Buyers into Showrooms," *The Globe and Mail* (New York Times Service), November 27, 1979.

207   Study by William L. Mercer Limited, Toronto, "With such a large ... be set," in Edward Clifford, "Easier Retirement Age Rules Forecast," *The Globe and Mail*, November 24, 1978. The ratio of retired people to people of working age was calculated from data in *Population Projections ... 1976-2001*, cited. This was also the source for the calculation of a shifting retirement age to suit the Big Generation:

	Retired dependency ratio	Proposed new retirement age
1976	22.7	65 (actual)
1986	24.7	56
1996	26.6	59
2006	28.5	62
2016	36.9	66
2026	48.2	70

208   Alex Comfort, "cease to be people ... and crazy," in Brenda Zosky, "There's a Crisis Coming as Baby Boom Grows Old," Toronto *Star*, June 4, 1977.

208   Thomas C. Desmond, "No matter how ... our society," in "The New Concern for Old Age," *Christian Century*, December 28, 1960, quoted in "Youth–the Young Go 'Boom'," *The Great Ideas Today 1961*, cited, p. 128. Sen. Croll, "The aging population ... retirement," in "Double Pensions, Let Old Keep Working, Senators Urge," *The Globe and Mail* (Canadian Press), December 20, 1979.

209   Ronald Blythe, "Old Age ... future-orientated existence," in *The View in Winter*, cited.

page

209 Report by International Social Security Association, "Europe in the year 2000 may become a continent of aged misfits unless something is done to change the attitudes of modern society toward its elderly citizens – and fast," in "Report Sees Europe Full of Aged Misfits," *The Globe and Mail* (Reuter), September 9, 1976. Trends in the timing of the marriage of a family's last child and the death of one spouse are in "Households and Families," *DataTrack 4*, Summer 1978, p. 13. The principle of the reverse mortgage was explained in Dennis Slocum, "Reverse Mortgages Ready," *The Globe and Mail*, March 16, 1979. "The ultimate . . . social revolution," in Alan Walker, "Rochdale – the College the Students Already Run," *The Star Weekly*, January 13, 1968.

210 A million more old women than old men: calculated from *Population Projections . . . 1976-2001*, cited, Projection 4. Prof. Revelle, "The life-styles . . . by the women," in Caroline Donnelly, "A Free-Spending, Job-Squeezed, House-Proud Future," *Money*, May 1976. Dr. Nancy Datan, "the emergence of the sensuous grandmother," in "Emergence of 'Sensuous Grandmother' will Squelch Stereotypes, Psychologists Say," *The Globe and Mail* (New York Times Service), September 1, 1977.

210-1 The cost of caring for very old people, in Mark Abrams, "The Future of the Elderly," *Futures*, June 1979, pp. 178-184. Future costs of hospitalization in Canada, in L.A. Lefebvre, Z.S. Zsigmond, and M.S. Devereaux, *A Prognosis for Hospitals: The Effects of Population Change on the Need for Hospital Space, 1976-2031*, Catalogue 83-520 (Ottawa: Statistics Canada, 1979).

211 "A nursing home patient-day is about one-fifth as expensive as one in a hospital: $25 versus $125 in 1976," in Lefebvre *et al*, *A Prognosis for Hospitals . . .*," cited. Victor Fuchs, "The subsidization . . . quantity demanded," in "The Economics of Health in a Post-Industrial Society," *The Public Interest*, Summer 1979, p. 10.

212 *Canada Pension Plan, Statutory Actuarial Report No. 4, As At December 31, 1977* (Ottawa: Department of Insurance, 1979).

212 "This position . . . will be honoured," in *One in Three . . .* cited, p. 40. Jonathan Mills, "Just wait . . . old age pensions," in letter to the editor, *The Globe and Mail*, August 13, 1979; see p. 198 of this book.

213 The number of pensioners 100 workers would have to support was calculated from the projected participation rates used in most labour force calculations in this book and from population data in *Population Projections . . . 1976-2001*, cited. "A substantial minority (42 per cent) of all current employees have 'hardly any confidence at all' that Social Security will be able to pay them the benefits they are entitled to when they retire," in "Americans Expect to Delay Retirement . . . ," *World of Work Report*, April 1979, cited.

213-4 CPP contributions would have to rise to 9%, in *Canada Pension Plan, Statutory Actuarial Report No. 4 . . .*, cited. CPP pay-as-you-go contribution rates up to 15.2%, in *One in Three . . .*, cited, p. 40. One third of GNP on public retirement programs, in *One in Three . . .*, cited, p. 28.

214 The disability pension was proposed in, e.g., George C. Sawyer, "Dwindling Pensions?", *Business Tomorrow*, October 1979.

INDEX

257

259